THE HUMAN AURA

By WALTER J. KILNER

B.A., M.B. (Cantab.), M.R.C.P., etc.
Late Electrician to St. Thomas's Hospital, London

WITH 64 ILLUSTRATIONS

FOREWORD BY LESLIE SHEPARD

The Citadel Press • Secaucus, New Jersey

Copyright © 1965 by University Books Inc.
All rights reserved
Published by Citadel Press
A division of Lyle Stuart Inc.
120 Enterprise Ave., Secaucus, N.J. 07094
In Canada: Musson Book Company
A division of General Publishing Co. Limited
Don Mills, Ontario
Manufactured in the United States of America
ISBN 0-8065-0545-1
5 6 7 8 9 10

FOREWORD

THE IDEA OF A HUMAN AURA, a radiating luminous cloud surrounding the body, is an ancient one. Sacred images from early Egypt, India, Greece and Rome used this convention before it became so popular in Christian art, and before the aura was considered an attribute of ordinary everyday mortals.

In the religious convention, the aura sometimes surrounded the head only, at other times the whole body. The distinction was clarified precisely in Christian art, where the luminous cloud round the whole body was termed an *aureola,* the luminous disk or halo round the head a *nimbus,* and a combination of both *nimbus* and *aureola* was known as a *glory*.

It is thought that the pre-Christian tradition derived from identification of divine personages with the sun and its rays, specifically in the Mithras cult and its widespread diffusion. It may well be, however, that the religious idea of a radiant emanation was also based upon the actual observations of seers. Throughout the Christian era saints have been credited with radiance at moments of exaltation; this might have been an intensification of an already-existing aura, visible only to gifted seers.

For centuries it has been believed that clairvoyant ("clear-seeing") people could actually see an aura surrounding ordinary individuals, and that this aura differed from person to person in color and character, expressing the health, emotional and spiritual attributes of the subject. The visionary Swedenborg wrote in his *Spiritual Diary:* "There is a spiritual sphere surrounding every one, as well as a natural and a corporeal one."

It is a long way from religious and occult traditions to a twentieth century doctor's consulting room, but Dr. Walter John Kilner bridged this gap in his bold move to establish the reality of the human aura as a physical phenomenon.

Walter John Kilner came from a conventional medical family. He was born 23 May 1847 at Bury St. Edmunds, Suffolk, England, the son of John Kilner, a Fellow of the Royal College of Surgeons. Both Walter Kilner and his younger brother Charles Scott Kilner

FOREWORD

studied medicine on established lines. Charles Kilner, for example, qualified as M.B., C.M. (Edinburgh University), D.P.H. (Cambridge University), and became Senior Medical Officer for West Suffolk General Hospital. Walter Kilner was educated at Bury St. Edmunds Grammar School, St. John's College (Cambridge University), and St. Thomas's Hospital, London. He took his B.A. in 1870, his M.R.C.S. and L.S.A. in 1871 and his M.B. in 1872. There is nothing in the least cranky or irregular in the standard medical background of both Walter Kilner and his brother.

Walter Kilner came to St. Thomas's Hospital as a student in 1869. Ten years later, in June 1879, he was appointed in charge of electro-therapy at St. Thomas's. This was the hospital's first official step towards establishing electrical treatment. Kilner held this post until about 1893. During this period he wrote several papers, published in the *Saint Thomas's Hospital Reports* series; these were careful medical contributions, such as: *The salicylates of calcium and bismuth in the diarrhea of children* (1879), *Some experiments upon, and explanatory of, the physical properties of muscle* (1886). His electrical interests are shown by the following two titles: *On the use of the continued current in diabetes* (1882) and *The effects of electricity upon the circulation, local and general* (1884). He became a member of the Royal College of Physicians in 1883. He had a private practice at Ladbroke Grove, London, then a fashionable neighborhood. In his spare time he was a keen and brilliant chess player.

Dr. Kilner graduated during an exciting period of scientific and medical discovery. In order to understand how he came to develop his concept of the human aura, it will be helpful to study the background of his time.

The sensational field of "animal magnetism" was now becoming respectable through the efforts of reputable physicians like Dr. H. Bernheim to establish hypnotism on a sound basis, while remarkable developments were taking place in electro-magnetism through the researches of scientists like Sir William Crookes and Professor Heinrich Hertz. The general trend was towards practical non-speculative science, and vitalistic concepts were becoming unfashionable. During this important historical period, one negative result was that some very interesting and worthwhile research was bypassed.

FOREWORD

In 1866, the brilliant German scientist Baron Carl von Reichenbach, celebrated for his fine work in chemistry, mineralogy and geology, had published his *Aphorisms,* based on hundreds of careful experiments with "sensitives"— nervous, highly-strung or psychic individuals who could perceive an emanation from magnets, crystals . . . and human beings. In one of Reichenbach's experiments sensitives described a luminous force that streamed from the fingertips. Reichenbach did not use the term "aura" but his "Odic force" is clearly comparable. He studied the characteristics of this force with minute care, only to have his findings ridiculed by dogmatic scientists of the period. Reichenbach died in 1869, a disappointed man.

In America, in 1878, Edwin D. Babbitt acknowledged his debt to the work of Baron Reichenbach. Babbitt was one of the most remarkable of men in the history of color and healing, and his book, *The Principles of Light and Color* remains as a classic in its field. He looked upon Reichenbach's "Odic" light as following the same laws and phenomena as visible light and as holding great value in revealing life forces. But Babbitt was dismissed as an occultist by the science of his day.

In 1895, Professor W. K. Röntgen made his monumental discovery of X-rays. St. Thomas's, where Kilner worked, was actually the first London hospital to have a practical demonstration of the Röntgen Rays in 1896, and in 1897 they had a busy X-Ray Department.

In 1903, Professor Blondlot of Nancy University, France, announced the discovery of new radiations, which he called N-Rays (N for Nancy). These were said to be emitted by many substances and also by human nervous activity. Blondlot was honored by the French Academy, but a few months afterwards was discredited by an American physicist, Robert W. Wood, who slyly removed a prism from Blondlot's apparatus while the latter was describing an N-Ray spectrum. According to Wood, this had no effect on Blondlot's observations which were therefore imaginary, and the ridicule which followed this "exposure" culminated in Blondlot's madness and death. Although the subject of N-Rays is now considered exploded, many reputable scientists like Professor Charpentier and Professor Becquerel had experimented with N-Rays and corroborated Blondlot's findings.

FOREWORD

Both Röntgen and Blondlot had studied the effects of their rays on phosphorescent substances such as potassium platinocyanide. Kilner had been reading about the action of N-Rays on phosphorescent sulphide of calcium, and it occurred to him that it might be possible to make human emanations visible.

Kilner was aware of Reichenbach's work, which he mentions in connection with seeing auras around the poles of magnets and the human hands. Kilner had also seen Theosophical literature on the aura and the etheric double, probably Leadbeater's pamphlet *The Aura: An Enquiry into the natural forms of luminous mist seen about human and other bodies,* first published in 1895.

It is also clear that Kilner had experimented with the "Sthenometer" of Professor Paul Joire, a simple instrument to measure human nervous energy. Kilner's somewhat ambiguous references to an instrument for measuring N-Rays by deflection of a needle are undoubtedly to a Sthenometer. This gadget was a lightly balanced needle with a calibrated dial, enclosed by a glass shade; the needle was said to respond to ambient human nervous force. Such devices have often been ridiculed, but some remarkable effects have been achieved with them under control conditions (see especially the article *An Instrument which is set in motion by vision or by proximity of the human body* by Dr. Charles Russ, in "The Lancet" 30 July 1921, pp. 222-4).

In 1908 Kilner conceived the idea that the human aura might be made visible if viewed through a suitable substance, and he experimented with dicyanin, a remarkable coal-tar dye. This dye appeared to have a definite effect upon eyesight, making the observer temporarily short-sighted and therefore more readily able to perceive radiation in the ultra-violet band. After many patient experiments Kilner published his findings in the first edition of *The Human Atmosphere* in 1911. The book was available together with diagnosis sheets and box of slides. Kilner described techniques for viewing the human aura, which he claimed had inner and outer components. The inner aura followed the body outlines, while the outer aura was more nebulous. Kilner said there were marked changes in the appearance of the aura in states of health and sickness, and that his viewing screen could be used for diagnosis.

There were unbelievers, of course. Kilner's book had a long

FOREWORD

review in the august columns of "The British Medical Journal" 6 January 1912, but it was distinctly skeptical. It opened: "Many of the readers of this journal will already be aware from recent notices in the lay press of the claims of Dr. Kilner of London . . ." and went on to state "Dr. Kilner has failed to convince us that his aura is more real than Macbeth's visionary dagger."

Undeterred, Kilner continued with his experiments. He had fitted up a dark room in his house in Ladbroke Grove and there he studied the human aura for diagnostic purposes. Sir Oliver Lodge became interested in his work. In 1914, however, the work was interrupted by the Great War. Kilner's dicyanin, produced by an elaborate process, was supplied by the German chemists Meister Lucius & Bruening, and during the war supplies were cut off. Kilner retired from his practice and returned to Bury St. Edmunds, where he assisted his brother Charles Kilner, who had a very large practice.

By 1920, a completely revised edition of Kilner's book was in the press; this contained many additional observations and inferences. This edition was sympathetically reviewed in "The Medical Times" February 1921, a very broadminded professional journal. Many reputable medical men endorsed Kilner's findings. In March 1922 there was also an enthusiastic review in the cautious journal, "The Scientific American."

But Dr. Kilner did not live to see these articles. He died 23 June 1920, at the age of 73.

Kilner's work was clearly too unconventional to make much impact on the professional medical world, in spite of his explicit disclaimer of any clairvoyant or occult preoccupation. Ironically enough it was the spiritualistic movement which quickly endorsed Kilner's work after his death. Mr. Harry Boddington, a noted British spiritualist, made a number of improvements to Kilner's cumbersome viewing screen. Kilner's viewer was a narrow box with a cell of optically ground glass containing an alcoholic solution of the dicyanin dye. There were obvious disadvantages. It needed a large amount of the dye solution, which was very costly, moreover the cell was awkward for viewing since it did not exclude light at the sides. Boddington devised goggles fitted with double glasses between which the dye solution was placed, very little being needed. These goggles were refillable, as the alcohol evaporated in the course of time. They were provisionally patented in 1928 under the trade name "Aurospecs" but Boddington later discovered that satisfactory results could be obtained by using glass of the same spectroscopic tint. These "Kilnascrenes" had a considerable vogue amongst spiritualists and are still in demand. (Curiously enough, Kilner's book does not appear to have been noticed by the British Society for Psychical Research).

Kilner's researches were further developed on scientific lines by Oscar Bagnall, B.A. (Cantab.), who wrote *The Origin and Properties of the Human Aura,* published in 1937. This is a sensible and practical extension of Kilner's work. Bagnall confirmed Kilner's claim that continued use of the dicyanin viewing screen corrected long-sighted vision (both Kilner and Bagnall were long-sighted) but suggested that the colors of the dye forced little used rods and cones of the eye retina to respond to a shorter wavelength of vision. Boddington concurred with this view.

Bagnall's main contribution was an improved viewing screen using a more stable and much cheaper coal-tar dye called pinacyanol in place of dicyanin.

More recently, Mr. J. J. Williamson of the Metaphysical Research Group in England, conducted a number of careful experiments to check and correlate the researches of Kilner, Boddington, Bagnall and others. In 1954, Mr. Williamson compiled a lecture giving a valuable detailed summary of the main points involved. In 1960 his associate Dr. M. K. Muftic published an excellent survey of the whole field.

The subject of the human aura is a complex one. On the one hand there are firmly based theories of cell radiation by scientists like Dr. George Crile, H. S. Burr and F. S. C. Northrop, on the other hand remnants of the Animal Magnetism concepts of the early nineteenth century which deserve reappraisal. Dr. W. E. Benham, a modern radiesthetist, claims that insects have auras that may be measured (a butterfly's being said to be 20 feet long, for example). Other sensitive persons can react to emanations at critical distances from the human body. The late William Norman Pogson, a gifted water diviner, even believed that it was possible to capture sections of an aura in a test tube and keep it bottled up for some months.

Certain gifted subjects actually radiate a curious energy from the hands, which can either heal diseases or mummify organic substances like fruit or meat. (For example, the well attested case of Georges Gaillard of Lyons, France, who mummified two mutton chops within a minute, simply by holding them in his hands). Amongst more extravagant concepts of the human aura was the case of Dr. H. Baraduc, who used to "clip" at a short distance around the face and body of his patients with large copper scissors, to free the etheric body from the physical part of the aura . . .

The occultists and Theosophists link the question of the aura with the *chakras* of Hindu *Yoga* and the spiritual development of the individual. Clairvoyants continue to see auras of various colors and shapes; it is quite possible that such vision has some physical basis. Meanwhile the existence of various kinds of bio-electrical currents in the human organism is well known, but largely uncorrelated.

Dr. Kilner went to much trouble to emphasize that his discovery was physical and not occult. Yet many people have failed to see the human aura through Kilner devices of one sort or another. It has been urged against Kilner's work that it is easy to mistake the effect of well known optical illusions that can arise under the special circumstances of viewing. Worst of all, several people claimed that Kilner himself was really a gifted clairvoyant and saw things through his screens which had no physical basis! It is only fair to say that many clear-thinking and reputable investigators confirm Kilner's researches, and today there is even evidence of a revival of interest in the earlier work of Reichenbach.

The subject of the human aura still veers uneasily between science and clairvoyance. Clearly it is premature to claim that Kilner's findings have been firmly established, yet one cannot discount his years of patient experiment and the considerable body of supporting evidence.

Kilner's important book has been a scarce out-of-print item for many years. Now it will be possible for many more people to experiment.

More experiment is needed. Newer apparatus is available to measure ultra-violet and infra-red radiation. Some attempts have been made to photograph the aura; it might be possible to show

FOREWORD

some components of the aura on a modified television screen. For the ordinary investigator, Aura Screens of various types are now available.

Meanwhile it is good that Kilner's careful pioneer researches should be available again.

Grateful thanks are due to the following individuals for their assistance during the compilation of this Introduction:

Miss Dorothy L. R. Kilner; The Assistant Librarian, Royal College of Physicians, London; The Library Staff of St. Thomas's Hospital, Medical School, London; Mr. J. J. Williamson, Metaphysical Research Group, Hastings, Sussex, England.

The following books will be found valuable for supplementary study:

BERNHEIM, H.	*Suggestive Therapeutics* . . . 1884-6 (reprinted as *Hypnosis and Suggestion in Psychotherapy*) University Books, New York, 1964.
POWELL, A. E.	*The Etheric Double and allied phenomena.* London, 1925.
CRILE, G.	*The Phenomena of Life. A Radio-Electric Interpretation.* London, 1936.
BAGNALL, O.	*Origin and Properties of the Human Aura.* London, 1937.
OUSELEY, S. G. J.	*Science of the Aura.* London, 1946.
BODDINGTON, H.	*The University of Spiritualism.* London, 1946.
WILLIAMSON, J. J.	*Seeing the Aura.* Metaphysical Research Group, Hastings, Sussex, England, 1954. (mimeographed).
MUFTIC, M. K.	*Researches on the Aura Phenomena* (Parts 1 & 2). Metaphysical Research Group, Hastings. n.d. (mimeographed).
BABBITT, EDWIN D.	*The Principles of Light and Color,* Babbitt & Co., New York, 1878.

London, England   LESLIE SHEPARD

PREFACE

SINCE the former edition was published a large amount of fresh material has been collected, with the result that new properties of the Human Atmosphere have come to light.

Although at present it is impossible to say exactly of what the aura consists, yet I feel positive that we are dealing with an ultra-violet phenomenon. Some women have the power of changing the colours of their auras by voluntary effort (no man or boy has as yet been found to possess this faculty), and these hues unquestionably do not belong to the ordinary visible solar spectrum, so we must be encountering a second and higher spectrum having shorter wave lengths.

The physical aura exhibits another interesting property inasmuch as it can be influenced by external forces such as electricity and chemical action.

Naturally a considerable amount of time and thought has been devoted in trying to discover how dicyanin affects the visual organs, but the explanation remains incomplete.

Although photography has not been mentioned in the text, yet occasionally the aura has been photographed to a slight extent but not by any means satisfactorily, nor have the necessary conditions for obtaining the impressions been determined. Nevertheless I am certain that a photographic picture of the size, shape and condition of the Human Aura is not only possible but will shortly be made, thus enabling the aura to become a still greater assistance in medical diagnosis. It has been my earnest desire

PREFACE

to achieve this object, but now, age with its attendant infirmities, superadded to other difficulties, almost precludes any hope.   However, the successful pioneer in this direction has in anticipation my sincerest congratulations.

W.J.K.

Hatter Street,
Bury St. Edmunds

CONTENTS

THE HUMAN AURA

CHAPTER I

The Aura of Healthy Persons

INTRODUCTION

HARDLY one person in ten thousand is aware that he or she is enveloped by a haze intimately connected with the body, whether asleep or awake, whether hot or cold, which, although invisible under ordinary circumstances, can be seen when conditions are favourable. This mist, the prototype of the nimbus or halo constantly depicted around saints, has been manifest to certain individuals possessing a specially gifted sight, who in consequence have received the title of " Clairvoyants," and until quite recently to no one else. This cloud or atmosphere, generally termed the AURA, is the subject of this treatise, in so far as it can be perceived by the employment of screens containing a peculiar chemical substance in solution. It may be stated at once that the writer does not make the slightest claim to clairvoyancy ; nor is he an occultist ; and he specially desires to impress upon his readers that his researches have been entirely physical, and can be repeated by any one who takes sufficient interest in the subject.

As long as the faculty of seeing the aura was confined to a few individuals, and ordinary persons had no means of corroboration or refutation, the door to imposture was open. Since this has been the case up to the present time, the subject has always been looked on askance ; but there is no more charlatanism in the detection of the human aura by the means employed than in distinguishing microbes by the aid of the microscope. The chief difference lies in the claim of some people that they are able to perceive the one through the possession of extra-normal eyesight, while no one has yet had the hardihood to assert that they have the power of seeing an object one-thousandth of a millemetre in length without instrumental aid. There cannot be the least doubt of the reality of the existence of an aura enveloping a human being, and this will in a short time be an universally accepted fact, now that it can be made visible to nearly every person having ordinary eyesight.*

It, indeed, would be strange if the aura did not vary under different circumstances, and there is good reason to believe that a study of its modifications will show that they have a diagnostic value in disease.

The writer asks the indulgence of his readers while he makes a few personal remarks. He has endeavoured to be as far as possible impartial and accurate in recording all observations and to avoid pitfalls and faults having their origin in uncontrolled enthusiasm and imagination. This, in one part of the subject is very difficult, as so much depends upon subjective vision. It is only fair to add that his sight is his most perfect sense ; and consequently he may be able to distinguish by its aid a little more than the average man, and may thus have perceived effects which escape the notice of other observers. Some of the deductions he has made may be thought, and perhaps rightly, too dogmatic, since they are founded upon such a small number of cases ; but the excuse advanced is, that they have been brought forward solely

---

*The author considers that ninety-five per cent. of people with normal eyesight can see the aura. One gentleman states that only one person out of four hundred, to whom he had tried to show the aura, was unable to distinguish the phenomenon.

with the intention of providing working hypotheses to assist in future investigations.

The discovery of a screen making the aura visible was by no means accidental. After reading about the action of the N rays upon phosphorescent sulphide of calcium, the writer was for a long time experimenting upon mechanical forces of certain bodily emanations, and had come to the conclusion, whether rightly or wrongly, that he had detected two forces besides heat that could act upon his needles, and that these forces were situated in the infra-red portion of the spectrum. There was a hitch in his experiments ; and in the early part of 1908, he thought certain dyes might help him. After considering their different spectra and, as far as he could, ascertaining their properties, he made a trial of several, and fixed upon the coal tar dye " Dicyanin," as the most likely to be useful. While waiting for this chemical, a thought flashed across his mind that the substance might make some portion of the effects of the above forces visible ; and should this be the case, he expected to see the human aura. He had heard about that phenomenon, but until that moment never had any intention of investigating it, as he believed it to be far beyond his natural powers.

As soon as the dye had been obtained, glass screens coated with collodion or gelatine and stained with it, were made, but were found entirely useless as decomposition took place almost instantaneously. Several other methods were tried with varying success, but the only one which gave really satisfactory results was glass cells filled with an alcoholic solution of dicyanin. Even these after a time change their colour from chemical decomposition, and should be kept in the dark when not in use. Two of these screens are needed for ordinary work, one being dark and the other light, but as will be mentioned later on, other screens quite different will be required for special purposes. Immediately a screen was finished, the writer looked at a friend through it, and instantly saw round his head and hands a faint mist greyish in colour, which he concluded could be nothing else than the human aura. In the course of his early experiments, it was not long before he noticed that he could for a few minutes see the haze without the intervention of a screen. This power only lasted a short time, but was found to be renewed by looking through a dark screen at the light, which, it is interesting to note, is the general rule. A minority of persons who are not able to see the aura, or only to a slight extent after gazing through the dark dicyanin screen at the light, will find that they can detect it more easily and distinctly if they examine it through the light dicyanin screen. Herein lies the main use of the second screen.

At first the aura had such a fascination that every free moment morning, noon, and night, was occupied using the screen for experiments, but the writer found to his cost, that dicyanin had a deleterious effect upon the eyes, making them so painful that it was necessary to cease work for some days. On this account it is recommended that the dark dicyanin screen should not be used for a longer time than about one hour daily. The action of the dye is apparently cumulative, so that the power of seeing the aura without any previous use of the screen is gradually acquired, nevertheless the writer deems it expedient to gaze at the light for a few seconds before inspecting a patient.

The aura can only be satisfactorily defined when certain conditions are fulfilled. In the first place the light must not be too bright. The requisite amount has to be determined at each observation, and experience is the only guide, as some persons can best perceive the aura when the light is much too bright for other people. Roughly, the body of the person under examination should be just distinctly visible after the observer has become accustomed to the dimness. The light should be diffused proceeding from one direction only, and illuminating the patient equally all over. The best arrangement is obtained when the observer is standing with his back to a darkened window while the subject faces it. An alternative method, and occasionally the only one that can be employed away from home, is to have a tent similar to the X folding portable dark room used for photography, except that it should be lined with a dead black material instead of the ordinary yellow fabric, and have the front curtains removed. Generally it is possible at a patient's house with a little manœuvring to place the tent facing the window, otherwise if a sufficiently large room can be obtained, it may be placed to, and about three or four feet in front of, a window, so that the person under examination will be illuminated. Every window in the room, except the one at the back of the tent, should be completely darkened, while this one must have the blind drawn down to a greater or less extent as needed. The important objection to this arrangement is, that the observer has to stand opposite the light, which is inconvenient for every part of the inspection, and is especially awkward for observations connected with the complementary colours as described later on. It is always essential to have a dead black background.

A large portion of the writer's work has been conducted in a room with only one window. This window is fitted with an ordinary blind at the top, and below another blind* consisting of two thicknesses of black serge, that can be raised to any desired height. The serge permits a considerable amount of light to pass through, in fact too much, except on very dark days ; but the illumination is further regulated by lowering the ordinary blind. This arrangement is

*In his present house the outlook is more open, so two blinds are installed.

convenient, as a slight gap can be left between the two blinds, allowing extra light to pass into the room when the patient is being examined through the deep carmine screen, and occasionally when the complementary colours are being employed.

Opposite about eight to ten feet from the window is a rod supporting black and white curtains, either of which can be utilized as required.

It is important to bear in mind that the patient should stand at least a foot in front of the background, to prevent any shadows or marks on it from producing optical illusions, and vitiating the observations.

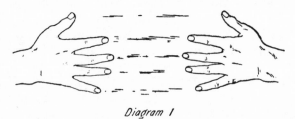

Diagram 1

Trouble from this cause, however, is not likely to occur, unless the investigator is fresh to the work.

As a number of people have tried to see the aura and failed, some through faulty arrangement of the light, some through straining of the eyes, and others again through various misunderstandings, all of whom have been able to perceive it quite easily under proper conditions, a short description of a few preliminary experiments may be of assistance in the early attempts at detecting the aura. When these have been carried out conscientiously and successfully, the observer will have overcome the main difficulties.

A beginner should get someone to hold his hands about a foot in front of the black background on the same plane and parallel with it, from eight to ten inches apart with his fingers extended as in diagram I. He must then peer through the dark dicyanin screen for about thirty seconds at the daylight (the sky if possible, but not directly at the sun). This screen *ought to be held quite close to the eyes*, to prevent all light impinging upon the retina unless it has traversed the blue fluid. Without this precaution the screen has little or no effect upon the sight. The influence of the screen usually persists for an hour or more, but sometimes on the first few occasions for a much shorter period, when the operation may be repeated as often as necessary. Next, the blinds ought to be so arranged that the hands to be examined are just clearly visible to the observer as he stands with his back to the window and shades them with his body. This position enables him to in- crease the light upon the hands to a greater or less extent with- out altering the blinds, simply by moving a little to the right or left. The observer will, as a rule, be almost immediately able to detect streaks proceeding from the fingers of the one hand to the fingers of the other, and

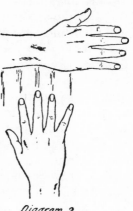

Diagram 2

a haze in the interval between the two hands. Directly he has perceived the haze and streaks, he will probably be able to see a similar, but not quite as plain, mist around the arm if bared. Now and then there is some slight difficulty at the first trial, which can be generally overcome if the other hand is held at right angles, and a short distance from the arm. (See diagram 2.) By this means the aura will be intensified, and when the hand is removed the observer will be able to see it round the bare arm. Needless to say, as the eyes become accustomed to the subdued light, the illum- ination will periodically require alteration.

A large percentage of persons after gazing through

the dark dicyanin screen at the light, are able to perceive the aura as described above, but a small minority find it impossible to detect it without the aid of the pale dicyanin screen. It stands to reason that when this screen is used the light will have to be increased a trifle.

After the aura around the arm and hand has been satisfactorily inspected, the observer may with advantage inspect it through the deep carmine screen. For this purpose it will be necessary to raise the blinds a short distance, until the arm and hand can be seen through the screen to the same degree as before. He will now find that the larger portion of the aura has vanished, while the part that remains encircles the limb closely, being usually from one and a half to three and a half inches in breadth. At a cursory glance the texture of this portion of the aura will appear more opaque, but when examined carefully will be found to be finely striated, looking as if brushed out with a camel's hair brush. At places which vary from minute to minute, the lineation can be more easily distinguished than at others. The striated portion has been named the *inner aura*, and the wide amorphous part, not seen when using the carmine screen, the *outer aura*. At times, but by no means always, a close scrutiny will detect an apparently void space between the body and the inner aura. This area is called the *etheric double*. All these different parts will be described in later chapters.

It is imperative that the hands and the arms should be viewed exactly as if looking at a picture; there must be no straining of the eyes. The more accurately the observer can focus his eyes upon the plane in which the hands are held, the more easily and plainly will he be able to discern the aura. Straining the eyes is not merely a hindrance, but frequently will entirely prevent the perception of the haze. The reason for this will appear later on.

Directly the observer feels that he will be able to see the aura fairly easily, he may proceed to examine it round a large portion of, or better still, the whole body. For the first trial it is preferable that the subject should be in good health and if possible robust, because the aura always loses in distinctness during illness. It is also useful to remember that the aura varies in clearness from day to day even in rude health.

While the subject is undressing and getting into position for examination, the observer, unless he has previously done so, should look through the dark dicyanin screen at the light for a few seconds. The light must now be regulated by drawing down the blinds, when it will be noticed that the amount needed is much less if the whole body is being in-spected than when the hands alone are looked at. Standing with his back to the window, and opposite to the subject (using a pale dicyanin screen if neces-sary), the observer ought to distinguish immediately, or certainly after a few seconds, a faint mist enveloping the body. This varies even in health according to age, sex, and individual peculiarities.

The first thing to observe is the texture, whether fine or coarse, as no two persons have identical auras. Note the colour, which is generally some shade of blue mixed with a greater or less amount of grey. A great help in determining the colour is to get the person to place the hands upon the hips, and at the same time to extend the elbows, when in the space between the trunk and the arms the aura emanating from the body will be reinforced by that proceeding from the arms.

At the commencement of a systematic inspection it will be advisable for the patient first to face the observer and the light. The aura round the head can best be seen as he stands or sits with his hands hanging down by the sides. Its breadth can be roughly measured by noticing the distance it extends beyond

the shoulders, and this position also permits comparison of the aura on the two sides, which is of great
importance because in certain cases of disease it will
be wider on one side than the other. At this stage
attention ought to be paid to the general shape of the
aura while the hands are hanging down, as there is
often a difference from what is seen when they are
raised to their full extent. During the greater part
of the examination it will be found advantageous to
let the patient stand with his hand lightly resting on
the top of his head, so that the aura from the axilla
down the trunk, thighs, and legs may be as little
influenced as possible by that proceeding from the
arms. This is also the time to determine the size and
shape of the aura, and whether it follows the contour
of the body, or whether it is wider by the trunk than
by the lower limbs ; and if so, how far it descends
before it contracts. Some abnormality of texture can
frequently be detected, which is best studied later with
special screens.

Occasionally the aura can be separated by its
appearance into two or sometimes three distinct
portions, but the further study of these must be
deferred to a later stage of the examination. After
all the information concerning the aura at the sides
has been obtained, the subject should be turned sideways to allow the aura at the back and front to be
investigated. Should at any time suspicion arise of
irregular illumination the aura must (in addition to
the foregoing inspection), be again scrutinized when
the back has been turned to the light, and again completed as the patient is standing sideways facing the
opposite direction to the one he had previously assumed.
This simple manœuvre eliminates a number of errors.

The aura envelops the whole of the human frame,
but on account of the delicacy and transparency of
its texture is only visible in sections ; consequently
when it is desired to investigate a portion emanating

from one particular spot, it becomes necessary so to turn the patient that this portion may be seen against the background.

The next stage of the examination is to separate the inner aura from the outer by means of the dark carmine screen. Should the patient have anything wrong with this aura, the defect will often become manifest through some change, such as want of definition, or alteration of texture, which may for instance be granular. Generally the impairments are merely local. The complementary coloured bands may now be used, and finally the aura between the body and the arms while the patient is posed with arms akimbo, may be investigated through different coloured screens.

In addition to the varieties in size and shape of the aura, both in health and disease, there are great modifications in the texture. The alterations are usually so subtle that to translate them into words is an impossibility, but any person who has inspected several auras would, indeed, be a poor observer, if he had not noticed how rarely two are alike. Although diagrammatic drawings may look alike, resemblance ends here. It would answer no good purpose to label auras fine, medium or coarse, as the differences so grade into one another, that it would be frequently impossible to decide the class to which a given aura should be referred.

Apart from factors such as ill-health, fatigue, depression, etc., which are known to affect individual auras, it has been found that all, or nearly all, auras vary in distinctness from time to time, being generally clearer on days which, as tested with the actinometer, are most favourable for photography. Temperature and humidity changes do not seem to be concerned. The true explanation of these phenomena remains obscure. The above teaches one important lesson, namely, the necessity for trying to see the aura a second time should the investigator fail at the first trial.

Examination of a number of people in good health, shows not merely individual variations which might be naturally expected, but also the existence of group differences. Males, independent of age, after making allowances for individual peculiarities, all possess the same characteristic aura. Quite the opposite is the case with females, because their auras undergo a veritable transformation at one period of their lives. In childhood the aura is identical with that of a male. In adults it is far more developed, while in adolescence —from twelve or thirteen up to eighteen or nineteen years of age—it slowly advances from the masculine to the more extended feminine type.

Inspection of a man shows that the aura enshrouds the head equally all round, usually being three to four inches broader than the width of the shoulders. When he stands facing the observer with arms raised and hands resting on his head, the outer aura will appear narrower by the sides of the trunk than round the head, and following the contour of the body, where it does not usually exceed more than four or five inches in width, or roughly speaking, one fifteenth of his height. Viewed in profile it will be seen down the back about as broad as down the sides, but barely as wide in front. It is always continuous down the lower limbs, though a little diminished in width. Around the arms it resembles that encircling the legs, but it is usually broader round the hands, and constantly projects a long distance from the tips of the fingers. The inner aura is generally from two and a half inches to three and a half in extent, and keeps the outline of the body all over.

The above description also applies to the auras of girls up to the age of twelve or thirteen years, but the texture is generally finer, occasionally making it difficult to distinguish the edge, as is also the case with boys. Children, therefore, are not good subjects for early observations.

The aura of a woman has a specific shape of its own. Above the shoulders, round the head, and down the arms and hands it is very similar to that of a man. The difference at once becomes evident when facing the observer, she places the hands on the head, for the aura extends further from the sides of the trunk than in males, and broadens out until at the level of the waist it has reached its full size. Hence it gradually contracts until it approaches the ankles. This is the most perfect form, the ovoid, but sometimes it appears to narrow higher up, but not in health before it arrives at the level of the lower part of the thighs, from which it proceeds downwards much the same in width or else only shrinking slowly. This gradual diminution is so difficult to describe in words that it is referred to as " following the outlines of the limbs," etc. Of course, this is a slight inexactitude, yet it gives a good general impression.

When a woman stands sideways, the aura will be seen wider behind than in front, and the broadest part is at the small of the back owing to the spinal curve. It ought to descend in a straight line from the shoulders to the nates (being an equal distance from the body at each of these places), and afterwards to follow the form of the thighs and legs. The haze is often more pronounced in front of the breasts and nipples, and this increase is evidently dependent upon the functional activity of the glands, as it becomes most definite during pregnancy and lactation, and occasionally also, only to a less extent for a short time before, during and after menstruation. When once the aura has been fully developed, age does not produce any alteration, but disease may. Figs. 9 to 18 are good diagrammatic representations of the auras of women in health.

Amongst healthy women auras may depart in shape from the above description. Modifications arise from differences in width by the sides of the trunk and the level at which full contraction takes place over the lower limbs.   At the same time it will be noticed that the breadth in front of the body varies, but not to the same extent.   At the back the variations are more frequent and marked, and are generally related to temperament.   With one person the outer margin of the haze is seemingly quite straight from the level of the shoulders to the most prominent part of the nates, and from thence it takes the outline of the thighs and legs.   Another person will exhibit an outward curve at the small of the back that diminishes as it reaches the middle of the thighs, or may nearly reach the ground before it has fully contracted.   In chapter 6 a detailed account of these bulges is given. The average breadth of the aura of a woman at the waist is from eight to ten inches, sometimes it does not extend to more than six or seven, while occasionally it may attain the width of fifteen inches.   The inner aura resembles that of a man except, perhaps, that it is not quite as wide.

At the approach of puberty the aura begins to expand, leaving the infantile form to acquire in five or six years the shape characteristic of the adult female.   The change generally commences a short time before menstruation appears, but only very rarely has the transitional stage been noticed before the beginning of external bodily development.   For example, a girl of fourteen years of age (case 10, figs. 7 and 8), had a marked transitional aura previous to menstruation.   The youngest child to exhibit any increase of the aura by the side of the trunk, was just two months over twelve years.   She was a big tall girl, precociously developed.   Another instance of early enlargement of the aura, was that of a well grown girl subject to epileptic fits, who at the age of thirteen had an infantile aura, but six months later this had commenced to develop.   A second girl of the same age possessed an aura in the transitional stage, and judging from its size, it must have begun enlargement before she had entered her teens. She was strong and healthy, and only properly developed for her age.

As far as it has been possible to determine, the general rule is for the aura to start expanding between fourteen and fifteen years of age, and with one or two exceptions all the girls who have been inspected between fifteen and eighteen have had transitional auras. One weakly girl nearly seventeen years old, who had never menstruated, retained a perfectly formed infantile aura. A woman twenty-eight years of age, whose faculties were far below the average, had an aura the size and shape of a child of sixteen. Her aunt stated " that her habits and mental powers were about the same as those of a girl of that age." On the other hand a well formed woman thirty years of age, with an undeveloped uterus, who had only menstruated four times in her life, was surrounded by a very distinct aura, larger than usually seen. Another woman, forty-two years of age, sixteen years after the removal of both her ovaries, had a fairly plain aura quite up to size by the sides of the trunk, and exceptionally broad at the back and front.

There can be no two opinions about the growth of the female aura at the period of adolescence, but it remains uncertain whether this is entirely dependent upon the functional maturation of the sexual organs or whether other changes taking place contribute to this growth. Anyhow, it can be confidently stated, as will appear later on, that menstruation has a subtle effect upon the aura, while pregnancy produces marked alterations.

For the present it will be sufficient to state, that the aura can be naturally divided into three distinct parts

First, there is a transparent dark space, which is narrow and often obliterated by the second portion.

When visible it looks like a dark void band, not exceeding a quarter of an inch, surrounding and adjacent to the body, showing not the slightest alteration in size in any region. This will be called the *etheric double*.

The second constituent is the *inner aura*. It is the densest portion and varies comparatively little, or even not at all in width, either at the back, front or sides, and in both males and females follows the outline of the body. It appears just external to the etheric double, but frequently looks as if it were in contact with the body itself.

The third portion or *outer aura*, commences at the distal edge of the inner aura, and is inconstant in size. It is the extreme visible outer margin of this haze that has hitherto been taken for the outside limit of the aura. When the whole aura is observed without the intervention of any screen, the two latter divisions appear blended together, but the part nearest the body looks the most dense. If, however, a pale carmine screen be employed, each of the factors can be distinguished, or should the screen be a dark one, and the light properly arranged, the outer will be altogether eliminated.

The following descriptions are selected from persons in good health, varying in age from early infancy upwards. They are arranged according to age, first the males and then the females.

Case I. A, a fine healthy infant, fifteen hours old, was inspected while lying on a black cloth on his mother's bed. Although seen under adverse circumstances, his aura was plainly visible, being of a grey colour tinged with yellow. As far as could be distinguished it followed the outline of the body. This was the youngest child yet examined, and it may be interesting to note that both the mother and nurse were able to see the cloud around him when they looked through the dark dicyanin screen.

He was inspected a second time at the age of four months under more favourable conditions, on a sofa with a black cloth under him. His aura followed the outline of the body and was slightly over an inch in width, with the exception of the part round his head, where it was broader. The colour had changed to a dark blue-grey.

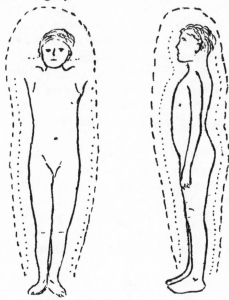

FIGS. 1 AND 2.   Healthy boy.

Case 2.   B, a healthy boy four months old, was examined when lying upon a black cloth with a black background behind him. The aura could be easily detected, and had a bluish grey colour. The outer looked about an inch wide, round his body and limbs, but by the sides of the head it was a little broader than the width of his shoulders. Through the dark carmine screen the inner aura was quite plain, about three quarters of an inch wide, and displayed well marked striation.

Case 3.   (Figs. 1 and 2.)   C, a strong lad, healthy,

five years of age, stood facing the observer. His aura appeared to be about six inches wide round his head. It came down by the sides of the trunk about three and three quarters of an inch in width, and a little narrower by the thighs and legs. The inner aura was conspicuous, being nearly two inches by the sides of the trunk and about one and a quarter by the legs. When he turned sideways, the outer aura was two inches in front, and the inner about a quarter of an inch less. Both these measurements were slightly diminished lower down. At the back the outer aura was about two and a half inches wide by the trunk, and contracted as it proceeded downwards. Here, too, the inner aura was about a quarter of an inch narrower than the outer. The colour was a blue-grey.

It is worth remembering that in children, especially in males, the inner aura is frequently almost as wide as the outer, and occasionally there is a little difficulty in separating the one from the other.

Case 4. D, a youth fourteen years of age, was rather tall and had always enjoyed good health. His aura was well marked and of a bluish grey colour. As he faced the observer, the outer aura was seven inches round the head, four inches by the sides of the trunk, and lower down three and a half. The inner aura was two inches in breadth all over the body. The etheric double was visible, one eighth of an inch in width. As he stood sideways, the outer aura was about three inches in breadth at the back by the shoulders and nates, coming down straight. It was three inches over the whole length of the front.

Case 5. (Figs. 3 and 4.) E, a professional athlete, thirty-three years of age. He was well proportioned in every way and robust in health. The colour of his aura was a blue with a little grey. The outer aura was eight inches round the head, and all down the trunk, arms, and legs five inches. The inner aura was extremely well marked, being three inches in breadth, and its striation was quite easy to see. A side view showed the inner to be the same width at the back, front and sides, but the outer aura was a trifle narrower in front than at the back. The etheric double was clearly defined, about a quarter of an inch

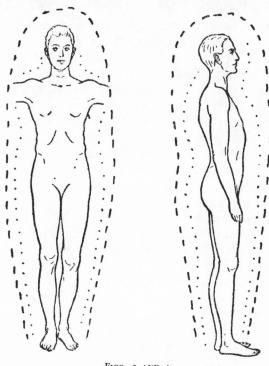

FIGS. 3 AND 4.
Healthy, strong man.

broad. This aura was unusually coarse in texture.

After considerable difficulty a full blooded negro, a native of the United States, was engaged for inspection.

Case 6. F, a healthy Negro man fifty years old, was examined in 1912. He was tall and well made— a typical specimen of his race. His outer aura was normal for a man round the body, where it was five inches broad, but was narrow by the head as it was only seven inches wide.   The width of the inner aura was three inches all over the body, and striation was present, although at first it was troublesome to distinguish.   The difficulty was palpably due to the colour rather than want of definition.   The hue was an opaque hazy brown-grey.   It did not stand out against the black background as distinctly as the ordinary blue-grey auras do.   On the other hand it was easily visible through a pale blue screen when the background was white.   The complementary coloured bands (see chapter 5), after making due allowance for the colour of the skin, were even all over the body and apparently normal.   The mutual attraction of the auras emanating from the subject and the observer's hands will be described later on.

Case 7.   G, a female infant lying on her mother's bed, was inspected when a week old.   The external conditions were unfavourable, but with a little difficulty the aura was perceived as a greenish haze following the outline of the body, being very narrow, but widest round the head.

When the child was four months old (compare A, case 1, and B, case 2), she was examined a second time under better surroundings.   The aura was exceedingly hard to detect as it was not nearly as distinct as was expected.   It only looked about half an inch wide by the body, and a little broader by the head.   The most interesting feature of this case was, that the colour had changed from a greenish to a grey shade.

Case 8.   H, a fragile child, was examined when she was four years old.   She was rather a small child, but in good health.   She had an extensive aura for a girl of her age and size.   The outer aura was three inches all over her body, except by her head, where it was five.   The inner aura was two inches in breadth, distinct and striated.   The colour was a true blue.

Case 9. (Figs. 5 and 6.) I, a tall girl nine years of age was recently inspected. She had only suffered from childish ailments. The colour of her aura was very peculiar—green, yellow, and grey intermingled but not blended. (See chapter 3.) The outer aura was eight inches round the head, which is extraordinarily large and exceptional for a child. By the trunk and limbs it had the usual infantile shape, and

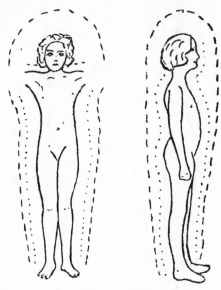

Figs. 5 and 6.
Young girl. Healthy aura.

was of average width, namely, three inches by the trunk and slightly less lower down. The inner aura was about two and a half inches broad, exhibiting striation plainly, exactly what might be expected for a girl in good health. The chief interest lies in the remarkable size of the aura round the head. (Compare with case 15 in an adult.) It is more than probable that when grown up she will be a clever woman.

Case 10. (Figs. 7 and 8.)   J, has always been very healthy, and her aura has been inspected from time to time, thus allowing the growth to be watched at different periods of her adolescence. When first examined in January, 1911, she was twelve and a half years old, and both her auras were distinct and normal

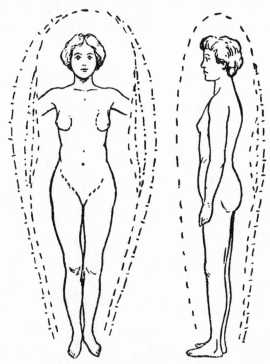

Figs. 7 and 8.
Transitional outer aura. Gradual development.

for a girl of her age.   The outer was six inches round the head, and as she faced the observer, it was three and a half by the trunk, contracting somewhat by the lower limbs. When she turned sideways, it was the same width down the back and front. The inner aura showed normal striation and was two and a half inches wide.

In December of the following year she was again examined, being fourteen and a half years of age. Her body had commenced to develop, and she had menstruated once or twice. The outer aura remained the same size round the head, but, as she stood facing, it had increased to five inches by the trunk, and made no change by the legs. A side view showed an enlargement of half an inch in front of the body, while at the small of the back it had become an inch and a half wider. No alteration had taken place in the inner aura.

After another twelvemonth the whole aura had expanded. It had reached seven inches round the head, six and a half by the trunk, and three and a half by the legs. Viewed sideways, it was three and a half inches in front, six at the small of the back, and three and a half by the legs.

After a lapse of another two years and a quarter, her aura was inspected a fourth time. Her bodily development was up to the proper standard for her age, nearly eighteen. The aura had attained the adult form, although it will probably still expand, but not to any great extent. The figures, as she faced the observer, were round the head and by the trunk nine inches, and by the legs four and a half, making a good ovoid shape. When she turned sideways, it was six at the small of the back, and elsewhere four and a half inches.

Case 11. (Figs. 9 and 10.) K. The following is an instance of a perfectly shaped aura of average width, enveloping a young woman twenty-three years old, an artist's model, her profession being a sufficient guarantee that she is well built. She is bright and intelligent, quite healthy, and has never suffered from any serious illness. When examined, both auras reached the average standard of distinctness and size, the outer being eight inches round the head and nine by the trunk. The curve of the ovoid commenced

over the head and ended by the feet, where it was four
inches wide.   It was quite symmetrical.   A profile
view showed the outer aura to be four and a half
inches in front of the trunk, contracting to four
by the legs, while at the back it was six, coming down

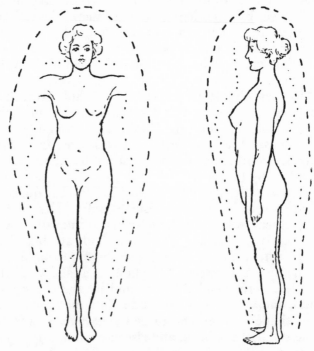

Figs. 9 and 10.
Healthy woman (average aura).

straight from the shoulders to the buttocks.   The
colour was a blue-grey.

The inner aura was distinct and lineation could be
easily distinguished.   It was three and a half inches
by the trunk, front, sides, and back, but only three
by the limbs.

As her aura has been shown to a number of medical
men, there have been opportunities for seeing some

curious effects. Once, when she was standing with
her hands down by the sides of her body, three bright
rays suddenly appeared simultaneously, all proceeding
a long distance beyond the visible limits of the outer
aura. No ostensible cause for this phenomenon, which
lasted a considerable time, could be discovered. On
another occasion, the room becoming a little over-

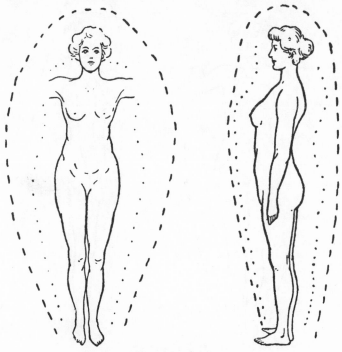

Figs. 11 and 12.
Healthy woman (very fine aura).

heated, the woman felt faint. The first intimation of
this condition was that both auras became dim ;
subsequently, as recovery took place, they gradually
returned to their normal state.

Case 12. (Figs. 11 and 12.) L, a strongly built
lady with intellectual faculties certainly above the
average, was recently inspected. She was robust and

very energetic, and her aura, as might be reasonably expected, was large and fine in texture. The colour was a good blue. The aura was nine inches round the head, twelve by the sides of the trunk and gradually contracted to five by the feet, making a perfect ovoid. A side view gave five inches in front, and eight at the

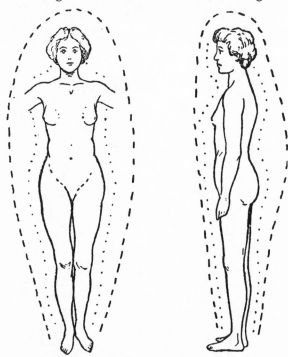

Figs. 13 and 14.
Healthy woman (narrow aura).

small of the back, without any dorsal curve. The lineation was unusually distinct in the inner aura, which was four inches wide all over the body and limbs. An interesting feature was that the definition of the distal margin of the outer aura had not the common sharpness, and gave the impression of an almost imperceptible haze beyond, a phenomenon rarely present except when the aura is wide. It has been called the Ultra-outer aura. (See page 47, chapter 3).

The next instance is an example of a low grade aura, the complete antithesis of the one just described.

Case 13. (Figs. 13 and 14.)   M, a diminutive, well shaped woman, twenty-eight years of age, had her aura inspected in 1913.   She had never suffered from any serious illness, but her mental powers were decidedly below the normal standard.

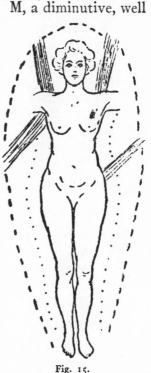

Fig. 15.
Healthy woman.   Rays.

The colour of her aura was a grey with hardly any tinge of blue, thus indicating an essentially low type.   In shape and size, although its full growth had been attained, it corresponded with the transitional form normally found among girls in their teens.   As she faced the observer, round the head and by the sides of the trunk the outer aura only acquired a width of six inches, and contracted to three by the lower limbs. viewed from the side, it measured three inches in front, but at the back it had a bulge, which was broadest at the level of the waist, where it was six inches.   The inner aura was about two inches all over the body and faintly striated.

Case 14. (Fig. 15.) N, was a married woman twenty-five years old.   The shape of her aura was quite ordinary for her age, but was remarkable for having several rays coming off from the body at the same time.   There were two, one from each shoulder, proceeding upwards, one descending from the right axilla, and another ascending from the crest of the ilium.   When she turned sideways, a fifth small ray could be seen emanating from a small fibro-adenoid tumour of the left breast.

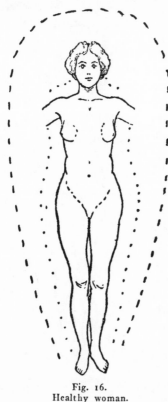

Fig. 16.
Healthy woman.

Case 15.   (Fig. 16).   O, a lady just turned twenty-three years, has had no serious illness, but has never been robust, and was suffering from the effects of overwork and not taking proper exercise.   She complained of having frequent palpitations and of great lassitude.   There was nothing organically wrong with her, and she soon recovered.   The main peculiarity was the shape of her outer aura, which was twelve inches by the head and eleven by the trunk, contracting to four by the feet, the curve being rather sharp.   A side view showed that the aura was normal in front, being four inches wide, but at the back at the broadest part it was eight inches, and was bow-shaped, commencing at the head to curve outwards to the level of the waist, from which it turned inwards to the feet.   The inner aura was two and a half inches all over the body, and did not display the usual distinctness owing to the state of her health ; nevertheless lineation could be detected.   In a subsequent examination her inner aura had regained its normal clearness.

There is another type of aura which is only occasionally met with among women. It is of the usual width by the sides of the trunk, and contracts very slightly by the thighs and legs, proceeding downwards straight. Generally the outer aura is equally broad at the back and front, and is even down the lower limbs. Its free margin is of the ordinary distinctness and there is no sign of the ultra-outer aura. The inner aura, too, is larger than the average. Taking it all round it approximates to an extra wide male aura. The following is a marked example.

Case 16. (Figs. 17 and 18.) P, a naturally strong young woman, well made, twenty-five years of age, came to have her aura inspected in 1918. The outer aura, as she faced the observer, was of medium size, being nine and a half inches by the head, nine by the trunk, and at the widest part by the thighs it was six inches, and continued the same breadth all the way down to the feet. This made the curve from the flank to the thigh small. A profile view showed the aura to be six inches wide in front without narrowing anywhere. At the back it came down straight, being at the thighs and legs six inches, and, of course, a little broader at the lumbar regions. There was nothing remarkable about the inner aura, which exhibited striation and was three and a half inches wide round the whole body. The colour of the aura was a grey-blue.

As heredity plays such an important part in determining the qualities of many constituents of the body, it would be, indeed, strange if some of the peculiarities of the aura were not transmitted by descent. The few cases of two or more individuals of the same family that have been collected show the surmise to be probably correct, but absolute confirmation will require long study and extended enquiries. A complete analysis of an aura should include observations on the texture as well as on the size and shape.   In practice it has been found impossible to directly compare the texture of the various individual auras even of the same family, as the inspection of two or more persons cannot be made simultaneously, and

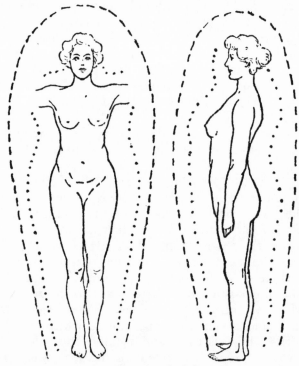

Figs. 17 and 18.
Healthy aura.   Masculine type.

generally a considerable time elapses between examinations.   It is fairly easy to compare the size and shape of adults one with another when they are of the same sex, but difficulties commence directly the comparison has to be made between the auras of a man and of a woman or of a woman and of a child, since the masculine type is so unlike the feminine.

Practically the only method is to measure the breadth of the aura over the trunk, as the subjects stand facing the observer.

For this purpose some scale is indispensible. It is quite certain that the height of a person makes only a very slight difference in the breadth of the aura, since a tall person's aura does not appear much, if any, wider, than a short person's, thus destroying any chance of finding a working ratio between the height of a subject and the width of the aura. Besides, it must be remembered that children have relatively broader auras for their heights than adults. To add to the difficulty, abnormalities will have to be taken into consideration. Similar deviations are found at times in several members of a family.

Since the ratio between the height of a patient and the breadth of the aura is precluded, there seems to be only one, and that not a satisfactory method, of obtaining a requisite standard. This is to fix arbitrarily the limits of the average dimensions of the aura, and to take any departure from them as abnormal. Thus all auras may be divided into three categories, namely, wide, average, and narrow. Roughly speaking, the aura of a woman may be called average, when it is from eight to ten inches broad by the sides of the trunk at the widest parts.

The standard for men is from four to five inches, and for children between two and a half and three and a half. As the auras of adolescent girls are changing from month to month, it will be necessary to consider each on its own merits, as no hard and fast rule is possible. These figures are the outcome of experience alone, and have no claim to scientific accuracy. It is frequently far from easy to decide whether a case ought to be classed as average.

One example will be sufficient to make this evident. Suppose that a woman's aura by the sides of the trunk is a little larger than the limits laid down for average width, and that it prematurely contracts down by the thighs and legs to below the normal, in fact is of the spatulate type (page 162), under which heading should it be placed ? The case must be treated upon its own merits.

The following tables contain all the examples of individuals of the same family that have been inspected up to the end of 1918. The first table relates to those cases in which two or more generations are involved, and the second to those belonging to the same generation. In two instances the same persons come into both tables. The ages are those of patients at the dates of their inspection.

TABLE I.—Parents and Children.

Name	Sex	Age	W	A	N	
N	F	25	w			Healthy.
Child	M	4 mths.	w			,,
U	F	30	w			,,
U,L	M	3, 5	w			,,
H	F	24			n	,,
Child	F	4 mths.			n	,,
D	F	28		a		,,
D.C	M	3, 5		a		,,
M	F	38		a		,,
M.K	F	5		a		,,
M.M	F	7		a		,,
X	M	58			n	Neurotic.
X.X	M	23			n	Epileptic.
X.B	F	23			n	,,
C	F	29			n	Married daughter. Healthy.
X.F	F	12.5			n	Grand-daughter. Healthy.
X.G	F	9.5		a		,,
X.E	F	7.5	w?			,,
Ca	M	59			n	Chronic Bright's disease.
Ca.D	F	23			n	Hysterical.
Cb	F	36		a		Healthy.
Cb.F	F	10		a		,,
Cc	F	35		a		,,
Cc.	F	6		a		,,
Na	F	36		a		,,
Na.G	F	6		a		,,
O	F	65		a		Hemiplegic.
O.O	F	28		a		Healthy.
G	F	26		a		,,
Child	M	4 mths.		a		,,
F	F	40		a		,,
F.A	F	15		a		,,
S	F	32		a		,,
S.IT	M	10		a		,,

TABLE I (Continued)

Name	Sex	Age	W	A	N	
B	M	55		a		Hemiplegic.
B.B	F	17		a		Healthy.
B.G	F	15		a		,,
Cd	F	56	w			,,
T	F	28		a		Married daughter. Consumptive.
I	F	29	w			Healthy.
I.D	F	4	w			,,
U	M	64	w			Very bad health.
Ba	F	34		a		Married daughter. Healthy.
Sa	F	31		a		,, ,,
Sa.B	M	12	w			Grandchild.
Sa.D	M	7	w			,,
J	F	24		a		Married daughter.
Ia	F	45		a		Healthy.
Ia.B	F	13			n	,,
Ma	F	56	w			Hysterical.
Ma.N	F	19	w			,,
Nb	F	38		a		Healthy.
Nb.B	F	8		a		,,
Da	F	30		a		,,
Da.R	M	5		a		,,
Db	M	57		a		Prematurely old.
Db	F	53		a		Bad health.
Db.E	F	29		a		Not strong.
Fa	F	56		a		Bad health.
Nc	F	30		a		Married daughter. Hysterical.
Dc	F	45		a		,,
Ba	F	73		a		Not strong.
Ba.W	F	29	w			
Nd	F	34		a		Healthy.
Nd.V	F	10.5		a		,,
Nd.G	F	11.5		a		,,
Ne	F	57		a		Bad health.
Ne.L	F	17		a		Epileptic.
Ne.P	M	10	w			

TABLE II.—Brothers and Sisters.

Name	Sex	Age	W	A	N	
Ta	F	37	w			Sisters.
Ua	F	35	w			
Dc.F	F	31	w			,,
Dc.N	F	25	w			Bad health.
Dc.E	F	23	w			
Dc.B	F	15.5	w			
Bb.G	M	19	w			Brothers.
Bb.I	M	14	w			
Ga.N	F	23	w			Sisters.
Ga.B	F	22	w			
Na	F	36		a		Sisters. Hysterical.
Nf	F	22		a		,, ,,
Ic.	M	5		a		Brother and sister.
Ic.N	F	8		a		
Ng	F	23	w			Sisters.
Ng.N	F	12.5	w?			
K	F	29	w			,,
E	F	20	w			
Fb	M	20		a		Brother and sister.
Fb.B	F	23	w			
Gb	F	27		a		Sisters. Healthy.
Gb.F	F	18			very n	Weak minded.
Ce	F	21		a		,,
Ce.A	F	21		a		
Dd	F	30		a		,,
Ea	F	26		a		
Eb	F	34			n	,, Epileptic.
Eb.E	F	28			very n	Neurotic.
Bc	F	37		a		,,
Nh	F	33		a		
Id	F	64	w			,,
Ub	F	58		a		

Since the type of a given aura largely depends upon temperament, itself a transmitted characteristic, it seems almost certain that the main attributes of auras are hereditary, and in a given case will be retained more or less unaltered during life, unless modified by disease. It will accordingly be found that the auras of quick intelligent children, however young and untrained, are more extensive than those of the dull and phlegmatic, although the latter may have the advantage in physique. The former, too, will probably possess auras above, the latter below the general standard of size, since in adults the same rule obtains, the finest auras surrounding the most intelligent people, and the smallest enveloping persons who are dull or of a low intellectual type. This is not only seen round the body, but becomes most obvious round the head ; and is more noticeable among men than women, as the auras of the former do not expand to the same extent round the trunk. Auras encircling women are more variable than those enveloping men, but the finest specimens will invariably surround naturally intelligent and energetic persons who have no tendency to neurotic complaints. In the above description perfect health is taken for granted.

Texture, the next character to receive consideration is more difficult to deal with, the delicacy of the modifications at times defy description. The inner aura will be found to be better · defined and broader in persons of both sexes who are naturally robust, and in good health, but fainter in weakly subjects, revealing that it is bodily rather than mental powers that are the chief energizers of this portion.

In general, the grain of the outer aura of men is coarser than that of women ; but after making due allowance for this, fineness and transparency may be considered a higher type than coarseness and dullness. Later it will be shown that the more grey there is in the colour of the aura, the duller and more mentally deficient is the owner.

Education is a factor that ought, theoretically, to have an immensely refining influence, but any changes induced by it are so delicate as to be imperceptible by our present means of examination.

The influence of heredity and temperament upon the aura is an exceedingly fascinating part of the subject, and it does not require a prophet to foresee that an enquirer in this direction will reap a rich harvest.

CHAPTER II

The Etheric Double

THE structure of the aura must now claim attention. It will, as might be expected, be found to be a composite not a simple phenomenon, and can be separated into three well defined divisions, with a fourth added for convenience. The names given to the different parts are respectively the *Etheric Double*, the *Inner Aura*, and the *Outer Aura*, while the fourth constituent is termed the *Ultra-outer Aura*.

The *Etheric Double*. Very soon after the aura had been detected one feature attracted attention, which at first sight was regarded merely as an optical illusion, but on further investigation proved a reality. This is the Etheric Double. It may be frequently seen through different coloured screens as a dark band adjacent to, and following the contour of the body, separating the latter from the true aura. Commonly it is from one-sixteenth to one-eighth of an inch in breadth, rarely more, keeping an uniform width all round the body. In disease this space will sometimes look much wider, but then it is presumably a pathological condition, and probably not identical with the natural phenomenon. The size varies with different people, and also with the same person under altered conditions. Occasionally it is so conspicuous that it can be seen at the most transitory glance ; at other times a very careful examination is requisite for its identification, while not infrequently a special screen is imperative. In instances where there is a difficulty in distinguishing it, the aura proper is apparently in close proximity

38

to the body, but even then careful observation will generally disclose a difference in structure, the details of which can be elucidated by means of coloured screens.

Experience has shown that people who most commonly show the etheric double plainly, are patients with a neurotic tendency, in whom the aura does not quite attain the average standard of brightness. Should the aura be more distinct on one side than the other, the etheric double is sometimes more pronounced on the fainter side, and may be only detected with difficulty on the brilliant side. The following case will exemplify these conditions.

Case 17. X.E., a girl eighteen years old. Her aura for her age was wide and spatulate, (page 162), showing a trace of the ultra-outer aura, which was more distinct by the lower limbs, thus making the shape to appear almost normal. This partial ultra-outer aura has only been seen a few times. The usual hysterical bulge was conspicuous at the back. The outer aura measured ten inches by the head and trunk, and was contracted sharply at the upper part of the thighs, and diminished to four and a half inches at the ankles ; viewed sideways it was six inches in front, and at the widest place, viz., the small part of the back, ten inches. The inner was striated throughout, but on the left side was by no means as bright as on the right, where it was normal. The etheric double, about an eighth of an inch wide, could be seen at the first glance all down the left side, but on the right and in front it could only be detected with great difficulty. At the back from the level of the shoulders to the middle of the gluteal region it was twice as broad, and from thence down the left thigh it resumed its previous width.

The simple experiments detailed below should be now undertaken with a subject showing a well marked etheric double. Complete success may not be obtainable at any given sitting, as undetermined conditions not infrequently exercise an influence. For this reason considerable time may have to be devoted to the experiments, but since the results are at present only of theoretical importance it will not be necessary to obtain them for diagnostic purposes.

Any portion of the body can be utilized, but perhaps the most convenient part is the arm and hand, as the investigation is longer than most people care to remain uncovered. The arm and hand offer a further advantage—the observer can, with very little trouble, employ his own. As soon as the subject has been placed in a suitable posture, it will be advisable for the observer to sensitize his eyes in the usual manner with the dark dicyanin screen.

Exp. 1. Inspect the arm and hand of a subject held in front of a black background through a dark blue screen. The etheric double will then appear as a dark band without any striation or granules, adjacent to the body and quite distinct from the aura proper.

Exp. 2. Replace the black background by a white one, and regulate the light accurately. The etheric double will then be perceived as a dark line.

Exp. 3. Employ a green instead of a blue screen. Against the black background the etheric double will be seen as a dark line, but not so clearly as when the blue screen was used. The aura, too, will be visible but less distinct.

Exp. 4. When the same screen is used with the subject's arm before a white background, in a subdued light, the etheric double is dark.

Exp. 5. If a yellow screen be next chosen, the etheric double will remain dark against either a light or a dark background.

Exp. 6. Frequently when examined through a dark red screen the etheric double will continue a black band round the body, similar to, but more defined than when other screens are used. Occasionally it will appear, instead of a void space, finely granular with a tendency to striation, but even then differing greatly in colour and texture from the inner aura.

Exp. 7. When the etheric double is examined against a white background through a deep carmine screen with the light properly arranged, it may become a rose colour, quite different to the carmine tint the white background has assumed. When carefully looked at this will appear lineated, and the fine striae to be the source of the colour.

The use of coloured screens has been found to be absolutely necessary for the detection of certain constituents, as well as the elucidation of some of the attributes of the aura, so that a few words on the action of the different screens will not be out of place, although the digression may appear very elementary. Since all the colours behave in a similar manner, red alone will be considered in detail.

1st. Upon looking through a dark red screen all white objects will seem red, red substances will become lighter in shade, and all the other colours are darker. This can be clearly seen if, in the ordinary daylight, a piece of white and a piece of black paper be placed side by side, and across them is laid a strip of red paper of a moderate shade, half on the one and half on the other. When this arrangement is examined through a deep red screen the red paper will be found to have lost nearly all its colour, and the contrast between it and the black paper will be increased. On the other hand the strip and the white paper will approximate in colour.

2nd. Keep the papers in the same position and view them through the pale red screen. The red paper will then have a darker tint, but the contrast between it and the white paper will remain unaltered, each having gained proportionately more red colour.

Theoretically, the red paper ought to show out more against the black, but the result depends upon the purity of the black.

Should the red paper have a very dark shade, the contrast between it and the black paper will remain unchanged, while that between the red and the white papers will be lessened.

The reason for these effects is obvious when it is recollected that white daylight is composed of all the colours of the visible solar spectrum, and that an object appears white when it reflects the whole of these colours in the proper proportions, but becomes coloured when it reflects a portion of the spectrum, absorbing the remainder. In the majority of cases a coloured object absorbs a limited amount of light, so that it reflects its own coloured rays with the addition of more or less white light. The shade depends upon the proportion of the white light mixed with the coloured rays, and is really a quantitative expression. If the white light which is being reflected by the coloured object has those rays, that are similar to the ones absorbed by the object, abstracted by any means, then the object will have a darker hue. This is what is done by the coloured screens.

As daylight is limited in quantity, a dark red screen will absorb the whole of it, with the exception of the red rays which are transmitted through it to the eyes. These rays are also limited in quantity. The white paper in the above experiments reflects practically all the daylight falling on it, including the red rays. These are the only rays not absorbed by the screen, consequently the white paper when seen through the red screen must appear red. The red paper, if not too dark, reflects the red rays mixed with a large proportion of others that are absorbed by the red screen. The red and white papers appear similar in colour when viewed through the red screen, because the former absorbs a portion of the white light which, had it been reflected, (as it is by the white paper), would have been absorbed by the screen. When a pale red screen replaces the dark one, all the red rays will be transmitted with the addition of a large quantity of the remaining rays of the spectrum, so that the red paper will have its colour intensified by being observed through this screen. It will be necessary to bear in mind that the light red screen will act precisely in the same manner in a dim light as the dark does in a bright. When these experiments are repeated, the results may not be exactly as described, on account of the differences in the colours used, and the amount of light employed, but the principle will remain.

One other experiment is needed. If a red hot coal, either in the dark or in the light, be looked at through a red screen of any shade, the red colour of the coal will appear intensified, as it is self-luminous, and thus colour is added to colour.

It is a fair inference to draw from these experiments, that the etheric double is quite transparent, and surrounds the body closely. When observed under very favourable conditions it is distinctly striated with delicate lines of a deeper hue than the encircling and apparently homogeneous stroma. It is probable that the whole of the etheric double receives its tint from these coloured lines. The hue is a beautiful rose, which certainly contains more blue than there is in carmine. It is difficult to understand how this rose tint can be seen against a white background coloured with the carmine screen, and as yet there is no satisfactory explanation forthcoming, unless the etheric double be self-luminous, or some phenomenon with the ultra-violet portion of the spectrum be involved.

CHAPTER III

The Inner Aura

THE aura proper lies just outside the etheric double. For some time it was considered indivisible, although the part nearest the body is evidently more dense, and has a different texture from the more distant portion; nevertheless, the one appeared to shade into the other too gradually to be treated separately. After many trials it was found possible to divide the aura into two distinct parts by the help of coloured screens, other than those containing dicyanin. These parts are known as the outer and inner auras. The new screens have made a great addition to our knowledge by opening up an increased field of observation in disease, and affording an explanation of several phenomena which were previously inexplicable.

The most useful screens for the present purpose are C, a deep carmine; Ca, a light carmine; and B, a pale blue, (methylene blue). After the patient has been inspected in the ordinary way without a screen, the aura may be examined through B. By its aid the two auras can be clearly distinguished. The inner will look denser and generally more granular, its outer margin more defined, but its structure incompletely differentiated. The outer aura stands out plainly, and its distal border can be perceived with tolerable accuracy, so that its size and shape can be noted. Next the screen, Ca, may be employed when the outer aura will be more or less eliminated, according to the light admitted and the tint of the screen. These factors should be so arranged that the two auras may be visible, to allow the width of the inner aura as seen through the screen, B, to be verified.

The last step is to survey the aura through the dark carmine screen, C, when much more light will be required. It might reasonably be expected that the screen C, would cut off some part of the inner aura as well as the whole of the outer. However, the conclusion arrived at, after repeated trials, is that no obliteration takes place if the light has been properly regulated. It is especially to guard against this error that the breadth of the inner aura has to be determined by the screens B, and Ca. The inner aura when seen through the deep carmine screen usually ranges between one and a half and three inches and a half in breadth, according to the age and individuality of the patient, being, perhaps, relatively wider, although absolutely narrower, in a child than in an adult. When the observer becomes expert, he may save time by omitting the examination through the pale carmine and blue screens.

In health the boundaries of the inner aura are determined by the distance the striae reach, when examined through the dark carmine screen. As a rule the breadth is uniform all over the head and trunk, and generally, but not always, slightly narrower down the limbs. Occasionally both in males and females it will become wider and coarser locally, but as striation can be discerned though perhaps with difficulty, there can be no uncertainty about limits. This is quite different to what takes place in local bodily derangements. The commonest position for the enlargement is at the sides of the waist in a woman, and the next is the small of the back in a man, but a granular appearance in this latter situation is generally pathological, and will be described later on. Females often show enlargements of the aura in front of the breasts and abdomen, and these will be alluded to in the chapter devoted to pregnancy.

As a rule the inner aura follows the contour of the body, its proximal border being in juxta-position to the etheric double, or in the majority of cases apparently to the body itself. The outer margin is free, irregularly crenated with large curves. The structure consists of excessively fine grains, so arranged as to present a striated appearance. The striae, too, are fine beyond description, parallel to each other, and running at right angles to the body. They show no intrinsic colour. They seem to be collected into bundles, with the longest lines in the centre, and the shortest outside. These bundles are massed together, and their shapes cause the outlines of the inner aura. In most people during health, striation is manifest, without the slightest difficulty, while in others of a delicate constitution or during ill-health, it can be only detected, if at all, by the most careful arrangement of the light, and the selection of a suitable screen.

Wherever this aura encroaches on the etheric double, it will almost always obliterate the latter, and this fact raises the issue whether its granules are not always present in the etheric double, although invisible, or whether they are driven outwards by some force emanating from the body, thus leaving it destitute of all granules and in consequence quite transparent. In the latter part of the last chapter, this question was considered when the patient was in good health, and the conclusion arrived at was that the etheric double contained no granules. In the last paragraph it was stated that the inner aura, as far as could be discovered, had no colour, and in Chapter II the striae of the etheric double seemed to be the origin of the rose colour occasionally perceived. If the striae of the inner aura and the etheric double are, as is very likely, continuous, the descriptions

are seemingly at variance. The descrepancy, however, is only superficial, as in the inner aura the faint
rose colour would be overwhelmed by the red shade
of the screen, and by the deeper hue the aura assumes.
Both ill health and local diseases alter all the conditions, and it seems probable that the granular
substance of the inner aura does at times invade the
etheric double. This subject will be discussed in
another chapter.

The outer aura commences where the inner leaves
off, and spreads round the body to a variable distance.
It has no absolutely sharp outline but gradually
vanishes into space, although in the majority of
instances its outer border is sufficiently obvious for
measurement. The above statement is not, however,
quite correct for all cases, because occasionally under
very favourable circumstances, an exceedingly fine
haze can be perceived extending outwards for a
considerable distance, which gives the impression that
one is more aware of its presence, than really able
to distinguish it. This elusive mist is presumably a
continuation of the outer aura, as on every occasion
it has been noticed, the periphery of the latter has
been less definite than usual. It has only been
observed in people with extensive auras. For the
sake of reference the phenomenon has been termed
the *Ultra-outer aura*.

At the end of 1915, a patient's aura was inspected
which gave most interesting and unlooked for results,
and was the first instance that seemed likely to afford
any assistance in elucidating the nature of the ultra-
outer aura.

Case 18. (Fig. 19). W.B., twenty-nine years of
age was first examined in 1914. She was a stout
largely built woman with rather small bones. Four
years previously she was thin but rapidly gained
flesh, and became fat and flabby. Her net weight
was one hundred and sixty-eight pounds. She was

anæmic and complained of weakness and shortness
of breath, and inability to walk any distance without
great pain in her back.   Heart sounds were normal
but muffled from fat.   Her thyroid was rather small.

The outer aura was of good shape, and round the
head and trunk could be almost classed as wide, being

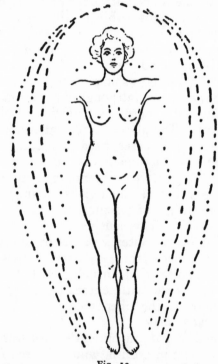

Fig. 19.

. . . .   Inner aura.
— — — — — —   Outer aura, when not well.
—.—.—.—.—.—   Outer aura, in good health.
—..—..—..—..—   Outer aura, after electrifying positively.

nine inches and a half in breadth, narrowing down
to four and a half inches by the ankles.   It was very
distinct but at the outer margin not well defined,
merging into a fairly obvious ultra-outer aura.   A
side view showed the haze to be four and a half inches

in front of the body and by the sides of the thighs
and legs, while at the small of the back it was six.
The inner aura, as might be expected from the state
of her health, was rather faint. It was three and a
half inches all over her body. The complementary
coloured band exhibited a yellow patch on her back
commencing as high up as the lower dorsal vertebræ,
and increasing in breadth over the sacrum. It is
interesting to note that the surface electricity (see
page 103), was even all over the body, and reached
a high intensity.

She was examined a second time in November of
the same year. This was fortunate, as details given
above were verified, and precluded any suggestion
of error in the previous inspection.

In May, 1915, the patient was in perfect health,
feeling strong and energetic, able to walk a long distance
without fatigue or pain in her back. Her weight was
reduced nearly a stone, and her flesh had become
firmer.

Both auras were very distinct, the outer being
twelve inches by the trunk, ten by the head, and five
and a half by the ankles. *Its distal margin was well
defined*, quite as much so as in ordinary cases, more so
than is usual with wide auras. Not the slightest
trace of the ultra-outer aura could be detected. The
inner aura was noted as being four inches in breadth.
Whether this aura had gained half an inch in width
is impossible to say, as at the first inspection, owing
to the state of her health, it was indistinct, and might
have been a little wider than stated, while at this
observation it was perfectly clear. There was no
doubt about the enlargement of the outer aura.

The woman was then placed upon an insulated
stool and electrically charged by means of the large
Wimshurst machine. The auras vanished in the
usual manner (page 91), but the operation was continued some short time after they had disappeared.

Subsequently the auras slowly returned, and when they had extended to their full amount, the outer had gained three inches in width. This was now fifteen inches in breadth, and the distal margin was fairly plain. Even this width was well within the observed outer limits of the ultra-outer aura seen on previous occasions. This experiment points to the correctness of the assumption that the ultra-outer aura is only an ill-defined extension of the outer.

Another instance is extremely interesting, as it affords additional information, and at the same time confirms the observations made in the last case.

Case 11 continued. In June, 1915, the artist's model previously referred to (case 11), was first scrutinized very carefully, to ensure that her auras were in their normal condition. Search was especially made for an ultra-outer aura, of which, however, not the slightest indication could be detected. The inner aura had the average standard of distinctness of health, and striation was clearly seen. She was placed then on an insulated stool and negatively electrified by the aid of a large Wimshurst machine. The effect was the usual one, but for some unknown reason the aura did not, and in all subsequent experiments has never disappeared as rapidly as it does with most people. The charging with electricity was persevered with for some minutes after the aura had vanished. A hand held near the woman's body, while there was no aura to be seen, induced a ray as usual, but there was no auric response. This fact was interesting as it was unknown whether a ray would reach the body without reinforcement. Whether it did absolutely come into contact could not be determined.

As soon as the electric charge had been got rid of, the aura began to return slowly. In a few minutes the measurements were taken a second time. The aura was ten inches by the head, fifteen by the trunk,

and six by the legs, and was a good ovoid in shape.
It was six inches in front, and at the small of the back
nine, and it proceeded down in a straight line from the
shoulders to the widest part of the nates, and was
six inches lower down. The inner aura was four
inches wide but indistinct. It was quite impossible
to decide whether striation existed at first, as the
changes proceeded too quickly to allow sufficient time
for examination. After the lapse of half an hour
another inspection was made. The inner aura still
remained unaltered, while the outer was found to be
still more extended, having gained another three
inches, while its margin was ill-defined, presenting the
appearance of an ultra-outer aura. The outermost
portion was similar to the true ultra-outer aura, but a
little closer to the body the haze seemed to be transitional between it and the ordinary outer aura, which
apparently proves that the former is merely an
extension of the latter.

If the ultra-outer aura be only an extension of the
outer, it is not unlikely that it may be always present,
whether the outer is wide or not, but too faint for our
existing means of observation. Auras of an average
breadth, and even narrow ones, can be enlarged by
statical electricity, as will be described later on.
(Page 93.)

The common size and shape of the outer aura has
been fully described in chapter I. It consists of a
faint amorphous cloud and appears entirely structure-
less, capable of being illuminated, but not, in the
ordinary acceptation of the word, auto-luminous.
(See page 78.)

During a prolonged inspection it will be evident that
the aura is not absolutely stable, as it constantly
undergoes changes in various parts. A portion may
become more brilliant and, after a few seconds or
minutes, fade back to its original state while some
other area commences the same cycle of changes.

Usually these fluctuations occur spontaneously or without any assignable cause.

Rays, the most frequent of temporary changes, may for practical purposes be divided into three groups :—1. Rays which proceed from one part to another part of the body, or from one person to another. 2. Streams which issue straight from the body into space. 3. Brighter patches entirely surrounded by the aura, which, as they seem to arise in the same manner as a ray of the other two groups, have been termed pseudo-rays.

The last group consisting of pseudo-rays will be considered first. They are always seen in close proximity to the body and nowhere else. They occur in the inner aura and are bounded by the body on the one hand, and the outer aura on the other. In their common form they are elongated, with their long axis running parallel to the body. Their shafts can usually be seen quite distinctly, but their ends gradually fade away. They generally appear suddenly, and vanish just as quickly. When examined through the dark carmine screen, striation in many instances may be recognized, but at other times granulation. These pseudo-rays are not as common as the rays in the other groups. They must not be confounded with the granular patches of the inner aura so frequently met with, although the writer must confess that for a long time he formed a wrong impression about them.

The rays of the first group are, perhaps, the most brilliant of all, and may be observed issuing from any part of the body, and running to any other, provided the two parts are sufficiently near to each other, and the angles between them not too great. They are generally emitted from irregularities of the surface rather than from smooth portions of the body. When the arm is held away from the body, one or more connecting rays may be seen. Here they apparently proceed from the trunk to the arm, rather in the reverse direction, because the rays are perpendicular to the former, and make different angles with the latter. Another good example, and one that is constantly occurring, is to be seen during the time the patient is standing with his hands resting on his hips and his elbows extended outwards, a ray may emerge from the axilla and pass' towards the wrist. An analogous effect may be obtained if the observer holds a hand a short distance from the patient, when rays will develop between the two, affording an illustration of the mutual attraction between the auras of different people. By careful observation it will be seen that these rays are formed chiefly by prolongations of the inner aura, and for some short time after the removal of the observer's hand, the inner aura will remain intensified. This phenomenon has already been utilized for demonstration purposes. (Page 7.)

A well marked case of external influence producing a ray will be described later on. On one occasion a ray passing between two people's hands was seen to change in a few seconds from a bright yellow into a liquid ruby red.

Rays of the second group are apparently projected into space at right angles to the body, without any deviation. In many instances they are only perceptible as far as the boundary of the outer aura, though it is by no means uncommon to see them prolonged into situations occupied by the ultra-outer aura, if existent, but whether they stretch beyond this region is impossible to ascertain. As the rays proceed outwards they generally fade away. The sides of the shafts are usually parallel (rarely divergent), and bluntly pointed. This is especially the case when they are derived from the fingers.

A straight line perpendicular to the body is evidently the natural direction of the rays, but under external stimulus they may be deflected, and proceed

at any angle from the body, but have never been seen
to curve.   It is quite easy to watch this phenomenon,
as rays emanating from the tips will appear continuous
with the fingers as long as nothing to attract them is
near.   If the fingers of the other hand be held eight
to ten inches away and moved about, all the rays
issuing from the one to the other will be quite straight,
although the movements will constantly alter the
angles made by them and the fingers on either side.
There will never be the slightest curve.   A pretty
illustration is provided by the following experiment :
Let a person hold his hands apart as just described,
and a second likewise only at right angles in the same
plane, one hand on each side of the above pair.   The
main rays will then form a cross, and secondary rays
will connect the adjacent hands.   Not one of these
rays will exhibit any curve.

The size of a ray varies much, and depends largely
upon its position.   For example, rays proceeding
from the shoulders are almost always broad, while
those emitted from the finger tips rarely exceed one
and a half diameters of a digit.` Although rays have
been seen springing from every part of the body under
favourable conditions, yet they have been seldom
noticed coming from the subject towards the observer
when the two are facing each other.   This fact is
explained by their extreme transparency, on account
of which their visibility depends upon a more suitable
background than the skin affords.   Foreshortening
also adds to the difficulty.   A black background is the
most efficient, because rays seen against it are made
as distinct as possible.   Even though rays emerging
from a patient towards the observer may be invisible,
yet their presence can sometimes be detected by
their causing an alteration in the complementary
coloured band, as will be described later on.

Besides the ordinary bluish colour, red, and yellow
have been noticed tingeing the rays.   Perhaps they

can take on other colours. They apparently do not arise from the outer aura, as they have never been observed affecting either its density or brightness.

As their structure resembles that of the inner aura, the conclusion is arrived at, that the two have a common origin ; in fact, a ray is composed of extended fasciculi of the inner aura.

Allusion has already been made to the circumstance that when one person holds a hand near to any part of the body of another, rays proceed from the one to the other. The structure of one such compound ray was elucidated by the following observation :

A Negro (case 6), came to have his aura inspected. This was very coarse in texture and of a hazy brown colour. When the observer's hand was held near his body, the usual conjoint ray was formed and could be easily analysed into light coloured rays interspersed with brown rays, each stretching the *whole distance* between the two persons without any amalgamation.

It is worthy of notice that these rays can be more readily obtained between two points than betwixt two large smooth surfaces. For example, if the observer holds one finger near the side of the person under examination, a ray will promptly appear, and will certainly be seen sooner and more definitely near the finger than the body. Afterwards it may or may not become equally brilliant throughout its whole length. Again if the observer holds a finger the same distance from a pointed part of the patient's body, such as the nose, chin, bended elbow, or finger, the rays are more quickly generated and frequently brighter. Thus, if the expression be allowed, the auric potential is greater at points than over a flat surface, in that respect resembling static electricity.

Again if the observer holds a bare arm parallel to a subject's body, the intervening auras will become brighter and will blend, showing that a mutual attraction exists between the two auras. In all these cases the distance between the subject and the observer should be sufficient to allow an interval of one or two inches between their visible auras. It is extremely important for both persons to be mentally as passive as possible. More will be said later on about the influence of the mind upon the aura, but the following observation is enough to show the necessity for caution. Let the observer hold his finger some eighteen inches from the subject. He will then find that the emission from finger tips of a ray towards the subject is so far under voluntary control, that by an effort the gap can be more or less easily bridged.

CHAPTER IV

Optical Problems

The human aura is invisible in total darkness, and can best and most easily be seen in a dim light, when the eyes are in an incompletely dark adapted state. As this condition is of great importance in relation to various problems that will require discussion, a short and concise account of it will not be out of place. Without taking into consideration any except the most elementary physiological facts, it is well known that in the normal and healthy eye the iris is contracted more or less in proportion to the brilliance of the light. (Changes relating to accommodation will not be referred to here.) The aperture of the pupil is consequently small and allows external objects to be focused as sharply as possible on the fovea. This part of the retina is composed of cones which are colour-sensitive to all the rays of the ordinary visible solar spectrum. Mixtures of these rays in certain proportions will cause the sensation of white light, while light of a single wave length or of mixtures of wave lengths other than in proportion to produce white light, cause colour-sensations.

In the dark adapted state the iris becomes more dilated and the eye more sensitive to slight changes of illumination. The larger pupil also permits more light to pass, which of itself is an advantage in a dim light, but what is still more important it allows a larger portion of the retina to be illuminated. This fresh portion of the retina differs from the fovea inasmuch as it contains a great number of rods far outnumbering the cones as the periphery is reached. The rods are considered colour-blind and their stimulation only produces a grey sensation. They are acted upon chiefly by *the shorter and more refrangible rays*. In the dark adapted state the point of maximum luminosity has been *removed towards the violet* end of the spectrum to the yellow-green.

It is highly important to determine, if possible, how the dicyanin screen enables the aura to be perceived. The solution of this question depends partly upon the attributes of the aura itself, but to a still greater extent upon the action exerted upon the chemical upon the eyes.

On one occasion before systemic examinations of the auras had been undertaken, a lady wished to see the haze round the arm and hand. A dark blue screen was given to her to look through at the light, but after using it she was quite unable to see the aura. In the meantime it had been noticed that a methylene blue screen had inadvertently been handed to her. She was allowed to use it without being informed of the mistake, because this was regarded as a good test of the comparative value of the two screens. She afterwards looked at the light through the proper screen, and immediately the blinds had been regulated, could detect the aura. Twice again at different times has the methylene blue screen been unconsciously substituted for a dicyanin one, and it has also been tried intentionally several times and always found inert.

Reichenbach, in his " Researches on Magnetism," gives instances of over fifty sensitives who were able to see light proceeding from magnets, etc., in total darkness. Unless all these people were frauds (and there is no reason to class them as such), they must either have possessed very acute sight, which enabled them to detect an illumination too faint to produce any sensation in ordinary men and women, or else that the quality of their sight was different, and permitted them to descry phenomena usually invisible. This latter supposition is probably correct, the force emanating from magnets, etc., producing vibrations situate at some distance beyond the ordinary visible Solar Spectrum. The same, too, may be true of the human aura. One reason for coming to the above conclusion is, that if the effective undulations are identical with those at any part of the visible spectrum, there should be a large number of people with sufficiently acute vision to have observed so remarkable a phenomenon at the poles of a magnet and the somewhat similar appearances here referred to as the aura. This argument will be still further strengthened if it can be proved that clairvoyants do not possess more than the average acuteness of vision for all ordinary purposes. A clairvoyant was consulted and kindly replied that " the gift was in no way connected with the ordinary sight," and in fact that some clairvoyants have inferior ordinary vision. Under these circumstances it may be safely concluded, that individuals who can see the human aura and the haze round magnets, etc., obtain their powers, not from keenness of sight, but from ability to see rays not included in the ordinary visible spectrum.

If some people are able to distinguish undulations outside the usual visible spectrum, there would seem to be no particular reason why, by the aid of some apparatus, or even by treatment of the eyes, others should not be able to do the same. This is exactly what is claimed for dicyanin.

Although from the very first it was recognized that dicyanin exerted a peculiar influence upon the organs of sight, yet for a long time the part of the eyes affected and the nature of the change brought about remained utterly incomprehensible, and any attempt at an explanation can even now be only hypothetical.

Nine or ten years ago, when the writer was investigating by mechanical means forces emanating from the body, a beam of light reflected from a small movable mirror (similar to those used for galvan· ometers) upon a scale was employed, and as it was necessary to read accurately the deflection at a distance of eight feet, use was made of a pair of opera glasses that required to be racked out to the full extent for clear vision. One day some years later, happening to look through the glasses, he found to his surprise that they did not need the same extension for perfect vision, even though the object was only half the distance away. The only feasible explanation that can be offered for this occurrence, is that the focal length of his eyes had in· some manner been shortened virtually or absolutely, and as no other cause was forthcoming, the effect could only be attributed to the constant peering through the dicyanin screen. That some alteration has taken place in his eyes, is confirmed by the fact that the time of the visual examination of the aura was commenced (over ten years ago), the writer was contemplating buying stronger spectacles, which. as he ceased to be troubled by his sight, he forgot to do and he has not done to the present day, moreover his reading distance has actually diminished, though accommodation, of course, has not improved.

Shortly after this discovery, a friend, a medical man, mentioned that a gentleman to whom he had been showing the aura by means of the dicyanin screen, did not need glasses for reading or writing for over twenty-four hours afterwards, although previously he could not distinguish print properly without their aid. These two cases led to the conclusion that it was quite possible that the dye might to some degree affect a number of people in a similar manner, and might perhaps furnish at least a partial explanation of the occular changes required before the aura can be seen. But before describing the experiments undertaken to put this idea to the test, it may be remarked that several other instances have been met with where persons after using dicyanin screens have taken up a book or paper and have proffered the information that they were able to see the print without glasses better than they could ordinarily. The two following are amongst the first recorded cases. A lady, while her husband was talking, took up a book and exclaimed " that she could read it quite easily without spectacles," which, by the way, she had left at home, " a thing she had not been able to do for years." In the second instance, a medical man, after an allusion to the property of dicyanin under discussion, tried to read a newspaper without glasses. In general, he could only accomplish this when he held the paper out at full arm's length, but now he found that he was able to read it when held six to eight inches nearer.

Every person who has remarked upon his or her sight being temporarily improved, was presbyopic, though not to any great extent. The effect has never been noticed in emmetropia or myopia.

As it seemed impossible that coloured screens could influence accommodation, all experiments were conducted from the point of view of the other functions of the eyes. For this purpose a microscope was used, on which the fine adjustment lowered or raised the objective 1/100 of an inch for each revolution. The wheel was divided into ten parts, so that each division corresponded to 1/1000 of an inch. In table 3 this unit is denoted by the letters mi (mille-inches). The lowest eyepiece and the inch and a half objective were employed. Screens were prepared by filling glass cells with weak aqueous solutions of different dyes — carmine, K yellow, methylene blue, and gentian violet respectively. The exact depth of the colours seemed immaterial provided they permitted sufficient illumination of the object on the stage, but this condition unfortunately introduced a disturbing factor, viz., the large amount of white light which passed through the screens.

The procedure adopted was as follows : The observer focused a selected bristle of the proboscis of a blow-fly (the object used) as sharply as possible by means of the coarse adjustment, the fine adjustment being placed at zero. Directly a sharp image had been obtained, he looked away for a second or two and then glanced at the object as quickly as he could, to determine whether the focus was correct. Further adjustment was made if required. This was done two or three times to ensure the elimination of accommodation effects.

A coloured screen was then inserted between the mirror and the object. The bristle had now to be focused a second time. This time the fine adjusting screw alone was used, with the same precautions as before. This procedure was repeated with each filter-screen in turn, the position of the fine adjusting wheel being noted for every observation and the results recorded.

The observer next looked at the light through the deep dicyanin screen for about thirty seconds, and then repeated the whole series of observations, focusing the object first in white light, and afterwards through each filter-screen in rotation.

The following is a detailed account of one experiment. The experimenter (A in the table) taking the precautions mentioned above, focused the bristle with the coarse adjustment, the fine adjusting standing at zero. The result was called O. A yellow screen was then placed under the object, which remained in perfect focus. Result O. The filter was then changed for a red one. The bristle was no longer in focus, to rectify which the wheel had to be turned one tenth of a revolution in the direction that lifted the objective

away from the object. The result was designated
—1 mi. A blue screen was now inserted, and the fine
adjusting wheel had to be rotated one division from
zero in the opposite direction. This made the objective approach the slide, and the effect was termed
+1 mi. With the violet filter sharp definition was not
attained until the wheel had been turned two further
divisions, altogether three tenths of a revolution, or
+3 mi.

The observer next peered through the dark dicyanin
screen at the light for about thirty seconds, and then
refocused the object without the intervention of any
screen, when it was found necessary to lower the
objective +2.5 divisions from zero, which result was
duly recorded. The red, yellow, blue and violet
screens were then inserted in turn, but between each
trial the observer looked at the light through the dark
dicyanin screen for a few seconds. The resultant
figures were for red +1 mi., yellow +1 mi., blue
+2 mi., and violet +3.5 mi. This observer was
tested on three separate occasions, and the readings
obtained showed no variations.

Most of the observers in these experiments were
medical men, and every one was experienced in the
use of the microscope. Only those results (fifty in
number) which passed the strictest tests as detailed
above were kept. One or two observers did not take
sufficient pains, but the cause of most failures was the
difficulty in overcoming accommodation. During
each series of experiments the focus of the microscope
was purposely disturbed two or three times, when
practicable, without the knowledge of the observer,
and unless the re-adjustes completely coincided with
the original readings, the series was rejected. Consequently not more than one series out of every three or
four was accepted.

It was interesting to notice that the greater the
alteration of the focus required after looking through

the dicyanin screen, the more easily was the aura perceived. In no case when the change for white light after the use of the dicyanin screen exceeded that requisite after the insertion of the blue screen alone, was there the slightest difficulty in seeing the aura. When the dicyanin produced a less effect than did the blue screen, the more nearly the readings approximated, the more readily did the observer perceive the aura. If a microscope be used for ascertaining whether a person is likely to see the aura easily, it will be unnecessary to traverse the whole series of tests. The following procedure will be quite sufficient : First focus the object in ordinary light, next with a blue screen beneath the object, and lastly again in daylight after looking through the dicyanin screen. Unfortunately, however, this method can rarely be employed, as few people are sufficiently conversant with the use of the instrument.

Some observers find it difficult to obtain a good definition when the violet screen is beneath the object. The trouble is due to the fact that the dye (gentian violet) used gives two bright bands with spectroscope, with one maximum between $4,000\,\lambda$ and $4,500\,\lambda$, and the other between $6,500\,\lambda$ and $7,000\,\lambda$.* (*Vide* Mees' " Atlas of Absorption Spectra.") The colours being so far apart in the spectrum are antagonistic to one another. The violet screen has only been retained for convenience, as very little importance can be placed upon results obtained by its aid. It ought to be borne in mind that the violet in the spectrum consists of wave lengths adjacent to each other, while all the violet pigments and dyes are merely mixtures of red and blue.

In table 3 the first three series were obtained by observers who were under the age of forty, the next three between forty and sixty, and the third over the

---

* λ is the symbol for Angstrom's unit, viz., 10^{-10} metre, or one-tenth millionth of a millimetre.

TABLE III

	WHITE	RED	YELLOW	BLUE	VIOLET
A	0 +2.5	−1 +1	0 +1	+1 +2	+3 +3.5
B	0 +3	−1 +1.75	0 +2	+2 +2	+4 +4.5
C	0 +2.5	−1.5 +0.5	0 0	+2.5 +2.5	+2.5 +2.5
D	0 +1	−1 +0.75	0 +0.75	+1 +1.5	+3 +3.5
E	0 +2	−1.5 +0.5	0 +0.5	+1.75 +1.75	+1.75 +1.75
F	0 +2.5	0 +1	+1 +1	+1 +3	
G	0 +1	−1 −0.5	0 0	+1.5 +2	+2 +2
H	0 +1	0.75 +0.25	0 +0.75	+1.75 +2	+1.75 +2
I	0 +1.5	−1 +0.5	0 0	+1 +1	
J	0 +2	−1 0	0 +1	+2.5 +2.5	
K	0 +6.5	−1 +2.25	0 +5.25	+2.5 +6	
L	0 +2.25	−1 +07	+0.09 +1	+2.4 +2.8	

age of sixty. The tenth observer was a medical student whose accommodation was temporarily suppressed by atropine, the eleventh that of a clairvoyant. The last readings are the means of fifty cases. The upper reading of each series is before, and the lower after looking at the light through the dicyanin screen. The figures explain why persons over the age of fifty years have greater difficulty of seeing the aura at their early trials than younger people.

The eleventh case is extremely interesting as the observer was a clairvoyant, and the writer was especially gratified at meeting her, because he had often wondered how far clairvoyant's eyes differed from the normal in ordinary respect. Fortunatey this lady was quite expert with the microscope and was painstaking. Her husband was the possessor of a very fine instrument which she was in the habit of using. It will be noted that before looking through the dicyanin screen, the coloured filters under the microscopic object only produced the average effect upon her eyes. The dicyanin had, however, a greater influence than in any other instance met with before or since. This was the lady previously referred to as being able to see better without her glasses than she had done for years. (Page 61.)

In order to appreciate these experiments to the full extent, it is necessary to recall a few details of elementary physics. Ordinary daylight is well known to consist of undulations in the ether of different wave lengths. The visible solar spectrum is divided into six main divisions (purposely omitting indigo), viz., red, orange, yellow, green, blue and violet. If a quartz prism be used there is a portion of the spectrum lying beyond the violet named the lavender-grey, which some people cannot see. The intensity of the luminous spectrum in daylight is greatest near the yellow region, from which point it gradually diminishes towards the red and violet ends. There is no physical reason why the yellow should be more energetic than any other colour of the spectrum, and the cause is purely physiological.

Although full of marvels the human eye is by no means a faultless optical instrument. It is imperfectly corrected for chromatic aberration, since the various colours come to a focus on different planes. The red being the least refrangible, has its focus furthest from, and the violet nearest, the lens. The focus of the yellow is about midway between the red and the violet, and in the normal eye the yellow rays fall exactly on the retina, while the other colours come to a focus a little in front or behind it. Correction is arranged for in the brain centres. Since the red rays are focused behind the retina, the lens would have to be moved slightly forwards in order to make them fall exactly on the retina. This is equivalent to moving the objective of the microscope a little further from the object. The blue and the violet rays on the other hand would require the lens to be shifted nearer the retina, tantamount to bringing the object glass closer to the object.

Thus when the object has been first focused in white light, and again after the coloured filters have been inserted beneath the object one after another, it will be necessary to move the objective further from the slide for the less and nearer for the more refrangible rays.

Now to return to the dicyanin screen. Before looking at the light through this screen in the experiments just detailed, red was the only colour negative to the white and yellow, while the blue and violet were positive. In the series fully described the observer A, after having peered through the dicyanin screen, found red, yellow and blue all negative, while the violet remained positive but only to a small extent. This becomes more evident if + 2.5 mi.* be deducted from each of the figures, making the corrected readings for red —1.5 mi., yellow —1.5 mi., blue —0.5 mi., and the violet —1 mi. These experiments prove that some alteration has taken place in the eye equivalent to a lengthening of the eye, or a shortening of the principal focus, which enables presbyopics to *read without glasses*. It would also appear that white and yellow rays, at or near the

*+2.5 mi is the amount of adjustment required to bring the object into focus again in the white light after peering through the dicyanin screen.

D line, come to a focus at the true principal focus of
the normal eye ; in the eyes after exposure to the
dark dicyanin screen, rays on the violet side, probably
in the yellow-green or green, come to a focus at that
point, and thus possibly the phenomenon is associated
with the extension of the visual powers into the
regions of the spectrum beyond the usual limits.   The
impression induced upon the sensitized eye by a visible
aura, etc., might then be the result, at least partially,
of the action of ultra-violet rays.   This, too, would
be the explanation of the colour variations and
changes as seen with or without screens or complementary coloured bands.   Great support is given to
this hypothesis by the fact that the greater the alteration produced by a dicyanin screen in the focusing
test of the microscope, the easier it is to see the aura.

It is evident from these experiments that dicyanin
has the power of shortening the focus of the eye, yet
there are very great difficulties in determining the
way this is achieved.   Accommodation, as it apparently remains unaltered, seems to take no part in the
transaction, and as yet no test has been devised, the
question must be treated entirely theoretically.   For
this purpose the eye has to be considered under three
different aspects, viz., the physical, the chemical and
the nervous.

The equivalent of shortening the principal focus
of the eye can be obtained by :—

1.   Increase of the curvature of the cornea or lens.
This proposition is so improbable that it requires no
consideration.

2.   By the increase of the refractive index of the
media.

If the change be due to this cause, the fluid media
will be the most likely parts to be affected.

a.   By the increase of solids in solution.

b.   By a greater tension.

c.   By a chemical change in the substance.

a. The first of these assumptions could not take place during the short time of peering through the screen.

b. The second would be merely an incipient glaucoma, and the repetition of the sensitizing of the eye might cause all the inconvenience of this disease. As no stage of this affection affords symptoms at all similar to those produced by dicyanin, this proposition gives no help.

c. It thus seems that a chemical change is the only possible explanation ot the production of an increase of the refractive index. What the alteration consists of cannot be imagined, but that a true modification has really taken place is strengthened by the peculiarities in the colour perception as will be considered later on.

Even though it is unreasonable to imagine that a shortening of the focus of the eye can be accomplished directly through nervous agency, yet there is good cause to suppose that dicyanin exerts an influence upon the nervous system of the eye ; either on the retina or the central ganglia, separately or in conjunction. Comparison between the two following experiments, one diminishing and the other adding to the efficiency of the eye, is instructive.

Exp. 1. Let a person look at a primary coloured band as directed in chapter vi, only colour-blinding one eye instead of two. If he then looks at a white screen with both eyes the complementary coloured band is visible. If he closes the unaffected eye the spectre still remains. If he shuts the colour-blinded eye no complementary coloured band can be observed.

Exp. 2. A lady who had never seen the aura tried to detect it under the most favourable conditions of light and background, but completely failed. One eye was sensitized with dicyanin in the usual manner, while the other was closed. The result was that she could immediately see the aura when looked for with both eyes. It was equally plain when she closed the non-sensitized eye. When she used the latter alone she could see the aura, but not so distinctly. After peering through the dicyanin screen at the light with both eyes, each eye was equally perceptive.

Exp. 3. A, failed to see the aura, but after sensitizing one eye by means of the dicyanin screen, he found both eyes were equally efficient, although not quite to the same extent as when he had subsequently peered through the screen with both eyes in the ordinary manner.

Exp. 4. P, was unable to perceive the aura. After sensitizing one eye only with the dicyanin screen, she remained incapable of detecting it, when either using one or both eyes. After looking at the light through the same screen in the ordinary manner with both eyes, she obtained the power of seeing the haze.

Exp. 5. G K, looked for the aura but could not see the slightest sign of it. He then looked at the light with his right eye for about thirty seconds through the dicyanin screen, while he closed and covered the left. Directly afterwards he could distinguish the aura with his left eye, but it was not quite as distinct as when the right eye was used alone. Sensitizing both eyes increased the efficiency slightly.

These experiments have been repeated several times with the similar results.

The inferences from these experiments are intricate and very difficult to interpret. The only explanation that seems to be forthcoming is that the observer has naturally a slight power of the perception of the aura, but so slight as to be latent until it has been aroused by some outside stimulation. This idea is strengthened to some extent by a lady who tried to see the aura without having peered through the dicyanin screen and completely failed. However, she persevered for some ten minutes, when she said that she thought she could see the haze but was uncertain whether the impression was not merely imagination. Her eyes were then influenced by the dicyanin screen when she could immediately distinguish the aura plainly, there being no difference to what she had noticed before except in distinctness.

The next step is the consideration of the conditions in which the aura can be seen. The most favourable is a dim light (not complete darkness), which is also best suited for practical work. The haze can often be seen round any part of the human body against a dark background in ordinary daylight when viewed through coloured screens.

The depth of shade required for these screens is dependent upon the brightness of the light. Advantage of this method has been taken for the examination of the inner aura through the red or carmine screen. (Chapter iii.) Many screens of different colours have been experimented with in order to obviate, if possible, the necessity or a dark room, but none have been found to be sufficiently satisfactory. Taking all in all, a dark blue screen is most efficient for seeing the outer aura, but it does not reveal the peculiarities of the inner aura as plainly as the red. Some people can see the aura in ordinary daylight to a greater or less extent.

The inference that can be drawn from the above statements is that a dark adapted state of the eye is not an absolute necessity for the perception of the aura, but that this phenomenon can be far better observed when the eye has been partially reduced to this condition. It must be borne in mind that the need of a dim light may be partially due to the delicacy of the aura, whose visibility is destroyed by a bright light.

It is well recognized that an object that affords only a slight colour stimulus, when first seen in the incomplete adapted state, is grey and gradually becomes coloured. The progressive development of colour depends upon the advance towards complete adaptation or on an increasing strength of colour stimulus. This tallies with the appearance of the aura, which at first looks grey and then shows an addition of some colour, usually blue or green.

It was mentioned a little time ago that one of the effects dicyanin had had upon the eyes was to confer the power of perceiving ultra-violet rays, and this supposition will be still strengthened by the study of the auric colours, which will now be done.

For our present purpose it is immaterial whether the undulations of different wave lengths are discriminated in the nerve centres, or whether they are separated in the retina by the nerve-endings of the fibres which convey the stimulus to and originate in the brain the perception of light, or by fluorescence of the media of the eyes.

These colours must be fully studied. Screens are necessary for their investigation, and it has been ascertained by experiment that deeply coloured ones are to be preferred, as by using them a fair amount of light may be allowed in the room ; otherwise the exact depth of colour is of no consequence. The screens employed are :—

Red ......made with a solution of carmine. (The same as used for defining the inner aura.)

Orange.....   ,,   ,,   yolk yellow.
Yellow ....   ,,   ,,   K yellow.
Green .....   ,,   ,,   napthol green.
Blue ......   ,,   ,,   methylene blue.
Violet......   ,,   ,,   gentian violet.

Other dyes will answer just as well.

Before considering the effects of these screens upon the aura, it will be advisable to say a few words about their action under ordinary circumstances.

According to a widely accepted theory, the eyes possess three sets of colour-sensitive nerves, that are excited by red, yellow,* and blue respectively, and all other colours are perceived as a consequence of excitation of two or more of these nerves in varying degrees simultaneously.

The spectrum of ordinary daylight decomposed by means of a prism consists of a vast number of undulations of different wave lengths, that produce rainbow hues (the visible portion of the solar spectrum), besides many others that are commonly invisible. From a physical point of view the undulations of each colour and each shade of colour are quite distinct, and the notion of primary and secondary colours is entirely physiological. While slight variations exist in different individuals, yet for all practical purposes the spectral colours about Frauenhofer's lines B.D. and F. (about 6900λ, 5900λ, and 4870λ, respectively), may be regarded as the three primaries with sufficient accuracy for the following speculations.

Suppose a ray of light consisting of undulations of 6900λ, or thereabouts enters the eyes, it will influence the red-sensitive nerves most, and will appear to the observer, red. As the wave lengths become smaller, say about 6400λ, they will stimulate both the red and the yellow-sensitive nerves, giving rise to the sensation of orange. The wave lengths when reduced to about 5900λ, will be seen as yellow. In like manner as the undulations lessen gradually in size from 5900λ, to 4870λ, the observer will perceive yellow-green, blue-green, and lastly blue one after the other. Indigo will be left out. Subsequently a most interesting colour will be reached, viz., violet which roughly extends from 4200λ, to 3950λ. These rays not only excite the blue-sensitive nerves, but also stimulate the red-sensitive ones. *Thus at one end of the visible solar*

*For the reason of choosing yellow instead of green see chapter vi. page 141.

*spectrum there exist red rays that excite the red-sensitive
nerves to a greater or less extent, and at the other end
there are undulations composed of very different wave
lengths, that influence the same red-sensitive nerves,
although in the intermediate parts of the spectrum as the
wave lengths diminish the stimulation of the red-sensitive
nerve endings lessens until it practically ceases.*

When a quartz prism is used to decompose sunlight,
a lavender grey colour is found beyond the violet.
The visibility of this portion is probably due to
fluorescence of the media of the eye, when the shorter
invisible wave lengths are converted into longer and
visible wave lengths. Beyond these again are undulations which cannot be detected by the unaided eye.

As a possible explanation of the visibility of the
aura and of the various colour phenomena associated
with it, the writer would suggest that the dicyanin
screen brings about some change in the eyes, so that
sensations not merely of light but also of colour, may
to some extent be evoked by at any rate parts of
the ultra-violet spectrum. It is not difficult to conceive that under such circumstances by an extension
of the processes which occur at the violet end of the
ordinary visible spectrum, when the red-sensitive
nerve endings of the retina are again and with diminishing wave lengths increasingly stimulated, there
might occur a more or less complete repetition of the
spectral colour series probably greatly modified in
many respects. In short a *second, higher spectrum.*
Violet bears the same relationship to blue and ultra-
violet red as orange does to the red and yellow.

Coloured objects reflect hues differing from those of
the spectrum, inasmuch as the colours perceived may
be the outcome of a combination of the various parts
of the spectrum, on account of certain undulations
being absorbed from white light. The reflected rays
are rarely simple, being usually mixed with white
light, because the object is generally unable to absorb

the whole of any one set of waves contained in the light falling on it. For instance, a green object may reflect :

1. Undulations of green only.
2. Undulations of blue and yellow mixed.
3. Either 1 or 2 with the addition of white light.

The resulting shade of green perceived being dependent upon the sum total of the action upon all the colour-sensitive nerves.

When objects are examined through various coloured screens, should the colour of the object and the screen differ only in shade, the former will appear darker or lighter in hue as the latter is paler or darker. If the object and screen are of the same colour and shade, the object will remain unaltered in hue. (See page 38.) Should the screen and the object be of different colours, according to the depth of the former, the latter will become much darker, or may be changed in hue from the admixture of the two colours. For example take a yellow object. This will look dark approaching to black if the screen be a very deep blue, while if light, it will change in colour, becoming greenish from the intermingling of the blue and yellow.

Almost every observer after using the dark dicyanin screen sees the aura as a blue or blue-grey mist. The question arises whether this blue colour is due to wave lengths of about 4200λ, or belonging to a region beyond the ordinary visible spectrum. If the former it must be due to ordinary reflected light, and should follow the ordinary laws when examined through the coloured screens ; if the latter some departure from the usual appearances might not unreasonably be expected.

The investigation demands that the observer should be able to detect the aura without using the pale dicyanin screen ; have no deficiency of colour vision ; and be capable of describing accurately the colours he sees; consequently an artist, if able to perceive the aura, is the ideal person. It is curious that when examining the aura through the various screens, no two experimenters give identical names to the colours they see. The cause may be sometimes due to imperfections in their descriptive powers, as the colours are constantly weird and almost indescribable, but the discrepancies at other times are so pronounced that it is impossible to doubt that their visual organs were differently affected, although under ordinary circumstances colours are correctly named. The weird effects seem frequently to be produced by the non-blending of two or more colours seen simultaneously. For instance blue and yellow are often seen as blue and yellow, not green as might be anticipated; and red and blue do not necessarily make a violet or purple. In some cases it is likely that a partial combination does take place, complicating matters still more, so that blue and yellow not only appear separately but also as mixed as green, making a strange jumble of colours.

These peculiar impressions may be explained by supposing that as whereas the sensations due to simultaneous stimulation by yellow and blue are combined into green by the brain, the colours seen in relation to the aura being outside ordinary experience are recognized with the curious results already mentioned.

An artist's model stood in front of a black background, with her hands on her hips and her elbows extended, while the auras in the interspaces between the arms and body were examined. O, an artist by profession, when not using any screens, described the aura as a haze of which the colour was a blue and grey. The appearance was the same throughout the spaces, except the part nearest the body (evidently the inner aura), which was rather more pronounced. He next examined the aura through coloured screens, and the results are tabulated in series 1 of table 4 (pages 80 and 81). The model was then asked if she could change the colour on the left side to red. She succeeded only in producing a red-grey colour. Afterwards in like manner a very good blue was produced on the right side. Through the screens O saw the hues mentioned in series 2 and 3 of the table. The model next tried to produce a yellow on the right side, but the resultant colour being unstable was not very useful for a series of tests. However, it appeared a warm green through the first screen employed, which happened to be a yellow. It frequently occurs that a change in the colour of the aura when brought about by voluntary efforts, is not sustained sufficiently long to allow of complete examination through all the screens.

At various times in connection with similar experiments the writer has inspected this woman's aura through coloured screens. The results are given in series 4 to 7 of the table Series 8 and 9 are the colours recorded by Q, and the writer, which without the intervention of any screen appeared a liquid French ultramarine.

The other examples in the table were chosen to illustrate the colours seen during health. During illness alterations of the colours of the aura when viewed through different coloured screens, especially the blue one, are very frequent, and in a large proportion of cases some shade of yellow is present.

The above observations suffice to show that the natural hue of the aura remains a blue when looked at through a yellow screen, instead of following the common rule of becoming a green ; that yellow in some shade is constantly perceived when a dark blue or a violet is employed—an impossibility under ordinary circumstances. Again when by voluntary effort on the part of the subject the aura has been changed in hue, the colours seen through the screens do not coincide with those that might naturally have been expected.

These investigations confirm the view that a radical change in the visual apparatus is brought about by the dicyanin screens. In connection with the above experiments the following points should be particularly noted :—

1. The comparative ease with which the colours of the aura could be changed to blue or green.

2. The difficulty this subject experienced in producing a yellow, and the instability of the result.

3. The bizzarre effects found on the examination of the green aura with screens.

During the examination of patients, several women, but no man, have been able to change the colours of their auras to a greater or less extent, some quite easily, who with a little practice could have given invaluable assistance. Most of these persons had an excitable temperament. Unfortunately all of them were unavailable for experimental purposes as none of them were artist's models.

The explanation of the aura is full of difficulties, some of which vanish immediately auto-luminosity has been conceded.

Elsewhere (page 51), it has been stated that the aura cannot be seen in complete darkness, and consequently is not self-luminous in the ordinary acceptation of the word. This statement requires qualification, and a criticism of the meaning of the term self-luminous. In general, the phrase " auto-luminous," denotes that an object can be seen in the dark through some inherent or acquired property of emitting rays roughly speaking between 7500λ, and 4000λ, the range of the ordinary visible solar spectrum. If, however, the substance emanates rays of say, 3500λ, which are usually quite invisible, it will be classed among the objects that are not self-luminous. If the human eye can by some means or other

be enabled to see these rays, then the substance would
be defined as auto-luminous ; consequently the term
resolves itself into a physiological conception.   Should
these postulates be admitted, it seems easy to advance
a step further, and to conceive that an object may
emit rays which would be visible if they were in
sufficient abundance to act as an effective stimulus.
Since appropriate stimulation may render effective a
stimulus otherwise subliminal, and such a result
appears to have been obtained in the case under
discussion, whatever the nature of the rays concerned,
the aura may be conceived as being auto-luminous in
this strictly limited sense.

The position of the aura is as follows :—

The aura appears as a faint cloud whose structure
and distribution is determined by forces emanating
from the body and which becomes visible in a dim
diffused light.

As soon as a certain change in the eye has been
brought about by the use of dicyanin screens, the
aura can be seen.   It is suggested that the alteration
is in the direction of retinal sensitisation to ultra-
violet light.

The aura cannot be discerned in total darkness,
therefore it either does not produce rays which can be
recognized by the eye, or if it does they are not sufficiently abundant to cause effective stimulation.

	COLOUR OF AURA	RED SCREEN	ORANGE SCREE
1	Blue with a little grey	0A. Carmine 1A. Carmine	Blue Warmer blue
2	Reddish grey by voluntary effort	0A 1A	Mauve Mauve
3	Bright blue by voluntary effort	0A 1A	Blue Red
4	Bluish grey	Plum	Reddish grey
5	Bright blue by voluntary effort	Red　Blue	Red　Blue
6	Yellow by voluntary effort		Yellow with red tinge
7	Green by voluntary effort		Red
8	Very fine blue	Dull carmine 　　　　The	Bluish grey inner aura the sa
9	Very fine blue	Carmine	Blue
10	Grey	Reddish grey	Grey 　Peculiar
11	Greenish grey	Reddish green	Greenish yellow
12	Blue with a little grey	Carmine　Blue	Yellow　Green
13	Bluish green and white	Red　Green	Red.　Green (Opaque)
14	Peculiar blue	Reddish blue	Orange blue

IV

D WITHOUT COLOURED SCREENS

LLOW SCREEN	GREEN SCREEN	BLUE SCREEN	VIOLET SCREEN
ie arker blue	Blue Purple	Brilliant Orange	Purple Dark yellow
mine luish red	Unable to tell the colour	Purple blue Orange	Violet Plum
ge Yellow Blue ot combined)		Blue Blue	Plum Plum
e		Yellow ochre	Yellow
e		Dirty yellow ochre	Ochre
		Yellow	Yellow
re	Ochre	Ochre	Ochre
low arker.	Green	Blue	Reddish blue
low Blue	Blue	Blue	Bluish violet
y grey			Ochre
ish yellow	Yellow and peculiar blue	Yellow Green Blue	Purple
en Yellow lue	Grey ? Yellow	Yellow Blue	Violet Green
n with a little ue	Green with a little blue	Green with a little blue	Blue
owish blue	Green	Yellow Blue	Blue

APPENDIX. CHAPTER IV

FROM the commencement of the recent calamitous war, it has been impossible to obtain any dicyanin, and at the present time the probability of a further supply seems to be very remote. It was formerly made in Germany, and the demand for it has always been limited, so that there does not appear to be any likelihood that the new dye works will attempt this particular compound until the more marketable colours have been produced to their full extent.

It is unreasonable to suppose that the properties attributed to dicyanin should be confined to a single dye, and probably others more or less efficient may be discovered amongst those that will be produced as soon as conditions become more settled. The necessary experiments must be made by other workers, as the author feels on account of age and growing infirmities unable to undertake them. He, however, thinks a few hints about the procedure may be useful.

First of all it is to be expected that a suitable dye will be found amongst those of a blue colour, and especially those which transmit the shorter wave lengths of the spectrum in the greatest abundance, with the least amount of the longer.

In the search of a suitable dye he would suggest the use of a microscope in a manner similar to that described on page 62, but the process may be considerably curtailed. Suppose the same microscopic power and the same object be employed, it would only be necessary to accurately focus a bristle of the blow-fly's proboscis in ordinary daylight, using the coarse adjustment, which must not be altered again. For the next step the observer should gaze at the light for from half to one minute through a screen containing a moderately dark solution of the dye to be tested. After this he should focus the bristle a second time with the fine adjustment. Should no alteration in the focus be required, probably the dye will prove useless for the purpose on hand, but should it be necessary to lower the objective towards the slide by two or more divisions on the wheel, then the dye may be practically tested by using it instead of dicyanin before looking at the aura. No further experiments should be carried out on the same day.

N.B.—It is extremely necessary that the plan mentioned on page 62 for obtaining the accuracy of the focus and eliminating the effects of accommodation should be strictly adhered to. A little practice makes this quite easy to perform.

CHAPTER V

In the last chapter proofs were furnished to demonstrate the great probability that auric visibility and colours depend upon ultra-violet rays, and that the power of perceiving them has not only been attained, but to a certain extent explained. The present chapter will be devoted chiefly to the investigation of various properties of auras, and to the forces generating them.

The aura has been constantly searched for in the dark without success, proving that it is not auto-luminous in the ordinary acceptation of the term. (Vide chapter iv.) It is now necessary to examine the conditions which govern its visibility. The best results are obtained in diffuse daylight, graduated to the proper extent. Endeavour has been made, without much success, to ascertain whether different coloured lights show up the aura more plainly, one than another. It can be detected to different extents through red, yellow, green and blue screens, which also give results that vary with the depth of colour. One important detail becomes more conspicuous when a red screen is employed, viz, the striæ of the inner aura.

At first sight the cloudlike appearance might suggest that the aura was some form of vapour. This is highly improbable for the following reason : the aura remains immovable whether the patient is hot or cold. The only conditions which would cause a vapour to seem stationary are such as govern the

84

cloud banners seen on mountain peaks, where in a given time the amount of mist added corresponds exactly to that lost by diffusion and evaporation. In this case, however, every variation of the wind alters the position or shape of the cloud, but draught however great and movement of the body can produce no such change in the auric haze. Its structure is so delicate that likening it to an ordinary mist would be analogous to the comparison of the finest cambric to the coarsest canvas.

The most probable interpretation of the aura that can at present be given, is that it is the outcome of force emanation from the body, which like all forces is invisible, but becomes perceptible through its action, as will be more fully discussed in a later part of this chapter. A moment's consideration of this conception will show that it is neither so far fetched nor so preposterous as might be seen at first sight, and that parallels can be found in the animal world. Everyone is conversant that the human body generates heat, and consequently disseminates it in part into surrounding space as radiant heat. This, as is well known, consists of infra-red wave lengths transmitted through the ether. Again certain insects, etc., such as fire-flies and glow-worms have the power of emitting waves which are perceived as light. It is unnecessary to multiply instances.

If animals emit wave lengths in the ether which include most of the heat and visible portions of the solar spectrum, there would seem to be no reason why ultra-violet undulations should not be similarly produced. When these latter are emitted from the human body, some of them may be the true source of the aura surrounding men and women. This statement does not imply any specific part of the ultra-violet spectrum.

The present is the best time to consider whether there are other forces which produce like phenomena in any way resembling the aura. It is by no means needful that the exciting force should entirely correspond to the one issuing from the human body. Fortunately magnetism, electricity (whether from a static machine or from the poles of a galvanic cell), and radio-activity will supply three different forms of energy all producing somewhat similar appearances which can be seen under conditions like those required to make the human aura visible.

The magnetic haze is not quite so easily perceived as the human aura. The best effects are obtained when the background is perfectly smooth and black and illumination arranged, and dicyanin screens used as for the examination of the aura. It might be reasonably expected that the visible clouds would follow the magnetic lines of force, but as far as has been observed up to the present time such is not the case, although possibly the apparent discrepancies are entirely due to imperfect experimental conditions and will disappear as these are improved upon.

The magnets used in the following experiments were a six-inch horseshoe and an eight-inch bar, the latter blackened all over. Lately a strong permanent magnet built up of five horseshoes has also been employed, but shows no appreciable differences except that the haze is more distinct. The above were chosen in preference to an electro-magnet, which on account of its composite nature was not suitable.

On looking at a horseshoe magnet closed by its armature, a bluish haze about half an inch wide will be seen encircling it evenly. The central space will also appear cloudy. Directly the armature is removed a great alteration comes over the shape of the haze, which while remaining round the magnet, will be seen to become denser near the poles, the effect commencing about an inch above them and culminating at a little distance beyond them. A similar change occurs in the central space, but as this has fixed dimensions the mist merely becomes thicker near the free ends. From the poles themselves rays project into space, often being visible for several inches, and with the compound magnet they have been detected nearly a foot in length. For some undetermined reason the magnetic mist may be far more conspicuous on one day than another.

The rays issuing from the south pole have little or no tendency towards expansion, while those originating from the opposite pole become slightly fan-shaped, and the two sets amalgamate a short distance beyond the poles. When a bar magnet is examined in like fashion, the cloud will be seen enveloping its full length, but broader and denser as it approaches the ends. With this form of magnet the rays projecting from one pole are uninfluenced by those from the other, as they are as far apart from one another as possible, and their arrangements can be accurately noted. If a tintack be placed point outwards on the pole of a magnet, the mist will be brighter by the side of the nail and will concentrate at the point. As might be foreseen, if the two horse-shoe magnets be held with their poles near to each other but not touching on the same plane, and one of them be rotated, the haze will be brighter when dissimilar poles are opposed to each other, and vice versa. Continuous rotation will thus give rise to alternating phases of brilliancy.

It will be unnecessary to say anything about the luminous cloud round the point of a highly electrified body, as everyone is conversant with it, especially as it has no connection with the present subject. However, the poles of a galvanic cell when disconnected are in a similar state, but owing to the very low potential, only a few people can distinguish the haze round them. The field of force becomes visible as a mist when searched for in the same manner as the magnetic cloud. As might be expected, the haze surrounds any conductor joining the poles. If a piece of wire be connected with the zinc element, and another with the carbon of the cell, and these two wires be so arranged that they shall be parallel with one another and about two inches apart, the whole intervening space will be faintly nebulous. If a non-conductor be placed between them, the cloud will no longer be so diffuse, but will concentrate round the wires. This haze has a bluish tinge.

A cloud, under similar circumstances, can be seen enveloping a radio-active crystal of Uranium Nitrate. The crystal first used was irregular in shape and the mist was massed at the smaller end, and was yellow in colour. On one occasion it was noticed that when the crystal was placed near a magnet, there was a mutual attraction between the clouds surrounding the bodies, which seemed to extend out towards each other a short distance, after which they lost their individuality, either because they actually blended, or because each nearer its own source masked the other as it grew fainter.

It would be superfluous to quote any more experiments, as sufficient have been mentioned to prove that under certain favourable conditions a haze can be visually detected round substances in which there reside certain forms of energy ordinarily demonstrable by other and less direct means.

If the aura be the outcome of a physical force proceeding from the body and acting on the surrounding medium, it would appear probable that external forces, other than the auric derived from a second person, would influence it, but in what manner, experiments alone can determine. Magnetism is the easiest force to apply, and consequently was the first used. The electro-magnet was found not to be nearly so convenient as a permanent one, and was therefore laid aside after several trials.

When the poles of a horseshoe magnet, after the

removal of the armature, are held from six to eight inches away from the body of a healthy person, the observer will almost immediately be able to distinguish an increase of brilliancy of the aura at the part of the body nearest the poles, and simultaneously the haze projected from the poles of the magnet will become more conspicuous. This will in a few seconds concentrate into a single streak or ray joining the body and the magnet, and will have the same width as the poles including the space between them. Theoretically there ought to be two rays emerging from the body, one from each pole, and also, if the aura possessed any polarity, one should be brighter and larger than the other. This does not happen, perhaps on account of the proximity of the two poles of the magnet. If the magnet be moved about slowly, the ray will follow it and appear to be derived from the part of the body nearest the magnet. Thus the site of emission of the ray will be constantly changing, but no diminution in size or brightness can be detected. The one exception seems to be when a ray emanates from one projection of the body, such as the nose, elbow, or nipple, when it will continue so to arise even though the magnet may be closer to a plane surface of the body, confirming the supposition that the auric potential is greater on points.

When, instead of a horseshoe, one pole of a bar magnet is held a short distance from the body of a patient, a corresponding display will be produced, only less obvious. As far as has yet been ascertained neither pole of a magnet exerts a greater influence over the aura than the other. Consequently it is conjectured that the aura is equally acted upon by both poles of the magnet, and *therefore as far as magnetism is concerned the aura does not possess any polarity.* The mutual attraction of two auras belonging to different people is more intense than that between a magnet and the aura.

One experience with the magnet is so curious that it is worth relating.

During the investigation of the aura of a woman, which had arrived at the stage of the c.c. bands, darkness due to a severe thunderstorm came on and the examination had to be suspended. It was hoped that the light would quickly improve, and to pass the time, the action of the magnet upon the aura was tested. The effect was surprising, because when the magnet was held near the patient, she screamed out and said that it caused her severe pain. She was tried in various ways, with her eyes shut, with the magnet covered up, etc., so that she should not know when the instrument was brought near her, but in every instance when the magnet approached her she felt it, never once making a mistake, so that it was impossible to doubt the genuineness of the sensation.

As it still continued dark the remainder of the examination had to be deferred. Three or four days later the patient returned for the completion of the investigation, when the action of the magnet was tried a second time. Not the slightest conscious sensation was aroused, and it was concluded that the peculiar conditions connected with the electrified state of the atmosphere must in some way have made her abnormally sensitive.

By a piece of good luck in the autumn of the year 1916, a thunderstorm commenced during the investigation of the aura of another patient. Although the thunder and lightning were frequent and not far distant, yet the storm did not attain the severity of the one just mentioned. Whilst at its height, the effect of a powerful magnet, composed of five sections, held or moved about near different parts of the patient's body was tried. The result as regards exciting any sensation was absolutely nil, which was the more interesting as this person though in good health was of definitely hysterical disposition.

It might therefore have been anticipated that she would prove more sensitive to influences of this nature than a non-neurotic individual.

The effects produced by static electricity are exceedingly interesting. For early experiments women, on account of the width of their outer auras, were chosen, but the same results are obtained with males and children, when due allowance has been made for the different shapes of their auras. There is a slight difference in the result according to the sign of the charge employed, and as the negative induces a change with an intermediate transitional stage, it will be considered first. One method of investigation will now be described.

The subject is placed upon an insulated stool with hands upon the head, to allow the observer to notice as accurately as possible the breadth of both auras, and to make a mental note of their brightness. As soon as these observations have been completed, a negative charge is given through a chain attached to the corresponding pole of a Wimshurst machine. Generally* within the fraction of a minute the outer aura will contract and grow more dense, while the inner will lose distinctness. From this stage onwards both auras decrease in brilliance, and in a short time the inner will completely vanish. Proof of this disappearance is furnished by watching the inner aura through a dark carmine screen, when eventually a void space will be discerned. The outer by this time will have contracted and become scarcely visible, only to be detected just outside the proper limit of the inner aura. If the charging be continued longer, the outer aura will also depart, leaving no traces. Directly the charge is dissipated the auras begin to return.

This experiment can be repeated so as to allow

*The time required for electrification to induce the changes described, varies on different days in the same subjects, and also with each individual.

an examination of the aura during the whole length of time through the dark carmine screen, which if sufficiently deep in colour, will of course obliterate the outer aura, previous to electrification, in the ordinary manner. As soon, however, as the operation of charging the subject is commenced, the auras begin to alter, the inner fading, but the outer becoming visible through the screen as a result of concentration immediately outside the edge of the inner aura, which now looks coarsely granular without presenting any signs of striation. No modification except condensation, which makes it more opaque and in consequence distinguishable through the coloured screen, has been detected in the outer aura. As soon as this stage has been reached, the two auras commence fading rapidly, and as might be expected, the inner aura vanishes before the condensed outer, which is the last to go. Directly the charge is lost both auras return simultaneously, and during the procedure the outer aura does not show any condensation. With the hands on the hips and the elbows extended, a similar series of changes can be demonstrated. In the interspaces between the arms and the body, the outer aura is surrounded by the inner, and when the former is concentrated, an opaque bright mass is collected in the centre, presenting a wonderful appearance. All the other alterations occur exactly as has been described. These experiments must be performed on different occasions, as a second one shortly after the first is never really satisfactory.

When a positive charge is used, there is usually no massing of the outer aura, although occasionally it exhibits a tendency in that direction. Both auras vanish simultaneously.

Two Wimshurst machines were employed for these experiments. One large with eighteen inch, and the other small with ten inch plates, the latter giving a longer, the former a much thicker and more powerful spark. The early experiments were performed with the small instrument, and completely successful results could only be obtained when the machine was working at its very best. The large Wimshurst only occasionally failed to completely disperse the aura, and was altogether much more reliable.

One remarkable after-effect is the enlargement of the aura, the increase often reaching an additional fifty per cent. The best results were obtained by the employment of the large machine. When the greatest expansion is required, electrification should be prolonged for some short time after the complete disappearance of the aura. After its reappearance the aura continues to expand for a time up to the maximum and then remains stationary. Moderate degrees of enlargement can be obtained with comparative small charges. As soon as this phenomenon had been observed, it was studied with people healthy or otherwise, of both sexes and of all ages, and was found to be universal, and to show no greater individual variations than might have been expected.

In addition to alterations in size above described other changes may be noted. Immediately after the reappearance of the auras, the inner is slightly bigger and a little less plain but still shows striæ. It, however, very soon resumes its natural aspect. Co-incidently the expansion is taking place, but, with few exceptions, it never attains its original brightness. It becomes indefinite towards the periphery and gradually fades away into nothingness. The impression given is that there is no real increment in the quantity of the haze, but that it has been distributed over a larger space. An appearance not identical with, but closely resembling the ultra-outer aura, is not infrequently produced. The temporary resumption of clothes makes no difference, as upon their removal the outer aura still remains expanded.

When a person showing an ultra-outer aura is

electrified, the whole of the outer aura, as usual, is augmented in size, extending into the space occupied by the former. In two or three instances the whole aura did not diminish in intensity at all, or at any rate not to the same extent, as in cases where there had been no sign of an ultra-outer aura. The explanation is very easy if it be conceded that the ultra-outer aura is only an ill-defined extension of the outer and already occupies the space that will be filled by expansion, the result of previous electrification.

Owing to the lack of definition at the outer limits, there is often a difficulty in determining the size of the aura round the head after a subject has been electrified, but over the rest of the body, as far as can be judged, the whole aura is generally augmented proportionally, and so it retains its natural shape. Any local peculiarities are generally accentuated. Case 20 is a good example of this.

Case 19. (Figs. 20 and 21). V. S., a well grown girl, eight years old, of excitable temperament, but who had never suffered from any illness, with the exception of the usual infantile complaints, was inspected during the summer of 1915. Both auras were plain for a child of her age, and normal except for a slight bulge at the back, which commenced at the head and ended at the feet and was widest at the lumbar region. The bow although easily seen was not well marked. The outer aura was seven inches round the head, four by the sides of the trunk, and three by the legs ; in front three inches ; at the back five inches diminishing to three by the legs. The inner aura was two and a half inches wide.

Whilst standing upon the insulated stool she was positively charged from the large Wimshurst machine, for about five minutes. The auras quickly vanished in the ordinary manner, and rapidly returned directly the charge was dissipated. After a lapse of about a quarter of an hour, her auras were again examined.

The inner had regained its natural state.   The outer
had enlarged.   Round the head it was unaltered, but
by the trunk it was three inches wider, and did not
follow the outline of the body as closely as it had
previously done.   It was also broader by the legs
being here four inches.   In appearance it was very
similar to the transitional aura of a girl fifteen or
sixteen years of age, except that it was slightly wider
by the thighs and legs.   There was also an increase

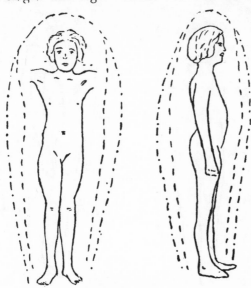

Figs. 20 and 21.
Young girl. Aura enlarged by electricity.

in size at the back and front.   The bow-shaped bulge
had become more conspicuous.

Case 20. I. S., a sturdy rather precociously
developed girl, fifteen years of age, was inspected in
July 1915, when in good health.   Both her auras
reached the average distinctness.   The outer exhibited the transitional appearance natural to her
time of life, being seven inches broad by the head
and trunk, and four by the legs, the latter part being

rather wide. A side view of the aura showed the breadth to be five inches in front, seven at the small of the back with the outer margin straight up and down, and four by the legs. Altogether it was a little broader than usual for her age. The inner was healthily striated and three inches in breadth.

She stood upon the insulated stool and was positively electrified for some minutes. The small Wimshurst

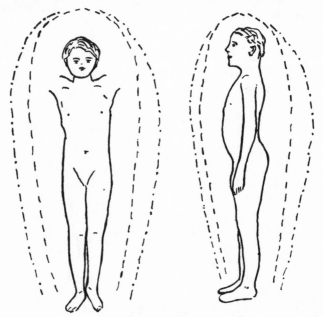

Figs. 22 and 23.
Boy's outer aura. Enlarged by electricity.

machine was employed. The whole aura disappeared and, a few minutes after returning, had enlarged to ten inches by the head and trunk, six in front, nine at the back and six by the legs. The loss of distinctness was slight. The writer considers the size and shape to be a forecast of the mature stage, which in her case will be probably attained soon after her eighteenth year.

Case 21. (Figs. 22 and 23). B. S., a schoolboy eleven years old, of excitable temperament but in good health, was inspected in 1915. Both auras possessed the average distinctness, and the outer was wide for his age, being as he faced the observer, seven inches by the head, five by the trunk, and four by the legs. When he turned sideways, it was four and a half inches in front, seven at the small of the back and four by the ankles. It was bow-shaped at the back, the curve commencing at the head and finishing at the feet. The inner aura was three inches wide and exhibited the natural striation. He was positively charged when insulated. The aura took rather a long time to depart, but afterwards, when it had completely returned, was found to be expanded while the bow-shaped curve was exceedingly plain. The figures were, as he stood facing, ten inches round the head, the same by the sides of the trunk, and six by the legs. A side view gave six inches in front and by the legs, and twelve at the small of the back.

Case 22. (Figs. 24 and 25). E., a tall, powerful, well made man, fifty years of age was examined in 1915. His outer aura was unusually wide and distinct. The inner was hardly as marked as had been anticipated from his physique. There was no sign of any ultra-outer aura. The outer aura was of good shape, ten and a half inches round his head, seven by the trunk and six by the legs. Sideways, it was six and a half in front and seven at the back. The inner showed striation clearly, being a little over four inches in breadth. Whilst standing on the insulated stool he was given a negative charge, and both auras vanished in the ordinary manner, only taking a rather long time. As an after-effect the outer was found to have considerably expanded, but at the same time had become proportionately less distinct and the distal margin was a trifle indefinite. There was no pesudo-ultra-outer aura. The size of the aura was fifteen inches round the head, ten by the trunk, nine by the legs, and the same width at the back and front.

It was at first taken for granted that the aura after enlargement by statical electricity soon resumed its natural state, but this was found to be an error when

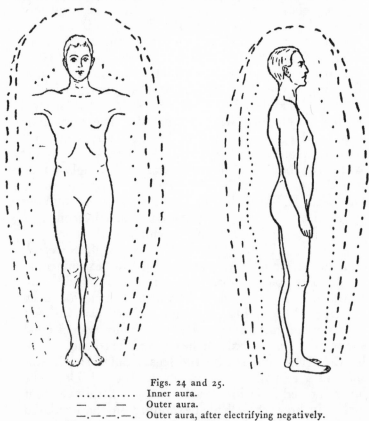

Figs. 24 and 25.
....   Inner aura.
— — —   Outer aura.
—.—.—.—.   Outer aura, after electrifying negatively.

examining a patient (case 48, which is described later on), who had been undergoing electrical treatment for curative purposes. On the first occasion the outer margin of the patient's aura was as sharply defined as usual, but on her third visit, (the aura was not inspected at the second), the outer had assumed an appearance indistinguishable from an ultra-outer aura, and which continued until the end of the course, although on one occasion an interval of a week elapsed, during which no charge was given and yet no contraction took place. In this case the ultra-outer aura appeared to be entirely the result of the application of statical electricity, but it had not been expected that a change in size induced in a minute or two would persist for several days.

A fortnight after the last charge had been given, the patient's aura was again examined and found to be of average distinctness, and to have returned to the dimensions noted at the first visit, except for a very slight haze four inches in breadth, which, however, did not in the least resemble an ultra-outer aura, and probably vanished within a few days.

The duration of the enlargement induced by a single application of statical electricity could be only determined experimentally, as was attempted in one of the two cases detailed below.

1. A patient received a just sufficiently large charge to cause complete disappearance of her aura, which on its return expanded to forty per cent. beyond its original size. Two days later she was inspected a second time for quite a different purpose, and it was found that the aura remained four inches wider by the trunk than it had been at the commencement of the previous examination, and exhibited all the features of the ultra-outer aura.

2. In May, 1918, M. W., a strong and healthy lady kindly volunteered to submit to daily examination of her aura during an experiment to determine how long the electrically produced expansion would persist. The outer aura which was of perfect shape and well defined, could be accurately measured, and was found to have the following dimensions : Round the head and trunk eleven inches, at the upper part of the thighs, seven, and lower down five inches ;

in front, seven inches contracting to five near the
ankles ; at the back, five inches by the shoulders
and buttocks, without a bulge in the lumbar region,
where it was eight inches. The inner aura was about
three and a half inches wide over the whole body,
except the thighs and legs, where it was slightly
narrower.

She was placed upon the insulated stool and charged
for three and a half minutes. The auras did not
completely vanish. After a few minutes the haze
was again inspected and measured. It had expanded
and no longer displayed well defined margins, but
showed a condition resembling an ultra-outer aura.
As near as could be ascertained the outer aura was
eighteen inches round the head and by the sides of
the trunk, eight by the thighs and six by the legs.
Sideways, it was ten inches in front, eleven at the
small of the back, and by the ankles, six.

Next day it was noticed that the aura had regained
its distinct margin, once more permitting of easy
measurement. Round the head it was eleven inches,
by the sides of the trunk fourteen, and by the thighs
and legs eight ; in front ten inches, and at the back at
the broadest part eleven, and at the ankles eight.
These figures show that the aura, although still
bigger than normal, was considerably reduced in
size, It had also recovered to a great extent its lost
brightness. On the following day, as promised, the
lady repeated her visit. Before examination it was
expected that the outer aura would be smaller than
on the day previous, but not exactly its proper size.
However, when the dimensions were taken and compared with those of her first examination, the two
completely tallied. In this instance the aura took
over twenty-four hours and less than forty-eight to
become normal.

If any conclusions may be drawn from two cases
it would appear that no definite time can be laid

down for the return of the aura to its proper size after augmentation, by electricity.

Enlargement of the aura by electricity can be obtained by other methods besides the direct charging of the patients when standing on an insulated stool. A quicker, and almost effectual way, is to hold an electric brush near a person under proper conditions. The brush used for this purpose consists of a thin brass rod nine inches in length attached to a glass handle, and with a number of tufts of tinsel fixed at right angles, which when spread out parallel with the rod form a large number of points in a row. When this is connected with a chain to one of the prime conductors of the Wimshurst machine and charged, a strong electric breeze is induced.

At the first experiment the electric brush was held near the spine of a patient and moved up and down, after which the aura was found to be increased in size, as is illustrated by the instance recorded below. It is of course impossible to conduct more than one experiment of this nature upon a patient in one day, owing to the length of time the aura takes to resume its normal state.

Case 23. C.E., not quite eighteen years old, had well-shaped outer and inner auras, without any abnormality, and rather wide for her age. The outer was eight inches by the head and trunk, and contracted to four by the ankles; five inches down the front and seven at the widest part of the back, where it was slightly bow-shaped. The electric brush connected by a chain to the positive conductor of the Wimshurst machine was held parallel to, and moved once down close to but not touching the vertical central line of the trunk in front of the body. No change in the aura could be detected. After a minute or two had elapsed, the brush was passed down the spine in a similar manner once, and the aura was again inspected. It had considerably enlarged, as round the head and by the trunk it had become twelve, and by the legs and in front eight inches, and at the small of the back twelve, the bow-shape still persisting. The girl was in due course placed upon the insulated stool and negatively electrified, when the aura vanished in the usual manner. After a period of some minutes, the aura was seen to have expanded still further, being two or three inches wider than before. Subsequent to both the application of the brush and to receiving a negative charge while standing on the insulated stool, the haze became less distinct, but especially in the latter case. The inner aura did not seem to alter.

The reason why the brush was held near the front and then at the back of the patient, was to determine whether static electricity influenced the aura directly by charging the granules composing it and thus causing them to repel each other, and bringing about expansion without any increase of substance ; or whether the enlargement was due to an alteration in the auric forces, produced by the stimulation of the central nervous system. If the latter, it was thought extremely probable that the electric brush would produce more effect when applied near the spinal cord than elsewhere.

With the same object in view another experiment was made with a girl eighteen years of age, who had a distinct aura, wide round the head but narrow for her age by the trunk. She was healthy and evidently clever, but late in bodily development. The electric brush negatively charged was held near but not touching her forehead for not longer than a couple of seconds. The aura was at once re-examined and exhibited a large extension all over, but with this increase in size there was a corresponding decrease in clearness. It is hardly necessary to give detailed measurements.

Except in two instances the supposition that the

electric brush would produce more effect when applied to the spinal cord, has always been confirmed. But these cases were not comparable, as the results were obtained under different circumstances.

In one case a gentleman remaining upon the insulated stool, as owing to an oversight he had not been asked to come down, while the brush was moved five or six times down and up the front of his trunk, when in addition to the local action aimed at, a charge was of course communicated to the whole body. In the other case the brush had been moved up and down the front of a woman for about one minute.

An electric charge resides on the surface of a charged body, and the human body forms no exception to the general rule. As apart altogether from electrified states produced under such experimental conditions as have been dealt with above, a surface charge varying from time to time in distribution and potential even on one and the same individual, investigations were undertaken to determine the relations, if any, existing between such local or general electrical states and the aura. Three artists' models, each on several occasions, and a number of other people, once or twice, have been examined, and some exceedingly interesting observations made, but only such as have any bearing on the matter in hand will be described.

The apparatus employed for the investigations consisted of ordinary single gold leaf electroscopes and proof planes. These instruments are so well known that there is no need for any description further than to state that the moveable gold leaf was about three inches in length and one-sixteenth in breadth. This size was selected after numerous trials as giving the best results. One electroscope (E.1.) was surmounted by a thin metal disc corresponding to the proof plane used. Sometimes the disc was replaced by a smaller condenser composed of two brass plates three quarters of an inch in diameter, insulated from each other by shellac. The upper plate was connected by an insulated flexible wire to the proof plane. Subsequently it was found more convenient to have a separate electroscope (E.2.), with a fixed condenser placed within the glass case. There was of course an attachment to permit the lower plate, which was in communication with the gold leaf, to be charged from the outside.

It is generally easy to charge an electroscope such as E.1. directly from the body, by placing the proof plane upon the extensor surface of the arm and then on the disc of the electroscope, and repeating the operation as many times as may be required to obtain the greatest divergence of the gold leaf. The sign of the charge will almost always be negative. Any part of the body may be treated as above, when, as frequently occurs, a sufficient charge cannot be communicated to the instrument, or it is necessary to economise time, it is preferable to employ the following method :—Charge the electroscope E.1. with electricity having the same sign, usually negative, as that of the surface electricity, till the gold leaf diverges a few degrees. If now the proof plane is held near to and above the metal disc*, after having touched any part of the patient, it will cause a still further divergence of the gold leaf. By repetition a rough comparison of the potential at the different parts of the body can be made.

When an electroscope of the pattern E.2. is used, the disc of the condenser connected with the gold leaf is charged from a static machine with electricity of the same sign as the skin possesses, while the proof

---

*A greater degree of accuracy may be obtained by attaching three or four small thin pieces of ebonite to the upper surface of the disc of the electroscope for the proof plane to rest on, thus allowing the distance between the disc and the proof plane to be always the same.

plane attached by the flexible wire remains in connection with the earth. By this arrangement, when the proof plane is brought into contact with the surface of the body and then removed, an increase in the divergence of the gold leaf will take place. Immediately the proof plane is connected with the earth the gold leaf collapses to its former condition. By this method observations can be quickly made. Unfortunately this instrument is not quite as delicate as the previous one.

These experiments, contrary to expectations, generally but not invariably, showed certain parts of the body such as the palms of the hands, nose, elbows, nipples, etc., most of them, it will be noted being points, to be almost if not entirely devoid of electric potential.*

Mrs. A., an artist's model, on one occasion after she had been undressed a considerable time and was consequently as free from external influences as possible, such as clothes, was found to be highly charged with electricity, and may be regarded as a typical case. Her aura was exceedingly distinct on that day. Her body was very carefully tested all over with the proof plane, at least once and in most parts several times, so that the results may be regarded as extremely accurate. (Figs. 26 to 28.) Except the forehead all the body showed a negative surface charge, which, however, was unevenly distributed. In front it was least on the central line of the thorax, but started increasing a little above the umbilicus, and gained its maximum just over the pubes. On the remainder of the front of the trunk, and on the thighs and legs it was as nearly as possible even. The sides and the greatest part of the back had the same potential, exceptions being over the seventh cervical vertebra where it was seemingly nil, and the sacrum

*As the skin, unless moist, is a very poor conductor of electricity, the increase of potential on points is not present as is the case with conductors.

where the potential increased from above downwards, until just above the gluteal cleft it reached the maximum for any part of the body. On two other occasions this woman showed no signs of a surface charge on any part of the body, with the exception of the lower part of the sacrum, where a considerable rise of

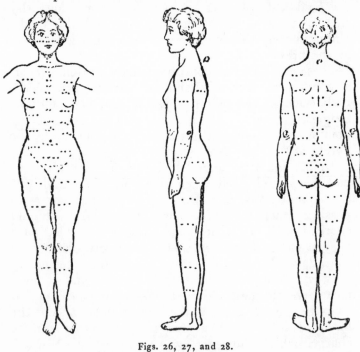

Figs. 26, 27, and 28.
Surface electricity.
Number of dots denote intensity.

potential could always be detected. On these days her aura was not less distinct than usual.

Another artist's model, whose aura was generally well marked, usually showed very little surface electricity, but on one occasion when the surface electricity was well pronounced and evenly distributed all over the body, except the lower part of the sacrum and just above the pubes, where it was most intense, her aura was not as plain as usual. This may, however, have been due to some peculiar weather conditions, as other people's auras hardly reached the ordinary standard of visibility.

Quite recently a very healthy woman was examined with great care, as peculiarities, previously never found in a sound person, were noticed in the distribution of a very considerable surface charge. The whole of the right side showed a higher potential, causing the gold leaf of the electroscope to diverge twice as much as did the corresponding parts on the left side. The charges were distributed as a whole evenly, on the two sides. A similar condition is not infrequent in some cases of disease, such as epilepsy and hemiplegia, when the aura is also asymmetrical.

The importance of this condition was at once recognized, and to make absolutely certain that the peculiarity was genuine, the investigation was made with first one and then the other electroscope, with similar results. The customary inspection of the aura was undertaken immediately afterwards, but not the slightest difference on the two sides either in size, shape, or texture or colour could be detected either before or after a static charge had been communicated.

In August, 1917, another instance of asymmetrical distribution of surface electricity was met with. The charge was negative, and as regards each side evenly distributed, but as in the previous case, it was greater over the right half of the body than the left. Although the patient has not been well for some time, being anæmic, nothing particular to account for this peculiarity could be discovered.

An interesting effect was noticed when this woman stood upon the insulated stool and was given a negative charge, when the outer aura massed more extensively and took a longer time to vanish on the left side than on the right, from which it was inferred that there must have been some difference on the two sides, too refined to be appreciated by the eyes.

Men and children only differ from women in the distribution of the surface charge, in that they have no places of maximum intensity over the pubes and sacrum. As a rule surface electricity is well marked on the back of the forearm, where it is probably due to the abundant hair in that situation.

A local change both in the aura and the amount of surface electricity was displayed by a woman, forty-four years of age, a short time before entering a hospital for operation on account of osteo-sarcoma of the humerus. Over the body the charge was small, but well marked on the upper arm above and below the tumour, while none could be detected over the diseased part. The inner aura was coarser here than elsewhere, but still exhibited striation.

The results of these experiments can be tabulated, and will show that there are great differences between auric and electric conditions, which appear independent of one another.

SURFACE CHARGE.	AURA.
Great deficiency or complete absence on points.	Most marked at points.
Very small on the forehead, palms of the hands, etc.	Well defined. Presence or absence of surface electricity makes no difference.
Usually negative but may be positive.	No polarity.
Increased by muscular movement.	Muscular movement causes no change.
Less on the flexor than on the extensor surface of the arm.	No differences on flexor or extensor surfaces.
Increased by friction of the skin.	Unaltered by friction of the skin.

Moisture of the skin prevents accumulation.	Moisture of the skin makes no difference.
	When the body is charged artificially the aura decreases or entirely vanishes. It usually enlarges afterwards.

The study of the aura has always had a great fascination for the writer, and one day when pondering over the subject, he wondered if it were possible by chemical means to induce alterations, either in size, texture, or colour, as he had previously noticed that the aura emanating from a part of the body which had been painted with iodine was different to the adjacent portions. If chemicals were applied to the body itself, pure effects might not be produced, and the interpretations of the results might remain doubtful, as factors additional to direct action on the aura might be concerned. The use of vapours applied at some distance from the body was therefore decided upon. As the first application happened to be made on the left side, this practice has generally been adhered to, though of course trials have been made on the right side, as well as over the whole body, to make certain that local differences do not exist. Besides, two different gases, such as chlorine and bromine, have been applied one on each side of the body, and the results have coincided with those obtained by the chemicals when employed separately on various occasions. These remarks, however, only hold good for a healthy subject with a symmetrical aura, and are correct for a single chemical, but not necessarily for mixtures of two gases.

Exp. 1. The first examination was performed with iodine in July, 1912. It is typical, and has been repeated many times with the same result, so that an account will be given in full. An artist's model stood facing the observer with her arms akimbo. The colour of the aura in the interspaces between the arms and body was a good blue and the same on both sides. The left side was fumigated with iodine vapour, obtained by pouring a few drops of Tinct : Iodid : Fort ; into an evaporating dish and warming it with a spirit lamp, at a short distance from the body, towards which the fumes were gently blown. Directly this was finished an examination was carried out in the usual manner, when it was found that the aura presented different colours on the two sides, and then as the subject turned slowly round, the lines of demarcation apparently corresponded with the median lines back and front. The aura on the right side still retained its blue colour, but on the left it was red-brown and opaque. The colour was very peculiar, and certainly contained some admixture of others. With the c.c. bands the shade on the left side was darker with the blue, red, and yellow, but lighter with the green. This last colour was especially noticeable in the extensions of the band beyond the body, pointing to its presence in considerable quantity. Through the screens the hues were dissimilar on the two sides. (See table 5, series 1.)

Exp. 2. An European lady with a strain of Malay blood in her veins, showed an aura of a blue grey mixed with white, giving it an opaque appearance which is by no means uncommonly seen through the different coloured screens, but is rare to the naked eye. With the arms akimbo, the aura in the intervals between the arms and the body exhibited more green than round the body, and this colour was even more in evidence with the various coloured screens, through which the aura appeared of a grey-green colour, instead of the more usual blue-grey. (See table 5, series 2.)

Fumigation of iodine on the left side turned the colour to a red-brown, while the aura on the right side remained unaltered. The difference between the

TABLE V.

	AURA.	RED SCREEN.	ORANGE SCREEN.	YELLOW SCREEN.	GREEN SCREEN.	BLUE SCREEN.	VIOLET SCREEN.
1.	Blue.	Blue & Green.	Blue & Green.	Blue.	Very fine blue.	Green-blue & little Green.	Yellow & Green.
	Brown.	Brown-red.	After fumigation with Brown with little red.	with Iodine. Brown.	Blue & Brown.	Blue & Brown.	Green & Violet.
2.	Green-grey.	Red & Green.	Red & Green opaque.	Green & little Blue.	Green and little Blue.	Green & little Blue.	Blue.
	Brown-red.		After fumigation with Iodine, All the colours were the same with the addition of red.				
3.	Blue.	Red-blue.	Green-yellow.	Green-yellow.	Blue-yellow.	Green & Blue.	Blue.
	Blue.	Colours unaltered	After the fumigation with through the different screens.	with Bromine.			
4.	Grey-blue.	Reddish Green-grey.	Blue-grey.	Grey-blue, opaque Chlorine.	Grey-blue.	Grey-yellow.	Blue & Yellow.
	Yellow-green.	Blue.	After fuming with Red-blue.	Red-green.	Blue & Green.	Green.	Violet & Blue.

two sides was very obvious. Examined through the different screens, the only alteration detected on the left side was the addition of red, which was especially marked when the red and orange screens were used. The effect of the chemical upon the size and shape of the aura was curious and interesting. The outer aura remained unchanged, but the inner receded from the body, giving rise to an appearance resembling an unusually wide etheric double. The inner was also undoubtedly diminished in breadth and less distinctly striated. Especial note was made of the fact that the two auras were obviously contiguous.

When a small amount of bromine is substituted for iodine, the alteration produced upon the aura is not always identical. Sometimes the haze will become a pure blue, at others an opaque green, while occasionally there seems to be an intermediate stage, when the colour is a mixture of blue and green without any blending. These chromatic effects were exhibited in the following three examples, in which the preliminary preparations were as nearly alike as possible.

Exp. 3. The aura of a tall well-made young man, twenty-three years of age, when facing the observer, with his hands on his hips and his elbows extended, looked bluish, but after the left side had been fumigated with bromine, the colour of the interspace was an opaque green, while the aura on the right side continued unaltered. Examination through the different screens showed the hue on the left side to be green, while the aura on the right side retained its normal colour. (See table 5, series 3.)

Exp. 4. B.F., a woman three and twenty years old possessed a wide well-shaped aura, of the ordinary blue colour mixed with a little grey. Fuming bromine was held near the left side of her trunk, and the aura on that size turned an azure blue, corresponding to the darkest shade in Rowney's specimen chart of paints. The inner seemed less distinct although its striation remained intact.

Exp. 4. D., a woman twenty-nine years old, manifesting undoubted signs of Raynaud's disease, had her aura on the left side fumigated with bromine. The colour, which was previously a blue-grey, became a pure blue mixed with green, the two colours not blending.

Until recently variations in the colour changes induced by bromine were attributed to some unknown differences in the auras themselves. This has been found to be incorrect, as the haze appears first to turn green, then blue and green, and finally becomes blue, according to the amount of bromine used. Unquestionably the aura of one person requires a much larger quantity of vapour before it arrives at the final blue stage than that of another. This may, perhaps, be due to idiosyncracy, but it is probable that the health factor must also be taken into consideration.

The above peculiarities of bromine were discovered accidentally. On one occasion a much larger quantity of the chemical than usual was inadvertently employed for the fumigation of an artist's model. The vapours were so abundant that the evaporating dish had to be carried immediately out of the room, but on the way it was held for an instant near the woman's side. Some of the gas reached her right side, which was unprotected, and of course there acted upon the aura, though to a less extent. No thought was given to the result, as it was taken for granted that the whole aura would be of the same colour, whether blue or green. Directly the examination commenced, however, a great contrast was noted on the two sides, the right being an opaque green and the left a blue. A further test was undertaken at the very first opportunity to corroborate this observation. The subject chosen was a perfectly healthy woman thirty years of age. Her left side was slightly fumigated with bromine, while the right was protected. The aura, previously a blue colour, changed to an opaque green. Subsequently it was dosed bountifully with the vapour, when it turned a blue of quite a different shade to the natural colour. After each of the applications, the aura was examined through the various screens, and in each instance showed considerably more green than before.

It is worth remarking that bromine is the only vapour which has been found to produce dichroic changes in the aura, though further investigation will probably discover other substances with similar properties.

As modifications in the colours of the aura take place upon exposure to the action of bromine and iodine, it would indeed be strange if their congener chlorine did not possess some similar influence, which was found to be the case, though contrary to expectations, this element was less active than the other two. The aura in every case without a single exception, when treated with chlorine, turned more opaque and a yellow green, the tint, however, not being identical with the one produced by bromine.

Exp. 6. A woman had chlorine applied to her left side. The gas was generated by the usual process, viz., the action of sulphuric acid upon a mixture of salt and di-oxide of manganese. The colour of the aura which was originally blue, now changed to an opaque green. Examination through the dark carmine screen showed that the inner aura had lost distinctness and striation, and could only be detected with difficulty. For the other changes noted, see table 5, series 4.

A green shade is the easiest to produce, and has been found when the aura has been acted upon by ammonia, carbonic acid gas, or the fumes of strong hydrochloric acid, as well as by chlorine or bromine.

It may with justice be objected, that the vapours

did not act directly upon the auras, as has been supposed, but that the skin was influenced and through it the auric forces, making the change of colour secondary. To obviate as far as possible this error, an artist's model was asked to resume her shift, and her side was then fumed in the usual manner with iodine. After disrobing, a result identical with the previous experiment was seen to have been produced. As in all these tests only a small quantity of the chemical was used, the greater part could never have been near the garment, and any of the vapour which did come into contact with it would, probably on account of the temperature, be deposited as a solid, so that, if by any chance some of the gas did permeate the meshes of the material, it must have been a very minute quantity. The chemical would afterwards have to traverse the air-space between the shift and the body, thus making the amount of iodine that could have possibly reached the skin so infinitesimal, that its action might be absolutely ignored.

It was always noted that when one side of the body had been treated with iodine vapour, the aura turned a red-brown, and this colour was confined to the same side, being limited by the middle lines of the body back and front. The other side remained either unaltered or changed in a different manner.

The next step would naturally be to apply the vapour to the spine. A few drops of the tincture of iodine was placed in an evaporating dish, warmed until fuming, and then moved down the spine of a patient twice, keeping as accurately as possible to the centre. The result was that the aura turned a red-brown, the colour being equally distributed on the two sides. This even distribution always took place when a large or moderate quantity of the chemical was employed.

The aura of a healthy woman was a blue-grey, the colour being exactly the same on the two sides of the body. Her back was fumed by passing an uncorked bottle of Tinct : Iodid : Fort : rapidly down, but not touching, the spine once. No change in the aura could be detected on the left side, while the colour on the right became the red-brown usually seen as the effect of this vapour.

This last experiment has been repeated a good many times upon different people, varied only by the quickness of the movement and the number of times the bottle was passed down. The results were :—with slow movements or when repeated several times, for the auras on the two sides of the body to be equally or nearly equally affected ; with one, or at the most, two quick passages of the bottle for one side to remain unaltered, and the other to become a red-brown ; and lastly, the aura on one side became the usual red-brown while the other was only partially converted, retaining more or less of its original colour. These results corresponded to the extent of fumigation. The deep colouration occurred as many times on the right as on the left.

In considering the effects of electricity upon the aura it was thought that the ozone might possibly have determined some of the alterations observed. For this and other reasons many experiments have been tried with this agent. The gas was generated by means of an ozone tube connected with the large Wimshurst machine. Sometimes the patient stood so that one side alone should be influenced by the gas, and at other times both sides were alternately exposed to its agency ; again at other times the subject was made to turn round several times slowly so that the whole body might be affected as evenly as possible.

A colour change was observed in every instance, and in many cases the haze became more distinct and sometimes more opaque. The hue attained was a red-brown, not very unlike that produced by iodine. The alterations caused by ozone were not exactly alike on every occasion, but generally the differences could be explained as depending upon either abnormalities of the aura due to ill-health, or the direct effects of electricity.

K.E., aged thirty-two had a very good shaped aura, the colour ot which was a blue-grey, but, when looked at through the deep blue screen, mixed with a small amount of yellow. She leaned over the ozone tube placed upon a chair, the inner tube only being connected with the electrical machine. No colour change was induced. Both tubes were then excited. The aura then turned a red-brown. On the opposite side the aura became more opaque and a whitish tinge was superadded to the original colour. Subsequently she stood upon the insulated stool, and was negatively charged and a few minutes later was examined again, when the outer aura was round to be enlarged in the usual manner. There was no further alteration in the colours, as the left side remained a red-brown, while the right was an opaque grey-blue.

Although static electricity had never so far been noticed to cause any alteration of colour, yet, as it was thought advisable to eliminate any chance of this change being overlooked, the air was first charged as above described.

It seems curious that when one side of a patient had been exposed to ozone, there should be any alteration of the aura on the other side of the body, but this phenomenon has been frequently found to occur. The same effect has often, only to a less extent, been noticed when applications of other chemicals have been made. At first it was thought that it might be caused by a minute trace of the gas reaching the opposite side. This supposition was, however, negatived by the application of a very small amount of the gas, which gave rise to no extra opaqueness and no heightening of the blue colour. The difference of the two colours on the two sides remained after the subsequenting charging proved that electricity had no action in inducing the colour change. The only explanation that can be offered is the asymmetry of the aura. (See page 209).

Attention must now be directed to the changes in the aura that can be brought about (1) voluntary efforts upon the part of the subject, and (2) suggestions to a subject in a hypnotic state.

In the investigation of the effects due to volitionary efforts, several essentials are necessary to ensure success. The patient should have well marked outer and inner auras ; must be in good health ; ought to take an intelligent interest in the subject ; possess great powers of concentration ; and, lastly, have perseverance if not at first successful.

Case 24. The first favourable opportunity occurred during the inspection of the aura of a young woman G., just under twenty ears of age, whose development had been delayed. Her case was interesting on account of the rapid growth of her aura, which in less than eighteen months had increased in breadth two inches by the side of her waist. Her natural functions had been established, and she looked a picture of health. Her aura was very distinct, perfect in shape, and even in brightness all over the body and showed no signs of rays—in short an ideal one for the purpose. Before commencing the experiment, she was allowed to see how the aura emanating from the tip of one finger could be voluntarily extended or diminished, and she was asked to reproduce the phenomenon in her own case. In this she almost immediately succeeded, and was then requested to try and induce prolongations from various parts of the body. The first place chosen was the crest of the ilium, from which, theoretically, rays should not unfrequently be observed to originate, though in practice, are rarely seen. In about half

a minute the inner aura on the selected part commenced to look brighter and then to gradually extend
outwards and upwards as far as the external margin
of the outer aura. The girl then relaxed her efforts,
and the ray rapidly receded.

The next point chosen was on the lower part of
the thorax, while she was standing in the same
position, viz, facing the observer. Rays of all kinds
(page 52) and also patches of light are not uncommonly seen in this part. The result was unexpected,
as instead of projecting outwards, the whole of the
inner aura from the sixth rib to the crest of the ilium
became bright without any extension, constituting,
in fact, a large pseudo-ray. The two shoulders were
the next spots selected. Here there did not seem
to be any difficulty, as the rays manifested themselves
almost immediately, running upwards and outwards.

The patient now turned sideways, and concentrated
her efforts in the projection of a ray from the tip of
her nose. The ray appeared at once, and stretched
out seven or eight inches, and was actually prolonged
beyond the limits of the visible outer aura. As by
this time the girl was evidently becoming tired, she
was requested as a last experiment to emit a ray
from one of her nipples. This she did immediately,
but the whole of the inner aura in front of the breast
became brighter.

It has already been pointed out that the aura over
prominences of the body is by far the most susceptible
to external influences, owing to the fact that the
auric potential is greater on points than on plane
surfaces. It is only natural to suppose that volitional
efforts would produce better results at these points.
The above mentioned experiments taken in conjunction with many other similar ones prove the
correctness of this supposition. But in coming to
this conclusion it must not be forgotten that the
concentration of the mind on a given spot chosen

for experimental purposes is comparatively easy, when a distinct portion of the body is selected, but the difficulty is increased when a small area in the midst of a large plane surface is chosen. In every instance it has been noticed that as the subject becomes weary, the power of concentration is lessened, and the effects usually produced diminish in intensity and become diffused.

In the above instance when a ray was desired from the nipple alone, the inner aura round the whole breast was also affected to a less degree. Had this effect been confined to a single instance, the diffusion might have been attributed to fatigue, but the same experiment has been repeated by different women always with the like result, even though the patient may have been quite fresh. The phenomenon is probably due to the intimate physiological connection between the gland and the nipple, which prevents the one from being affected without a corresponding change in the other.

As soon as the investigation had proved that the emission of rays from the inner aura was, at any rate to some extent, under the control of the individual, the enquiry was naturally pushed in the direction of voluntarily induced colour changes, which, it was thought, might prove not merely of great interest, but of considerable importance in the support of the theory advanced in chapter vi., viz, that colour alterations were frequently the foundations of the lighter and darker patches seen in the complementary coloured bands. In order to carry out the necessary experiments, the services of an artists' model, who was the subject of many ordeals until she emigrated, were requisitioned.

Case 25. A widowed woman, twenty-seven years of age, the mother of two children, had her aura examined in the ordinary manner. It was distinct and of a grey-blue colour. As she faced the observer, the outer aura surrounding the head and trunk was about ten inches in width, but narrowed a short distance below the level of the pubes and became four by the ankles. When she turned sideways, the aura in front of her trunk was five and four inches lower down. At the back it was four inches by the shoulders, bulging outwards until it became eight inches at the small of the back. It contracted suddenly just below the buttocks to four inches, keeping nearly the same width down the extremities. The inner aura was three inches by the head and trunk, and a little less further down. The complementary coloured band showed only one patch on the sacrum, otherwise was even all over the body. With her hands resting on her head, the extensions of the band by the sides of the body were alike on the two sides. As she stood facing the observer, with hands upon hips and elbows extended, the auras in the interspaces were similar in colour and density on the two sides. She was in excellent health, but, as might be surmised by the shape of the aura, of a hysterical temperament.

It was thought advisable to commence with attempts to project rays from different parts of her body. This she accomplished without much difficulty, but as the experiments differed from the ones quoted in the last case by only minor variations, they will not be described. It is worth recording, however, that the first ray took longest to appear, while each successive one was more and more prompt, until the last one flashed out almost instantaneously. She could perceive her own aura easily, and see rays quite distinctly, sometimes even before the observers.

She was now directed to make attempts to induce colour changes in the aura. As the use of colour names would have introduced not only an unavoidable source of uncertainty and error, but also a factor of unknown importance involving additional strain and probably the waste of a considerable amount of energy, precision was obtained for any instructions given, by drawing the woman's attention to any object, e. g., a book, of the colour required.

Exp. 1. As she stood with her hands upon her hips, she was first requested to make the aura in the left space of the same colour as a certain red book (darker portion of crimson alizarine of Rowney's specimen sheet of colours).*

In about a minute she said, " she could see the aura change in hue, becoming a scarlet red, but could not make it the same colour as the book." Afterwards she pointed out scarlet-vermilion as the colour attained. The observer's impressions were as follows : At first there was no alteration in the aura, both sides being alike ; soon an indefinite and almost indescribable change took place, and ultimately the whole aura seemed to vanish, leaving the space black ; the haze then re-appeared and disappeared two or three times, when the space became red-grey (grey and vermilion), instead of being as at first a blue-grey. At the commencement of the change only the inner aura was affected, and the part nearest the axilla was decidedly the most coloured and densest portion. The woman was asked to maintain the altered condition until the black background could be exchanged for a white one, to allow of examination with the complementary coloured bands. With the blue complementary coloured band the right extension preserved exactly the same hue as it had prior to the experiment, but the left extension was much darker with the blue and yellow complementary coloured bands, while with the red it was at first darker and, as the subject became fatigued, lighter. In order to eliminate errors due to uneven illumination, she was turned with her back to the observer, but

*The names of all the colours mentioned in this book are taken from Rowney's sheet of colours.

this made no difference in the colours. It is interesting to notice that on two or three occasions, different observers have seen and remarked upon the disappearance and return of the aura as above described.

Exp. 2. She was now requested to change the aura on the right side to a blue colour, which she accomplished with comparative ease. The colour attained was the darkest shade of permanent blue. After raising her hands and placing them on her head, the aura on the right side continued blue, while on the left side it retained the red tint (experiment 1) even down the thighs and legs. The effect produced by the different colours on the two sides was weird and bizarre in the extreme.

Exp. 3. While standing with her hands up, she attempted to alter the colours of the aura on the left side to yellow. She said " she could plainly see that colour," but for the observer, although the hue had changed somewhat, it never became a true yellow. The nearest colour on the chart was the darkest shade of Roman ochre. Of the colours red, yellow and blue, she found the last the easiest, and the yellow the most difficult to produce.

Interesting as these experiments undoubtedly are, they were considered only as a prelude to the following, which, not so striking, are more valuable. The chief aim all along was to obtain a coloured ray emanating, not from any projection of the body, but from a circumscribed area, part of a large plane surface. For this purpose certain new conditions were necessary, first that the aura surrounding the ray should not be affected in any way, or at the most to only a slight extent. This meant that the subject should be able to concentrate his or her mind upon a very limited area. A second condition was that the rays should issue at right angles from the body and proceed straight towards the observer. In all probability this would cause the ray to be invisible in the ordinary way, as the skin makes a bad background.   And lastly that the subject should be able to keep the ray constant for sufficient time to permit a critical examination with several complementary coloured bands.

The writer, aware of the many inherent difficulties, was agreeably surprised at the results of the first trials, which were not a little due to the painstaking efforts of the model, who before they were finished, was beginning to lose the power of concentration from sheer weariness.   Her power of perceiving the coloured rays was of the greatest assistance, as she could give the signal when to look for them.

Exp. 4.   A small area, half on the breast and half on the sternum, was chosen for the first trial, and the model was asked to turn the aura at this place red. Within a minute she said " she could see the spot red," while it still remained invisible to the observer. However, with the complementary coloured bands a patch was seen darker with the yellow, but lighter with the red.

Exp. 5.   In the next test the woman was asked to emit a red ray from a small space over the abdomen, not exceeding an inch in diameter, without mentioning or otherwise indicating its exact position.   As soon as she was ready, the abdomen was examined with the blue complementary coloured band, and the spot, a little above and to the left of the umbilicus, was immediately detected, and the writer placed his finger upon the exact centre of the place, over which the change had been produced.

Exp. 6.   Mrs. A. then attempted to alter the hue of the aura over an unknown place on the thorax, choosing yellow for the colour.   When she was ready the spot was searched for by the aid of the blue complementary coloured band.   A patch about two inches in diameter, darker than the rest of the band, but not clearly defined, was discovered upon the upper half of the left breast, and the writer put his finger on the centre of the dark patch. This, instead of coinciding with the middle of the place upon which she was concentrating, was only on the edge of it, about half an inch from the true centre. The diffuseness of the colour change evidently arose from fatigue.

The effects of suggestion while in a hypnotic state will now be considered. The differences between these effects and the phenomena recorded above is by no means as fundimental as might have been imagined, since in the one case, the results are brought about by the individual's own efforts, while in the other an outside suggestion is accepted and put into force. In the hypnotic state the objective mind has been cut off from the outside world, allowing the subjective mind to exert more active control. The writer believes he is stating the point correctly, but confesses that his main interest centres in the physical aspects of the results obtained.

Dr. A. Douglas suggested that it might be interesting to ascertain whether changes take place in the aura during hypnosis, and with this object brought a lady who had kindly consented to place herself at his disposal for the necessary investigations.

(Case 26.) A thorough examination of Miss X.'s aura was made prior to any experiments. Her outer aura was spatulate in shape, rather broader above the shoulders than usual, but had no other peculiarities. The inner aura was a little wide. Striation could be easily seen, but by the right side of the thorax and in the small of the back was coarse. The blue complementary coloured band in these regions was darker, which was also the case on the left side of the thorax between the sterno-xiphoid and subcostal planes, following the contour of the ribs.

Exp. 1. Dr. Douglas induced a hypnotic sleep of the first degree. The outer aura diminished in size round the body and became less distinct, while the inner, although retaining its natural width, was by no means plain. Above the shoulders both auras were increased in size and clearness, but striation was less marked. The inner aura could be clearly seen above the head, a rather unusual circumstance as the hair greatly interferes with its recognition. Directly Miss X. was roused from her lethargy, the auras commenced to return to their normal state, which was reached in a few minutes.

Exp. 2. Dr. Douglas then put her into a cataleptic state, as she stood facing him. Her left arm was lifted and her hand placed upon her head. The condition of her aura was the same as in the last experiment, except that the inner was much brighter and more opaque round the arm and hand, where also no striation could be detected. The moment she was recalled, the aura quickly regained its original condition.

Exp. 3. She was now passed into the trajectory state. Almost immediately the inner aura all over the body disappeared, leaving a dark void space nearly two inches wide. (Compare page 91.) Just outside this empty space the outer aura was massed, looked opaque and at the same time contracted. Nothing remained visible in this dark space through the deep carmine screen. When the screen was laid aside and the room darkened, a bright ray was observed proceeding from the patient's left elbow towards Dr. Douglas, who was standing about two feet away. This ray was nearly three inches wide and quite straight. Near its termination it spread out a little. As soon as she began to revive, the inner aura commenced to return, but had not completely regained its normal condition before another test was initiated.

Exp. 4. The last experiment was repeated. The inner aura was greatly diminished, but did not this time completely vanish. The outer aura was in the same condition as during the last experiment. Suddenly the inner aura increased in brilliance, and coincidently the woman regained consciousness, although not recalled by Dr. Douglas.

During the time Miss X. was in the hypnotic sleep, if a hand was held near her body, the mutual attraction was not as strong, nor did the aura turn as bright as usual, while the interval before any change could be detected was considerably longer than under ordinary circumstances.

A week later Dr. Douglas brought the same lady a second time for investigations with coloured screens in the various stages of hypnosis.

Exp. 5. Miss X.'s aura was inspected and presented the same appearances found at the preliminary examination described on page 125. The details of further examination with coloured screens are set forth in the table. (See table 6, series 1.)

Exp. 6. Hypnosis of the first degree was induced. For general details see page 125. For screen colours see table. (Table 6, series 2.)

Exp. 7. Dr. Douglas, without rousing her, then passed Miss X. into the trajectory state. The larger portion of the inner aura had vanished, but what remained was investigated through blue and violet screens and presented quite a different colour to the outer aura. While the inspection was in progress, a sudden change came over the auras, both becoming brighter, more especially the inner. Dr. Douglas said that she was returning to consciousness of her own accord, without having received any instructions from him. He had scarcely finished speaking before she was full awake.

Exp. 8. As Miss X. was standing in the same position, during examination through the dark blue screen, Dr. Douglas, without the writer's knowledge, again induced a hypnotic state of the first degree. An immediate alteration in the auras was noticed, and while it was being described to him, Miss X. passed into the trajectory state. This, too, the writer

TABLE VI.

Series.	Aura.	Red screen.	Orange screen.	Yellow screen.	Green screen.	Blue screen.	Violet.
1.	Normal. IA. Blue. OA.	Greenish Red. Blue.	Blue. Blue.	Blue.° Blue.	Blue. Blue.	Ochre. Ochre.	Yellow & Violet. Yellow & Violet.
2.	1st stage of hypnosis. IA. OA.	Bluish. Bluish.	Red. Red.	Blue. Blue.	Blue. Yellow-green.	Yellow, Blue, and Green. Bright Blue.	Violet. Violet Blue.
3.	2nd stage. OA. IA.	Red-blue. Red-blue.	Blue. Blue.	Blue. Blue.	Blue. Blue.	Blue. Grey-yellow.	Blue & Red. Blue & Red.
4.	Arm flaccid. Aura less plain.	Blue.	Greenish.	Blue.	Blue.	Greenish yellow.	Yellow-blue.

instantly discovered. As normal consciousness returned, the auras increased in brilliance.

Exp. 9. Miss X. was next sent into a hypnotic sleep, and a suggestion was made to her that one arm was flaccid and could not be moved. It was placed in the same position as in the previous experiments, only her hand was supported against her hip by her garments at the waist. She was then awakened. The experiment was devised to imitate as far as possible complete paralysis of a limb.

The auras, especially the inner in the space between the arm and the trunk, were not as bright as those on the other side, which were normal. The colours as seen through the screens are noted in table 6, series 4. Immediately permission was given to move the arm, the auras reverted to their normal condition.

Exp. 10. The subject now stood with her hands resting on her head, and while in that position the aura was again inspected, and found to be normal. Without putting her to sleep, Dr. Douglas made passes along the internal surface of the upper arm and forearm, in which region alone the aura became less conspicuous but did not completely depart. This portion was also devoid of sensation, as was demonstrated by pinching or pricking. As soon as the passes were discontinued, sensation gradually returned, and the aura became *pari passu* normal.

It is very interesting to note that there was no such intensification of the aura round Dr. Douglas' hand, while he was making the passes, as is generally seen when the motions are imitated by other people.

Exp. 11. Miss X. when in her waking state was requested to change the colour of her aura, either locally or on one half of her body. The result was a dismal failure. She was afterwards put into a hypnotic sleep, and was instructed to alter the colour of the aura on the left side to red. She was unable to do this, but after some time the aura turned a dirty grey-ochre. Miss X. was then asked to make the aura on the right side blue. This she accomplished tolerably well. When she raised her arms, there was a contrast between the colours of the aura on the two sides. When she was turned, it could be seen that the auras on the two sides were dissimilar, and that the lines of demarcation were the vertical median lines back and front. This was what might have been anticipated.

Exp. 12. She was next desired to tinge a small portion of the aura on her chest yellow. This little patch, invisible to the naked eye, when examined with the blue complementary coloured band, showed up instantly. These experiments demonstrate that Miss X., in her natural state, had no power whatever to change the colour of her aura, but when in a hypnotic state, was, to a slight extent, capable of following the instructions given to her.

On a third occasion Dr. Douglas brought another lady who kindly offered her services for experimental purposes.

Mrs. Y.'s aura was examined in the usual manner, and was found to be well shaped, wide, and blue. The outer aura was of average distinctness, but the inner barely reached the standard of clearness for health, although striation could be easily seen. There was a well developed ray proceeding from her right shoulder upwards to the limits of the outer aura.

Exp. 13. While this lady was facing the observers, Dr. Douglas sent her into a slight hypnotic sleep. The outer aura then diminished in brightness and showed a tendency to mass just outside the inner. This latter did not contract, but became less marked.

Exp. 14. She was now passed into the trajectory state. Both auras became still more indistinct, but neither completely vanished. During the time she was in this condition, a ray proceeded from her left elbow and reached to the crest of the ilium.

Exp. 15. A suggestion was then made during her sleep, that the aura over the left side should separate from the body so as to leave an interval between it and the body. The aura showed no change on the right side, but on the left side, in response to the suggestion, seemed to contract and to mass about six inches from the trunk, but left no void space between the body and the aura, and whenever Dr. Douglas ceased prompting, it immediately returned to the same state as on the right side. A curious phenomenon occurred during the experiment, viz., that the aura on the right side turned a brighter blue while the left took on a greenish hue. Directly Mrs. Y. became conscious, her aura regained the natural shape, but the colour alterations persisted for some time. It was noticed that this lady's aura did not disappear during hypnosis to the same extent as Miss X.'s under similar circumstances. Another interesting fact was elicited. When a hand was held close to the subject's body during hypnosis, the rays proceeding from the observer's fingers were normal, but the subject's aura did not respond with the usual alacrity or to the same extent as when she was in her normal condition.

Exp. 16. Mrs. Y. was next given a negative charge from the small Wimshurst machine while standing on the insulated stool. Her auras were greatly diminished but never quite obliterated. Afterwards, when she was charged with positive electricity, the whole aura disappeared. In both cases the return to their natural condition was slower than usual.

Exp. 17. Mrs. Y. was next requested to make an attempt to turn her aura red on the left side. There was certainly some little alteration in the right direction, but it was not very definite. This was a fair result for a first attempt, and there is little doubt that she could have succeeded if she had practised for a short time.

Dr. Douglas proposed that she should be hypnotized

and the experiment be then repeated. Under these conditions a change to purple, not red, was obtained. She was next instructed to turn a small spot on the chest red. The colour changed sufficiently to be detected by means of the complementary coloured bands. A second trial was made during the same sleep. This test was more successful as the patch could be distinguished by the unaided eye as having a different colour. She also complained of having a peculiar sensation at the affected spot.

The greater portion of this chapter has been devoted to a comparison between the aura and the hazes that surround certain inorganic substances, and to the effects produced by various agencies. It is now necessary to see how far the details collected can assist in the recognition of the force or forces generating the aura, and the differences of these from other forces. But in order to allow a comparison to be made, it will in the first place be necessary to outline the main characteristics as far as known of the forces underlying the phenomena connected with the aura.

The force or forces that give rise to the human aura are probably generated in the body itself. It seems hardly possible that the two auras can be the products of one force, when it is recollected, firstly that the inner aura is striated, and that its margin is fairly well defined, and that it is frequently prolonged into rays passing into or even through the outer aura without any concomitant alteration in the latter. Again occasionally in disease, the inner aura disappears locally in toto, or what is more common, leaves a partially void space. This empty space, when it does not include the whole width, is situated close to the body, superficially resembling a very broad etheric double, while the residue of the inner aura may retain its lineation, or may become granular. In none of these cases does the outer aura invade the territory of the inner, but it may be simultaneously affected. The inner aura can be made to vanish by artificial means from every part of the body, leaving a void space, as when acted upon by electricity or by a chemical. (See pages 91 and 113.) Secondly, the outer aura is entirely nebulous with an indefinite distal margin, its visible proximal edge coinciding with the outer border of the inner aura. The presumption that there must be more than one force concerned, is thus further strengthened by the crenated appearance of the inner aura and the phenomena associated with the production of rays. Were both auras produced by one and the same force, it would be reasonable to expect that the outer aura would also show a tendency to adapt a wavy outline, the results of varying activities in adjacent areas, and would also participate to some extent in the production and emission of rays.

Thirdly, the outer aura is more developed round the trunks in females from the age of puberty upwards than in males, and there is no corresponding increase or modification of the inner aura.

It must, therefore, be concluded that there are at least two forces at work, one of which, that originates the inner aura, may be called the inner auric force, or shortly I.A.F. ; and the other that gives rise to the outer aura, the outer auric force, or O.A.F. Even should it be eventually proved that the two auras are only two different manifestations of one and the same force, for practical purposes it will probably be advantageous to treat the subject as if two forces were present.

I.A.F. apparently acts intensely across a very circumscribed area, and the distribution of lines of force can be easily detected, and the part of the aura in which these lines are made manifest has been termed the inner aura. Whether I.A.F. affects the aura beyond the visible striated portion is unknown. If not, the division is a natural one, otherwise it is empirical. On the whole this force is distributed fairly evenly over the whole body, but the breadth of the inner aura by the sides of the trunk shows that it must be rather more powerful in that situation than over the limbs. Although continuous the force is not constant, as projections in the form of unstable rays are common, and these beams are continually changing their positions.* They pass through the outer aura, but their transit cause no alteration outside their direct route. This is so easily modified by any local affection of the body, as to make the inner aura an extremely sensitive tell-tale, even though the deranged tissues may be some distance beneath the surface. It is, also, more or less under voluntary control; its activities being more easily augmented than inhibited.

O.A.F. has certainly a wider range of action than I.A.F., and shows no visible indications of lines of force. As one result of its action is produced round the whole body a nebulous haze, which displays greater range in size, shape, and texture than does the inner aura, and whose outer limits are impossible to determine accurately. At times this outer aura must reach out a considerable distance, especially when accompanied by an ultra-outer aura, or when it has been expanded after the dissipation of a communicated electric charge. Compared with the inner aura, it is far less under its owner's control, which has indeed only been demonstrated in the case above recorded

*These rays afford a solution to a problem that greatly puzzled the writer when he was experimenting with mechanical means for the detection and measurement of N rays. The difficulty was that sometimes a large deflection of the recorder was obtained, too great in fact for measurement, even though the rays encountered obstacles of the most diverse nature, while at other times, under the same physical conditions, the results were negative. It can now be easily understood that a deflection took place whenever one of these rays fell upon the needle, and that when no ray was present the needle remained stationary. The writer ceased experimenting along these lines after having come to the conclusion that whatever the issue might be, there seemed to be no prospect of its being useful for diagnostic purposes, as he had at first hoped. Directly he held in his hands the means the aura could be made visible and submitted to examination, he felt that better and more comprehensive could be obtained by studying the seen rather than the unseen.

of a lady in the hypnotic state, and in a few instances in which more or less complete colour changes were produced by voluntary efforts. Even these changes always commence and are more evident in the inner aura.

Different states of ill-health, either general or local, react upon the forces and indirectly on the two auras, altering them, but not of necessity in the same manner. With a local affection it is by no means uncommon for the inner aura to lose all its striæ and to be transformed into a denser and more opaque mass, of a different shade or colour to the adjacent portion, or its striæ may become coarse and in appearance quite unlike the fine lines of health. Occasionally a space utterly devoid of inner aura may be seen. Whenever a change takes place over a large portion of the body, the inner aura may or may not be correspondingly narrower on one side than the other. When a contraction of the inner aura takes place, it is accompanied by some modification of texture, and constantly by further ill-defined changes, which will be referred to later on. The outer aura varies less than the inner. Its colour, texture, and distinctness may change, but as a rule the chief alteration is in breadth ; it contracts but never entirely vanishes, except under the influences of some external force artificially applied. Pathological changes, involving large portions of the body or affection of the nervous system, may cause wide-spread alterations of this aura, which in certain circumstances are diagnostic. The outer aura may be contracted while the inner retains its proper breadth, but the converse does not occur, as the outer never maintains its normal size after the inner has shrunk.*

---

*Case 42 is, up to date, the only apparent exception to this statement, and in all probability would have been found to comply with the rule, had not the presence of an ultra-outer aura rendered impossible the exact determination of the outer limits.

The writer has been repeatedly asked whether the origin of the aura is electric or magnetic. Although he himself at first believed in the electro-magnetic origin of the phenomena discussed in this book, he was particularly careful to return very guarded answers, and preferred, in the absence of exact knowledge, to designate the forces concerned as " auric " —a term involving no claim to any real understanding of their nature, cause or action. As soon, however, as attempts were made to identify the auric forces with either electricity or magnetism, difficulties arose.

Consider, first, the case of magnetism. The haze round a magnet possesses polarity which, as before mentioned, can be demonstrated by placing two horseshoe magnets close to, but not touching, each other in the same plane. On rotating one, it will be found that the haze between the magnets is brighter when dissimilar poles are in opposition and *vice versa*. On the other hand, by no known means can magnetic polarity be shown to be a property of either aura. The outer aura is uninfluenced by a magnet ; the inner is acted upon by either pole in precisely the same manner, and seemingly with the same intensity, and no repulsive or inhibiting power has yet been discovered. This alone is sufficient to demonstrate that auric and magnetic forces are not identical.

Again it would have been expected that if the auras were of electro-magnetic origin, they would have shown local and general disturbances or inequalities referable to the amount and distribution of surface electricity. That such do not occur has already been pointed out, and it has not been found possible to establish any relation between the natural surface electricity and the aura ; in addition to which the nature of a communicated charge makes no apparent difference in the effects produced.

It has been suggested that the aura is due to radio-activity. The conjecture appears to the author to be very improbable, in fact almost impossible, but he feels that unless some reference is made to the subject a certain number of readers will consider that one possible origin of the aura has not been studied.

Radio-activity is to a slight extent a universal property of matter, and it would be astonishing if the human body showed no traces of the phenomenon. For the comparisons between the human aura and the mist surrounding a radio-active body, it will be needful to employ some substance possessing the property to a marked degree. Uranium salts seem to be as suitable as any.

The cloud enveloping a crystal of uranium nitrate differs from that round a magnet, inasmuch as it is irregular and composed of rays which run out to the margin, and are more numerous where the haze is widest. It does, indeed, bear a superficial likeness to the inner aura, which, moreover, it attracts and is attracted by. Probably all resemblance stops here. Radio-activity is due to the disruption of atoms, and is met with to any appreciable degree, only in certain elements with the highest known atomic weights, which, if they occur at all in the human body, are present in the very minutest traces. Iron (Fe—55.9) is the element with the highest atomic weight which is at all plentiful in the body. It, however, is possessed in ordinary circumstances of none of the properties under consideration. It seems, therefore, impossible that the aura should be caused by the radio-activity of the elements which enter into the composition of the body, and the difficulties in accepting such an explanation of its origin become insuperable when it is considered that in life the aura is to some extent under voluntary control, while after death it disappears entirely.

Whatever the true nature of the auric forces, there can be no doubt that the phenomena to which they give rise are intimately connected with and dependent upon the activities of the central nervous system, as the following examples will show :

1. The electric brush applied to the spine produces instantaneous enlargement of the aura, while applied to the median line of the body in front it has no effect. (See page 102.)   The reason is obvious, as the spinal cord and the large nerves proceed from it near the surface at the back, and can be easily stimulated, but there are no great nerve centres near the front.   The same effect is produced by holding the brush close to the forehead.

2. Changes in the shape and size of the aura occur as results of severe nervous disease, e.g., epilepsy, hysteria, hemiplegia, and when fully developed remain constant ; while if due to a transient nervous disturbance, such as sciatica, herpes zoster, etc., on recovery the aura gradually returns to its normal condition.

3. All kinds of impairment of mental powers automatically causes a diminution in size and distinctness of the aura, which is also narrower in the weak-minded.   These facts afford support to the contention that the higher brain centres are intimately concerned with the output of auric force.

4. When a patient becomes faint the aura loses a good deal of its brightness and is reduced in size.   The changes are probably the result of temporary nervous exhaustion.

Temperament, or the sum total of the mental and physical powers of individuals, has already been noted as exercising a great influence upon the aura—an influence mainly proportional to the mental endowment.   The aura is affected not only in volume, but also in quality, as is illustrated by the coarse-grained, grey auras of dull and unintelligent people.   It is unnecessary to enlarge further on the existence of an intimate connection between the central nervous system and the aura, a better understanding of the nature of which will prove the key to the solution of many problems.

Answers are also required to many questions, such as the causes determining the actual shape of the normal aura, and the sexual differences ; the mechanism of the discoloured patches seen with the c.c. bands ; the nature of the striæ of the inner aura, and the changes associated with granulation, etc. At present little more than the descriptions of observations actually made can be attempted.

This is, perhaps, a good place to answer an enquiry constantly made, as to the existence of the aura round a dead body. Although inspection of a corpse has always been repugnant to him, yet the writer has on several occasions made such an examination, but has in no instance observed any trace of an aura. It is only right to state that in each case several hours had elapsed since death. The time of the departure of a human being has always been felt too solemn an occasion to be occupied with experiments, however pregnant with interest.

The disappearance of the aura is only what might have been expected in view of the results obtained in hypnotic states, and the diminution of distinctness seen when a patient in a bad state of health is examined.

CHAPTER VI

COMPLEMENTARY COLOURS

Soon after the discovery of the aura, a friend called attention to the fact that if a light were gazed at, and the eyes were first turned to one side and then the other of any person, the colours of the spectre were often not identical. Having convinced himself that this peculiar phenomenon did manifest itself, the writer thought it possible that the apparition might be made an aid to diagnosis, but that for that purpose investigations must be carried out methodically. Experiments were commenced by gazing at gaslight, not that for a moment was it thought that such a crude plan could be satisfactory, but in the hope that the discovery of its defects might assist in future trials. It was noticed that the resultant phantom was complex, as the main portion was of one hue, and was surrounded by another entirely different. The inconvenience of having to work with two or more colours was immediately apparent, and this, coupled with another insurmountable difficulty arising from the constant changes in the colours of the spectre, which were initiated by the slight movements of the eyes for comparing the two sides of the patient, caused accurate results to be impossible. It was also recognized that if any benefits were to be derived from this process a monochromatic image was essential. After many experiments it was concluded that for obtaining this, pieces of paper of different colours answered the purpose as well as any thing else, though they were afterwards replaced to a great extent by transparent coloured screens, which will be described later on.

This chapter will be devoted to the problem of the effect of the aura upon complementary colours, than which a more extraordinary property can hardly be conceived. The monochromatic spectre is modified by the aura so that its colour is changed to a lighter or darker shade or its hue altered under certain conditions. It is needless to say that the whole topic is difficult and complicated, but the explanations that seem most useful will be given. Some of the theories put forward may appear far-fetched or even heteodox ; nevertheless they are advanced for want of better hypotheses. As the subject is entirely dependent upon colour vision, a few preliminary remarks will not be superfluous.

One widely accepted theory postulates the existence of three sets of colour-sensitive nerves in the eyes. White light is the outcome of an equal stimulation of all the colour-sensitive nerves, or, perhaps, it would be more accurate to say a stimulation proportionate to that which occurs with sunlight. The withdrawal or weakening of the stimulus to any set will produce a colour sensation which is thus derivable from the excitation of one, two or all of these sets of nerves, either separately or in combination. When more than one set of nerves are excited, they are usually unequally stimulated.

The writer has for many years considered that each person has their own proper primary colours, and accordingly sees a coloured object differently to any one else, but as a result of education every one calls the colour* by the same name. For instance, let two persons A and B look at an object of a colour usually designated as a shade of yellow. This colour might

---

*A simple test for obtaining one's own personal primary colours is to press the closed eye, when there will be generally seen small yellow dots covering the whole field of vision. Intermingling with these are much larger discs of blue, and lastly red points intermediate in size between the yellow and blue discs. The yellow are the most numerous, the blue next in number, and the red fewer and far more difficult to obtain.

only stimulate one set of colour-sensitive nerves of A, and would be to him a pure yellow. On the other hand, with B, not merely the yellow-sensitive nerves be excited but to a slight extent the blue-sensitive ; he would see a greenish yellow tone. But as both A and B have been taught that the colour is a certain shade of yellow, which, whenever they see, they will call by the same name. Nevertheless if A saw it with B's eyes he would designate it differently. Both would be correct. It follows as a corollary, that each individual probably sees in nature hues unlike those perceived by his neighbour. It is unnecessary to enter into this matter more fully except to state that the writer's primary colours are at the present time red, yellow, and blue, although thirty years ago the blue discs were a purple-blue. It is not proposed to consider any other theory, as this one will answer the purpose of explaining the action of the complementary colours.

Putting aside all speculations, it will be found that when one set of colour-sensitive nerves is exhausted to the utmost extent, the observer will on necessity be temporarily to the corresponding colour blind. If the red-sensitive be the nerves fatigued, he will be red-blind, although still able to perceive all the colours that do not contain red ; in addition he will be able to see any colour that has an admixture of red, but as if all the red has been removed. Taking a simple example, purple would be more .or less blue. This artificial colour-blindness evidently causes the eyes to become hyper-sensitive to many colours and shades of colours that do not contain red, as red helps to obscure a very faint tinge of other hues. The following experiments have been tried by many people, and will furnish a proof of the above remarks. When a band of light tinged with carmine, is thrown upon a white screen from a magic lantern, it will have a certain visibility, but should the observer previously look through a red or a blue glass at daylight for a minute or so, he will see the band having more blue, or more red respectively, although, perhaps, not quite as brilliant. Similar effects can be obtained after the eyes have been fatigued by looking at a blue or a yellow strip of paper (*vide ultra*), when the observer has for all practicable purposes become temporarily blue-blind or yellow-blind. Were it possible for two sets of colour-sensitive nerves to be inhibited for some short time, the observer would be completely mono-chromatic. This extreme proceeding is never requisite for the present investigations, and in practice it has been found impossible by this method to induce total red, blue or yellow blindness. However, the remark that "the eyes have become abnormally sensitive to certain shades of colour" remains correct. It is quite reasonable to suppose that this colour hyper-sensitiveness of the eyes permits the rays of the aura which are probably ultra-violet, otherwise invisible, to be perceived, and that this is one of the explanations why the different coloured patches can be seen within the complementary coloured bands.

In ill health, as will be noticed hereafter, the aura frequently contains more yellow than during good health, and this colour is especially pronounced in circumscribed areas from local disturbances. These patches are usually seen as yellow places in the midst of the blue complementary coloured band. The rationale of this penomenon is probably as follows: when the eyes have become sufficiently fatigued for the successful induction of the blue complementary coloured band, the yellow-sensitive nerves are only able to convey to the brain sensations of that colour to a limited extent, while they still retain their power intact for the shorter wave lengths of the ultra-violet yellow. Possibly these latter exert a greater influence from not being obscured by the more easily perceivd yellow of the ordinary visible solar spectrum. Another factor which very likely assists in the perception of the auric colours, but to which too much importance must not be attached, is that the body assumes as a whole the hues of the complementary coloured band and thus affords a better contrast to the yellow or other colours the aura may locally possess. (Page 170.)

Every one knows that if he gazes intently for a short time at a coloured object and then looks at the ceiling, or at a white screen, etc., he will see on it a spectre of the same object similar in shape but of a different hue. This secondary colour will for an equal amount of stimulation always have the same tint, which is dependent upon the hue of the object, and is termed complementary to the primary colour.   For example, after a yellow object, has been gazed at, the hue of the virtual object will be blue, the exact tint being governed by the shade of the yellow employed, and to a certain extent by personal idiosyncracies.

When an investigator has looked at a yellow object sufficiently long, the time varying accordingly to the brightness of the light, and the steadfastness of the gaze, etc., he will always see the after-image at first of the same blue tint, but this will gradually become lighter, and will more frequently blend with red, turning purple or plum coloured.   In these cases the complementary colour always includes a red tint, although it is at first masked by the intensity of the blue colour.

Should he, however, at first see a plum or purple coloured phantom, he may be sure that his eyes have not been adequately fatigued by the original yellow colour, or else that there is a larger amount of white light in the room than usual.   These modifications show the advisability of being conversant with the varying tints the spectre undergoes, but at the same time they do not make all the difference that was at one time imagined.   After a short time the phantom will vanish, but will be sure to return with an altered hue. This secondary change may as a rule be neglected, because the employment of the complementary colour is rarely continued sufficiently long for its advent. However, the secondary changes may at times be useful, as the following instance exemplifies.

After the examination of a woman by means of the complementary colours had been completed and the blind drawn up, in full daylight while the writer was speaking to her, a new after-image became visible upon her body, and in the middle of the band there was a yellow mark about the size of a shilling on the upper part of the left mamma about two inches from the sternum. It had been overlooked in the prior examination. The spot was quite invisible directly the coloured band had disappeared, but as soon as the eyes had been re-influenced in the ordinary manner for obtaining the complementary coloured bands, the patch became again perceptible and very distinct. Here was an unrehearsed effect which up to the present has never been repeated.

One other self-evident inference still remains, viz., that when the background is not white the complementary colours will not always appear in their true shades, but as if blended with the hue of the background.

Since these complementary colours are entirely subjective, they will receive the names of pigments which afford the best matches, these being sufficiently accurate for all descriptive purposes. After a large number of experiments had been made with the colours usually termed primary, the conclusion arrived at was, that they did not give such good results as mixed ones. As a consequence of the trials, the following colours have been chosen as the most useful.

1. Gamboge, complementary colour, Prussian Blue.
2. Antwerp Blue   „   Gamboge.
3. Carmine,   „   Emerald Green.
4. Emerald Green   „   Carmine.

Each observer should if possible select by experiment what colour or colours suit him best.

In routine work, use can be made of strips of coloured paper three inches long and three quarters of an inch in width with a black dot in the centre, pasted on black board. Experience has shown that this is the largest size that can be conveniently employed, since a longer object does not yield the complementary colour perfect to the ends. With a patient standing a few feet in front of the observer, one of these strips will give a band of the complementary colour which, when used transversely, will be wider than the body, allowing the ends that are projected on each side beyond the body to be compared with one another, and also with the central portion of the body itself.

In winter or foggy weather, especially in London, the difficulty of using paper strips for obtaining the subjective complementary colours is great, and it is occasionally impossible to make a thorough examination from the inordinate time required, which is exceedingly trying to both the investigator and the patient. To overcome this defect an apparatus has been devised, which can be used in daylight or, in an emergency, even by gaslight. It consists of a cylindrical mask about six inches long and five in width, with one end shaped to fit the face, while the other has a revolving cap in which there is an oblong slit three quarters of an inch in breadth. The slit can thus be turned either horizontally or vertically to the eyes at pleasure. Behind the slit is placed a piece of ground glass, and at the back of this again a transparent screen, which may be either a cell containing a fluid, or else a piece of stained glass. The mask ought to be blackened inside or else lined with velvet. A small mark can be made on the ground glass to act in a similar way as the dot on the coloured papers. The distance between the eyes and the screen will be about correct for emmetropic sight, but for presbyopia and myopia the reading glasses worn by the observer will be needed. The writer's personal apparatus has a removable diaphragm with lenses of the same focal length as the spectacles he usually employs.*

To use the apparatus, it is only necessary to hold it in front of and close to the face, and to gaze at the light, keeping the eyes fixed on the mark on the ground glass. In a few seconds the eyes will have become sufficiently affected, and the complementary coloured band can be perceived in the same manner as if the coloured papers had been used. The apparatus requires more skill in using than the coloured papers, as the screen needs alterations in depth of colour according to the brightness of the light.

As soon as the patient is ready for examination, he should stand in front of a white background opposite the light and illuminated evenly all over. Should there be any shadows on the background they must be made to correspond on the two sides. Preferably the light should be brighter than when the aura itself is being inspected, but almost always it will be necessary for one blind to be partially or wholly drawn down. After everything has been properly arranged, the observer must look at the sky through the transparent screen in the mask, or stare at one of the coloured paper strips, keeping his eyes fixed on the dot from twenty to thirty seconds according to the brightness of the light.

When coloured strips are used a brilliant light is required, so it will be necessary to pull aside the blind to allow the paper to be fully illuminated. The observer then turns towards the patient and looks at some pre-determined spot on the median line of the body, when, if used transversely, the complementary

*The distance between the eyes and the screen is rather less than the ordinary reading distance, producing a slight strain of the eyes which has been found beneficial in practice.

coloured band will be seen reaching across the body and extending to the background on either side, the whole being simultaneously visible. He is thus enabled to notice variations in the shades of the colour in every part of the band. The tints of the extensions of the band prolonged beyond the trunk can be compared with each other, but of course not with the portion on the body itself. The above-mentioned method, although simple, requires a considerable amount of practice, and the mastery of one or two details, trifling in themselves, will assist greatly in speed and comfort. First, while looking at the coloured strip, it is indispensable to fix the eyes on one particular spot and keep this in exact focus the whole time, as unless this is properly done there will be blurring and an increase of time needed for obtaining the requisite effect. A slight exercise of will is required for this, but practice will soon make the effort almost involuntary. Secondly, a novice often experiences a difficulty in keeping his eyes on a given place on the patient's body, owing to the proneness of the complementary coloured band to wander, often out of the field of vision, and for the eyes to follow it, thus completely destroying the value of the observation. When the habit of keeping the eyes stationary on one point has been acquired, the complementary coloured band will remain fairly motionless, and should it move away will return to its proper position of its own accord. As dexterity can only be attained by exercise, it is a good plan to train the eyes upon some inanimate object before proceeding to the examination of the human subject.

For the future, unless otherwise specified, the yellow strip of paper with its blue complementary coloured band will be the colour implied, and also for the sake of brevity, the letters c.c. will be employed instead of " complementary colour," and p.c. will indicate the colour of the strip itself.

As there are natural variations in the colour of the skin, and shadows on the body of a patient, the observer ought to notice every modification, however insignificant, before inspection with the c.c. band. With care, judgment, and a little experience, most of the difficulties from these causes will disappear. In its simplest form the c.c. band projected upon the body of a person in good health will be equal in tint all over, if due allowance has been made for any variations in the colour of the skin, and the extensions of the band beyond the body will generally correspond in hue with each other.

When the extensions of the c.c. band show on a healthy subject a tint on one side unlike that of the other, the difference is rarely great. This dissimilarity of shade is the simplest form of alteration of the c.c. band, and may only be the consequence of improper lighting ; however, all doubt can be dissipated by turning the patient completely round, when, if correct, the different tints will have changed places, this being proof positive that the alteration depends upon the aura itself.

Another very characteristic effect can often be elicited as follows :—note which extension of the blue band has the deeper shade ; then gaze at the blue p.c. strip of paper to induce a yellow c.c. band. More frequently than not the latter will have a lighter shade where the blue c.c. band was darker, and *vice versa*.

An occasional change in the c.c. band, when projected upon the body of a patient who at the time is not in good health, and standing with his face to the observer, is for one side of the body to be darker than the other. When this happens, the shades may blend gradually into one another, or a sharp line of demarcation may divide them. In the majority of instances when the division is sharply defined, it will take place at the median line of the body, but there are many exceptions to the rule, and the line of separation may occur at any distance to the right or left. If the c.c. band (on one side of the body light and on the other dark), be continued beyond the body, the extension on the light side will invariably have a paler shade than the extension of the dark portion of the band. This change seldom if ever occupies the whole of the trunk, and occurs most frequently between the levels of the mammæ and umbilicus. Sometimes one thigh has a different shade to the other. The dark part generally overlies a deranged portion of the body, and it will be found that this place is absolutely of a deeper hue than the rest of the band. On the other hand the affected portion of the body may cause the c.c. band to become lighter, instead of darker.

There is another variation slightly different, but much more common, in which instead of the c.c. band across half the body being changed in shade, a patch either large or small is lighter or darker than the rest of the band which surrounds it. When the patch is large it occasionally takes the outline of an organ in whole or in part. The smaller patches, not exceeding an inch or two in diameter, do not in themselves determine what organ is affected, though they generally point to some disease or local disturbance and almost invariably to the seat of pain or tenderness.

A third constantly occurring alteration of the c.c. band consists of patches or spots of a colour different to that of the rest of the band. Some shade of yellow seems the most frequent, and the interpretation, with very few exceptions, is that the patient has at the time, or has had recently, pain and tenderness at that place. The colour does not necessarily denote anything abnormal, as it has often been seen on the epigastrium when there has been no dyspepsia to account for it, and it is then apparently dependent upon active digestion of food partaken a short time previous to inspection. Elsewhere it generally points to some pathological change.

Four p.c. strips of coloured papers or four transparent screens have been chosen, each possessing advantages not presented by the others. These advantages seem to be generally dependent upon obscure causes connected with the patient. For ordinary observations the p.c. strip giving rise to the blue c.c. band is the most useful, and generally the only one needed, since it is more sensitive to changes than the yellow c.c. band, which is as its complementary especially valuable as a control to the blue c.c. band, if the change in tint be only slight. There are, however, occasions when it is better to work with the yellow c.c. band rather than the blue. Perhaps the most sensitive of all the c.c. bands is the green, but unfortunately it does not undergo so many variations as the blue, and the changes are more fleeting in character. In cases of doubt, its delicacy of action will determine a question of fine differences of colour. The choice of the colour for the c.c. band is usually unimportant, when it is borne in mind that occasionally owing to individual idiosyncrasies better results can be obtained with one colour than with another.

A prolonged examination will fatigue the observer's eyes, and as no amount of will power can render any assistance, he must either leave off the inspection for a few minutes or else change the c.c. band. The former, when possible, is preferable, as the latter is only a makeshift to be used when time is of consequence. The opposite c.c. band will then be the best to employ.

A most pertinent question and one most difficult to answer now arises. What is it that causes the band to be altered in colour ? In the first place for reasons already stated, it seems more than probable that the eyes of the observer are hyper-sensitive to certain colours after gazing at one of the p.c. strips of coloured paper, and can differentiate tints so nearly alike as would baffle ordinary perception. Next, theoretically, there seem to be five agencies that can alter the shade of the c.c. band ; firstly the skin ; secondly the thickness of the aura ; thirdly a change in the texture of the aura ; fourthly the colour of the aura ; and lastly rays.

Each of these propositions will be considered in turn. After making all possible allowances for any variations in tints than can be appreciated in the ordinary manner, it is quite within the bounds of reason to imagine that there may exist hues in the skin that can be distinguished only under exceptional circumstances. This has been kept constantly in mind and instances have been sought for that would settle the question, but up to the present time without any success, so that although possible, this agency must be so extremely rare as to be negligible. One fact that especially militates against the skin being the cause of the change, is that when the c.c. band is discoloured up to the edge of the body, the extension will be in like manner affected, being lighter or darker as the case may be. Under no circumstances can the latter change be due to the influence of the skin, consequently there is nothing to which it can be attributed except the aura, although it hardly seems possible that such a transparent, colourless, almost invisible cloud should have so powerful an action upon the c.c. bands.

Secondly is the thickness of the aura competent to induce any change in the c.c. band ? As the aura is composed of highly attenuated material (the word is used advisedly), it would be necessary to acquire an enormous thickness before any perceptible alteration could be produced. Everything points to a negative answer to this proposition. One case illustrates the fact in the strongest manner. A woman, when standing sideways to the observer, showed an aura in front of the abdomen quite four times as wide as by the thorax, yet when she turned facing, no difference could be detected either directly or with the c.c. band, which was uniform in colour over both the thorax and abdomen. Pregnancy supplies analogous cases, as the aura is in front of the abdomen much wider than before the thorax. Never has this extra breadth been observed to make any change in the shade of the c.c. band unless accompanied by some alteration in colour or texture.

The first two theoretical agencies that might cause a change in the shade of the c.c. band have thus been discounted, and there remains a third and fourth, which offer better chances for a solution of the problem.

Thirdly, can an alteration in the texture of the aura induce a sufficient change in the c.c. band to account for variations in their tints ? When the writer first began to employ the c.c. bands, he imagined that after gazing at the p.c. strip of coloured paper and then exploring the body through the light dicyanin screen, he was able to distinguish shades of colour better than without the intervention of the screen, and consequently this method was habitually used. Unfortunately this was a mistake, as it led to patches that could be seen discoloured without the intervention of a screen, being attributed entirely to an alteration of the texture of the aura, consequently giving a greater prominence to that condition than it merited. It is highly probable that in the majority of instances an alteration of the texture and chromatic changes go hand in hand. There remain, however, cases in which no traces of colour can be detected, so that modification of the texture of the aura is the only explanation left. If with each of the c.c. bands employed in succession the patch continues to be either darker or lighter than the surrounding tint of the band, the presumption is that the change of the shade is the result of some peculiarity in the texture of the aura. On the other hand, should one of the bands show a light patch which appears dark with the rest of the bands, then it is likely that there is some other change. (See page 155.) It is quite on the *tapis* that two of the bands may disclose a light patch which others show dark. This probably means that the patch is caused by two auric colours, which primarily due to ultra-violet radiations, for some reason do not blend in the ordinary manner. A good illustration as to what may be taken as an alteration of texture producing a dark patch, is as follows :

Case 28. C., a man fifty-three years old, was inspected in October, 1914. He was not really strong, but made the most out of every ailment. He had just recovered from an attack of lumbago brought on by rowing when not accustomed to that exercise, and afterwards getting a chill. He had been subject to indigestion and also addicted to taking too much alcohol. His aura had a blue-grey colour. The outer which was quite plain and distinct, had a breadth of eight inches by the side of the head, four and a half by the trunk, five at the back, and three by the thighs and legs. The inner aura was below the average in clearness, about three inches wide, granular at the small of the back, and also by the right hypochondrium as he stood sideways, but otherwise healthy. *All the four c.c. bands showed a dark patch* on the back, over the two lower dorsal and all the lumbar vertebræ, which reached to about two inches from the edge of the body on each side. This patch did not seem to be derived from any local colouration of the aura, as tested by the c.c. bands, so that there was nothing to which it could be assigned except the texture. In front with the blue c.c. band there was a dark patch over the liver, and a yellow one over the epigastrium. He had pain and tenderness in all these places. As he stood facing the observer with his arms akimbo, when the aura in the interspaces between the body and the arms was examined by means of the coloured screens, no yellow was found. Had this colour been seen, probably the patch on the back would, although dark with the blue c.c. band, have looked lighter with the yellow.

A patch may be produced by two or more colours. A good-sized patch was seen on the sacrum of a patient of a pinkish hue when the blue c.c. band was used. As the colour was uncommon, this area was examined with three other c.c. bands. With the yellow it looked rather darker than the rest of the band. It certainly was not a pure yellow, as it contailed a mixture of other colours, that could not be dissociated. With the red and green bands the colour was red ; the tint differed in the two instances, but it was impossible to decide the particulars of the variation. Each band also made a slight alteration in the size and shape of the spot.

The only feasible explanation was, that the patch was multi-coloured, being composed of two, if not of more, colours (certainly red and yellow were there), and that the different c.c. bands resolved them. Unless the pink patch consisted of ultra-violet rays, its appearance in the red and the green bands would be incomprehensible.

When using the blue c.c. band it is not an uncommon occurrence to meet with dark and yellow patches upon the same person, but light patches accompanying the yellow are infrequent. On only one occasion have there been seen, when using the blue c.c. band, yellow dark and light patches on the same individual. The patient was a hysterical lady, of whose case a description is given in another chapter.

The pathological alteration of the texture that gives rise to a dark patch in the aura when seen by the aid of the c.c. band, always consists, so far as has been noticed up to the present time, of a coarsely granular state of the inner aura, but it is undecided whether the outer aura assists in any way. In no instance where the blue c.c. band has been employed and a light patch become visible, has it been possible to exclude all chromatic alterations of the aura, so as to be fairly confident that the change was wholly due to a textual modification. Theoretically an alteration of the substance may have taken place, but it is extremely difficult to obtain unequivocable proof of it, as the observer's eyes so often become tired before the examination is completed, and besides, patients naturally object to a too prolonged inspection, having usually come not for experimental but for diagnostic purposes.

The fourth agent, viz., the colour of the aura, has a much surer foundation, as patches of different colours to the surrounding c.c. band are being constantly perceived. When employing the blue c.c. band, yellow is the commonest colour, and next in frequency an indefinite pink. The shades of the yellow range from a transparent lemon to the darkest shade of Roman ochre. Besides a pink which varies a good deal, there are a number of hues that defy description, as they are evidently mixtures of ultra-violet colours. If these colours are naturally but merely locally present in the aura, an explanation is needed why they cannot be perceived except during the use of the c.c. bands. This has been partially given on page 151. On rare occasions it has been possible to detect them in the aura over (not by the side of), the body, but never as yet sufficiently distinct to describe. It is quite possible that better trained or more peculiarly adapted eyes may have the power of resolving them. At one time it was thought possible that the use of coloured screens might have revealed these patches without having to resort to the tedious process of partially colour-blinding the eyes. There was nothing but failure for reasons given a little later on.

In chapter iv., when discussing the likelihood of a secondary spectrum, an account was given of the inspection of the aura in the interspaces between the body and the arms of persons when standing facing the observer with their arms akimbo.   The results are extremely interesting, but the discrepancies so great as to render impossible any attempt to tabulate them in a useful form.   However, when the aura is investigated through the different coloured screens, two important facts stand out : First, during good health a blue tint is predominant.   Secondly, during indifferent health the aura constantly has an addition of yellow.

In good health the aura as a rule retains its natural colour, blue or blue-grey as the case may be, when examined through the yellow or orange screens, but it generally receives a tinge of red or violet when very dark screens of these colours are employed.   With the green screen the natural hue remains, or else the aura becomes a pure blue.   The action of the blue screen when dark is not that which would have been naturally expected. as it almost always causes the aura to assume a blue colour of a different quality and not resembling that of the screen.   At times when seen through any of the coloured screens, this blue may be mixed without blending with red, yellow, or green, but they are seldom distinct.   The auras of patients who are constitutionally weak, who have been debilitated from any cause whatever, or who are ill at the time of examination, are commonly more or less changed when looked at through the different screens, for the most part by the addition of red, yellow, or green, either singly or together.   The yellow is rarely absent and generally predominates over the other colours.   It may be a bright yellow, but the worse the health the patient has, the more nearly the hue approaches to the deepest shade of Roman ochre.

The blue screen is the most useful, and the only one needed to show the yellow when time is of importance, but when possible all the screens ought to be employed, as sometimes very bizarre effects are obtained.   The aura in the interspace between the arm and the trunk may be altogether blue, but usually the inner aura has a different shade to the outer, being as a rule darker or warmer. The inner may be yellow while the outer remains blue. A further variation is for the outer aura to exhibit an admixture of yellow or to be entirely yellow. The outer aura never contains yellow as long as the inner continues blue, nor is this colour ever more pronounced in the former than in the latter, so that it may be safely inferred that the inner aura becomes yellow more often and to a greater extent than the outer. It has been remarked elsewhere that the inner is the part of the aura that is most frequently changed locally, and in consequence very liable to assume a yellow hue in patches.

When an observer is investigating the aura in the interspaces between the arms and the body for colour, he is working under advantageous conditions, including besides a greater depth of the aura, a black background, but when examining the yellow patches on the body the conditions are by no means as favourable, because the body makes an inferior background, so that a yellow patch is harder to see, and consequently can only be detected by sensitive processes. This is the reason why too much importance should not be attached to the hue the body takes from the c.c. band. (See page 144).

On various occasions when using the transparent screens for the inspection with the complementary colours, the band instead of being projected directly on the body, had the appearance of being advanced several inches in front of the patient, and if horizontal, seemed curved towards the observer. This phenomenon has always occurred unexpectedly, and the writer has never been able to induce it voluntarily by focusing his eyes on a plane in front of the patient, nor when it once presents itself, is he able to throw the bands back on the body, without gazing through the p.c. screen again to induce a fresh after-image. This peculiar type of image, moreover, is quite useless, as the c.c. band, instead of being sharply defined, has always a weird and foggy look and never showed the slightest sign of any patch.

As the complementary colours are invisible in mid-air, and require a background for their perception, their appearance a little distance in front of the body of a patient has a peculiar interest. It proves that there must be some substance allied to a vapour or a gas which constitutes a background. There is only one thing that this background can possibly be, viz., the aura.

CHAPTER VII

The Outer Aura in Disease

If the theory that forces generated within the body give rise to conditions surrounding the body which can be seen under certain circumstances, and are known as the auras, be correct, it is reasonable to anticipate that these forces will vary and cause results varying in health and disease. In the former condition, after making due allowance for age and sex, the auras, both outer and inner, are within well defined limits very similar, all variations being due to individuality. It is extremely difficult to imagine any departure from health that can occur without in some manner influencing one or more of the auric forces, and in consequence the aura itself. If the ailment be only local, then probably there will be merely a circumscribed change in the aura ; but should the patient suffer from a general disease, the whole aura is liable to become affected, but as recovery takes place, it may return to its pristine state. (See cases 18 and 48.) The alteration in the aura occasionally does not seem nearly commensurate with the severity of the illness, as many of the modifications are far too subtle to be detected by the crude methods of observation at the present time available, but it must be postulated that future and more delicate processes of investigation will disclose a greater number and variety of defects. The changes most likely to be discovered at the present time are differences in size and shape of the aura accompanied by alterations of the colour and texture.

The auras of every one enjoying good health are

invariably symmetrical when they are standing facing or with their backs to the observer. One case mentioned elsewhere (case 51) is the only exception*. Down the front and the back of a person standing sideways, there is no equality. When a patient in ill health is being inspected, it is impossible, as long as the proper shape of the aura is retained, to determine whether the measurements of the aura are the same as when the patient was in good health, unless by any chance an examination either before or afterwards had taken place. (See cases 18 and 48.) It must be recollected that even it the patient had been inspected during health, a variation from the correct dimensions of his aura may be only apparent, consequent upon some change of texture, as it and visibility are closely associated.

In this chapter attention will be confined to instances in which the whole or a large portion of the aura is modified in shape from constitutional causes. The first departure from a typical aura that has been selected, is one constantly occurring, and more pronounced in women (solely on account ot the natural size of the aura), than in men. In the type under consideration, the aura is symmetrical, but instead of gradually diminishing and reaching its narrowest limits not lower than the lowest part of the thighs, as in health, it suddenly contracts, almost to its fullest extent, either at the level of, or a short distance below the nethermost portion of the trunk. Using a botanical term, this shape has been named " spatulate." Seen sideways, the aura in front is of average width or even broader, while at the back there is an outward bulge in the lumbar regions. The expansion usually commences near the level of the shoulders, and contracts sharply at the same horizontal plane as at the

*In the first edition of this book two cases were quoted of symmetrical auras in persons enjoying good health, but one of them had previously had an epileptic fit, which was not at the time admitted.

sides of the trunk, and then follows the contour of
the body. The inner aura apparently retains the
shape and size that is possessed by persons in good
health.

The spatulate type of aura is strongly presumptive of a hysterical temperament, and the more
pronounced the shape the more certain is the correctness of the diagnosis. Though most common in
adult women, it is not confined to them, as it has
been noticed in a girl eight years old, in boys of six
and twelve, and in men. All these cases exhibited as
perfect a spatulate aura as the natural shapes of the
hazes of young girls, boys and men would permit.
In every instance the mist was wider by the sides of
the trunk than normal, while by the thighs it was
natural in breadth or even narrow. These examples
suffice to demonstrate that the hysterical form of the
aura may occur in either sex. It is rarely detected
in girls under the age of puberty, or in boys, nevertheless it is possible that this deviation may have
been occasionally overlooked, owing to the difficulties
of distinguishing characteristic alterations. It is
exceedingly hard to decide whether the aura of a
girl when in the transitional state, especially during
the early period, is spatulate or not. Probable the
intermediate stage in girls is that at which the aura
usually commences taking on the abnormal form by
the sides of the trunk. It is doubtful whether at
birth the aura ever shows the increased breadth at
the waist or the narrowing above the upper third
of the thighs as is found in the typical hysterical
states. In one promising case, the aura of a girl
who was twelve years old and precociously developed,
was carefully examined, and was found to be in the
early stage of the transitional state. As she at that
time displayed hysterical tendencies, it was expected
that at least an abnormal bulge of the outer aura
would be present in the lumbar regions at the back,

but no trace of one, and not the slightest sign of spatulate aura could be detected.

An outward curve at the small of the back seems to be present in every instance of spatulate aura. This typical bulge usually begins about the level of the shoulders, convex backwards and then curving inwards beneath the buttocks, and is almost pathognomonic of hysteria in both sexes, whilst in the male or young people it is sometimes the solitary change that can be detected.

Girls who are more emotional than normal, and who are constantly described by their relatives as " slightly hysterical," although they have never suffered seriously, show a tendency towards the spatulate aura. On the other hand women not naturally hysterical, who through grave anxiety or trouble, exhibit auras having this special feature. A well marked instance (case 35), that of a young lady will be mentioned later on.

Case 29. (Figs. 29 and 30). D. X. was a girl two months under the age of seventeen years when inspected, rather tall, a perfect skeleton who five months previously had been plump. Emaciation had gradually progressed without any obvious reason, as all her organs were healthy. Menstruation, which commenced at fourteen years of age, had been in abeyance several months. She was depressed and lethargic but complained of no pain. Her family history was far from good, as she was the only child of neurotic parents. Her aura was grey tinged with a little blue, indicating a low type. Round the head the outer aura was seven inches wide, by the sides of the trunk eight, which would have been quite the average breadth for her age had not the shape been spatulate, and contracted as it reached a short distance below the lowest part of the body, where it became four and a half inches, and further decreased to three by the ankles. Sideways, it was not quite

four inches over the trunk in front and diminished
down the thighs and legs ; behind it was four inches
at the level of the spine of the scapula, but from this
point it rapidly curved outwards and again inwards
regaining its former width just below the nates, and
contracting slightly lower down.   The greatest extent

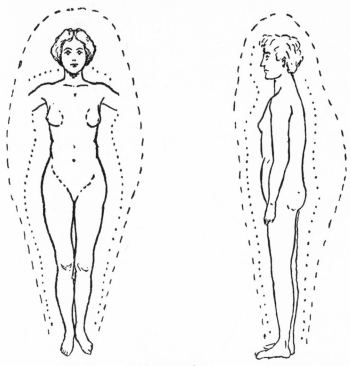

Figs. 29 and 30.
Hysterical aura.
Spine wanting natural curves.

the bulge attained was nine inches, which in itself
was remarkable for a girl of her age, especially as her
spine was peculiarly straight.   The inner aura was
naturally striated, about three inches broad over the
trunk, and a little less over the lower limbs.   The
colour in the interspaces between the arms and the

body, as she stood akimbo, exhibited through the different screens more yellow than was compatible with health.

Here was an ideal spatulate aura, so conspicuous that her aunt who accompanied her could easily distinguish its configuration. She was advised general massage, feeding up, etc. One visit only was paid, but her friends subsequently wrote to say that she

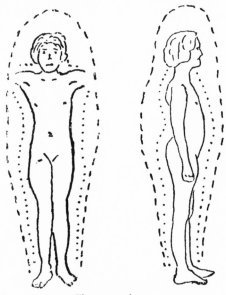

Figs. 31 and 32.
Young girl. Hysterical aura.

had regained her proper weight and appeared in good health.

Whilst examining some children for the effects of heredity upon the sizes of the aura, an early instance of the spatulate aura was discovered.

Case 30. (Figs. 31 and 32). E. X., a girl not quite eight years old was inspected in 1910. She was a bright and clever child, very excitable, but had a neurotic parentage on both sides. (See Table I.)

Her aura was bluish grey in colour. The inner was about one and a half inches wide displaying striation. On the left side over the whole of the trunk it was bright, being a good example of a pseudo-ray. (Page 52). In a short time this ray faded and the aura assumed its natural condition. There were areas of local brightness which gave the impression that rays were being emitted from various parts of the body, but none were absolutely developed. Round the head the outer aura was a little broader than the width of the shoulders. When the girl placed her hands behind her neck, the haze was four inches by the sides of the trunk, narrowing to a little less than three inches at a short distance below the pubes, from whence it proceeded regularly downwards. It was not easy to determine the exact width as the margin, especially by the lower limbs, was ill-defined. Seen sideways, the outer aura was barely three inches deep in front of the body, but at the back it bulged out, from the level of the shoulders to six inches at the lumbar region, and curved inwards a short distance below the nates. The c.c. band was even all over the body. This child had a wide aura for her age, which is all the more singular as the other members of the family had narrow ones. It was a typical specimen of an infantile spatulate aura.

Case 31. The next example has been chosen as the patient exhibited a very distinctive aura of this class. The boy was twelve years of age, far from robust, naturally quick and excitable, and had never suffered from any serious illness. His father had the same temperament, and his mother inclined to hysteria. He had been the victim of some peculiar attacks, one two years before, another about a year later, and a third a week previous to inspection. Each attack was sudden in onset, and consisted of a loss of individuality. He comprehended everything that was taking place, but all seemed a long distance away, and quite outside his sphere of action. The attacks vanished as quickly as they came on, and afterwards he felt none the worse for them. He gave a very good account of the seizure which happened a few days before his visit. It occurred when he was at school. He knew everyone and all that was being said or done. He repeated his lessons in a parrot-like manner, but was absolutely incapable to learn anything fresh. To him, the most curious symptom was his conception of time, half an hour seeming at least three hours.

His aura exhibited a blue colour, and was seen quite easily. The outer was six and a half inches round the head, as the boy stood facing the investigator, and five inches by the sides of the trunk, being symmetrical on the two sides. It curved inwards acutely at the level of the lowest part of the trunk, where it became only three inches, and continued this breadth down the thighs and legs. Sideways, it was about three inches in front of the body, but at the back there was a bulge six inches wide, commencing at the level of the spine of the scapula, and ending at the same level as the inward curve of the aura by the sides of the trunk, and then following the usual course downwards. The inner aura was about two inches all over, and striation could be easily distinguished. The c.c. bands were even over the whole body.

The above description is so nearly the counterpart of spatulate auras in adult males, that it would be useless to quote further cases in detail.

Allied to these cases of hysteria, there are others which exhibit certain resemblances but have one important difference, viz, that they apparently develop after severe shock to the nervous system, or an injury. The name traumatic hysteria designates the complaint sufficiently well. It would be interesting to know whether the auras of these people displayed the spatulate shape before the exciting injury occurred. Such is probably the case, although up to the present time no absolutely conclusive evidence has been obtained. It is undoubtedly instructive that one out of two or three dozen people, all of whom have met with somewhat similar accidents, should develop these nervous symptoms, while the rest remain immune from them. This fact strongly points to there being a constitutional predisposition. The youngest child whose aura displayed a perrect spatulate shape coming under this heading, was a boy six years of age. (Case 34). The early appearance of this condition after an accident, especially as it was accompanied by a rash ot nervous origin, strengthens the argument for previous neurotic tendencies.

Case 32. (Figs. 33 to 35). N., a retired officer, was wounded during the South African war in the shoulder. The shock of this injury apparently induced tunctional heart derangement of a severe type, which necessitated a complete rest for a considerable time before he was able to return to duty. Subsequently he was invalided once or twice, and finally had to leave the army altogether. After his retirement he went from bad to worse, until at the time he came for inspection he was unable to stand without the support of a stick. Both bodily and mental exertion tired him very quickly. He had consulted many leading surgeons in London.

The outer aura nearly reached the healthy standard of distinctness, but, for a man, was extraordinarily spatulate. It was nine inches by the head, and six by the trunk, as he stood facing the observer. It curved inwards just below the level ot the body, and became three inches by the legs. A side view showed it to be three inches in front, but at the back there was a bulge commencing at the shoulders and finishing just beneath the buttocks, being at the widest part seven inches, while lower down it was only three. The inner aura was far too indistinct for health, and striation could be detected only with the greatest

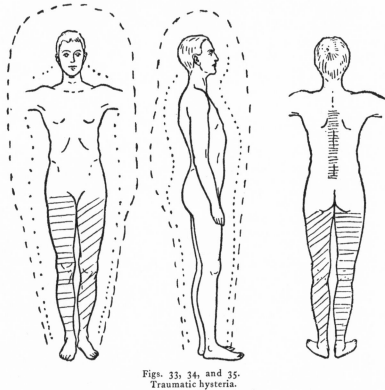

Figs. 33, 34, and 35.
Traumatic hysteria.
= Dark with the c.c. bands.
/////// Light ditto.

difficulty. It was three inches by the head and two and a half inches elsewhere.

The c.c. band was even all over the body with the exception of a long narrow patch over the spine, about two inches wide, and reaching from the fourth dorsal to the lower edge of the second lumbar vertebra. The whole of the right thigh and leg was darker than the trunk, while the left was lighter, and the extensions beyond the limbs corresponded, being paler on the left and darker on the right. Examination had to be carried out very quickly owing to the patient's inability to stand more than a few minutes. His

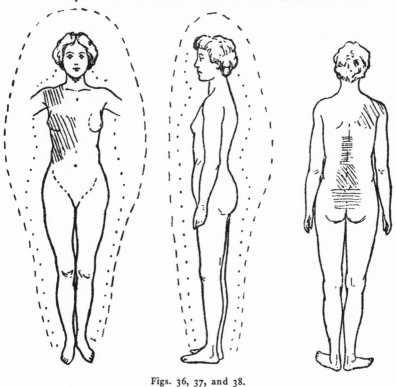

Figs. 36, 37, and 38.
Traumatic hysteria.
= Dark with the c.c. bands.
////// Yellow ditto.

right leg was weaker than his left. Knee jerks were excessive and equal on the two sides.

Case 33. (Figs. 36 to 38.) D, a thin spare woman, forty-five years of age, had been a servant in one place for twenty-seven years. Her mistress considered that she was excitable, but not, as far as she knew, hysterical. She enjoyed good health until January, 1914, the date of an accident, when she fell off a chair and hurt her back. It was expected that she would recover in a short time, but unfortunately such was not the case. She had been treated at two or three different hospitals, but became worse rather than better.

Inspection, which was made before any question was asked or any examination in the ordinary manner disclosed a spatulate aura, narrow, but of quite average distinctness. It was seven inches by the head and eight by the trunk, contracting to three by the legs. The inner aura was two and a half inches all over the body, except by the right side, where it was coarsely. granular, and appeared to be four inches in breadth. This granular portion could be seen extending round from the front to the back. Probably this apparent extra breadth of the inner aura was not genuine, but due to the outer participating in the derangement. No lineation could be detected at this place, but everywhere else it was visible. As is customary in hysterical causes, the c.c. band disclosed a good many local disturbances. There was a large multicoloured patch on the back extending from the sixth dorsal vertebra to the lower part of the sacrum. The centre portion of this patch was yellow, while the upper and lower parts were dark. On the right shoulder, both back and front, there was a yellow patch, and in front by the right side of the trunk there was another yellow patch reaching from the level of the thoracic to a short distance above the umbilical plane. The internal boundary was abrupt at the median line of the body. She complained of excessive pain in the spine and the right side of the thorax.

Case 34. A. I., a boy six years of age was examined in the early part of 1916. Until the previous July he had been healthy, rather excitable but not what would be commonly called a nervous child. A very peculiar circumstance had frequently been noted in connection with this boy ; as the result of emotion or some trivial indisposition, such as a cold, a rash would instantly break out over a portion of his body. It would be out of place to describe the rash more fully than to say it occurred in large patches and somewhat resembled Lepra Rubra. When it accompanied a cold the rash would last some hours, but if caused by excitement would vanish in from a few minutes to half an hour.

In July, 1915, he fractured his arm near the elbow joint, and was taken to a hospital, where a good deal of interest was aroused by the rash. Since the accident he had become very nervous, starting at the slightest noise, afraid of being left in the dark by himself, and incapable of doing things that he had been accustomed to do, being altogether a changed boy. Neither of his parents had shown any neurotic tendencies.

Both auras were quite plain, and the outer resembled in appearance the transitional state seen in girls of sixteen, except that it curved inwards more sharply at the level of the body. It was found to be five inches by the head and trunk, less than four by the thighs and legs, four inches in front, and at the back in the lumbar regions six and a half, being on the whole a wide aura for a boy of his age. The c.c. band was even over the whole body, with the exception of one yellow patch over the back of the neck, between the third and seventh cervical vertebræ. Query, had this patch any connection with the rash ? (Compare cases 77 and 78).

Although in every instance of hysteria that has been examined the spatulate aura has been present, yet in some allied conditions where this shape has been confidently anticipated, it has been absent. The following is a remarkable example :—

Case 35. H., a young lady twenty-five years of age, when she was eighteen attended an invalid relative for a year and a half, during which time she had not a single undisturbed night's rest, although working all the day. As a consequence, after the death of her relation, she had a nervous breakdown, and from being a bright girl became dull. By nature she possessed an amiable disposition, fortunately this part of her character did not change. Outwardly she was a well formed woman, but she had an undeveloped uterus, and had only menstruated three times in her life. She had undergone an internal operation in the country, the nature of which could not be ascertained. All round her eyes the skin was deeply pigmented, of a violet hue, giving at a short distance the impression of two black eyes. When first seen she was suffering from functional hemiplegia on the right side, with almost entire loss of sensation from the clavicle downwards, and was only able to crawl a few steps without the aid of a stick. Under treatment she soon regained the use of her limbs, and sensation became normal.

One peculiarity of her case was that the affected thigh measured two inches in circumference more than the healthy one ; the leg was also bigger but not to the same extent. This enlargement, due to increase of fat and not to anasarca, disappeared in a few months after her recovery, when both her lower limbs became symmetrical. A year later she had a slight relapse, which was of short duration. During her illness she was always desirous of getting well, did everything she could to help, and never showed any undue craving for sympathy.

Her aura was first inspected in January, 1909, and again in November, 1915. A description of the first examination will not be given as at that time the inner aura could not be separated from the outer. On the second occasion the outer aura was found to be almost identical with that seen at the first examination.

The patient was in good health when inspected in 1915, but was still slow in her movements, although she seemed mentally normal. Both auras were distinct. The inner, however, hardly attained the healthy standard of clearness. It exhibited striation which could be seen without difficulty, and in breadth it reached three and a half inches by the trunk, and a little less by the limbs. The outer aura was of the ovoid type. It was nine inches and a half round the head, eleven by the trunk, and gradually contracted until it was four and a half inches by the ankles. In front it was five inches all the way down, and at the back it was four and a half inches by the shoulders, and at the widest part seven, coming down straight without any bulge. The c.c. band was even all over the body, showing no discoloured spots. Nothing unusual was seen in the colour of the aura when examined through the different screens.

Case 36. A patient lately seen possessed an extremely interesting aura, as the front view seemed normal, but the profile showed it wide in front, while at the back there was a well pronounced bulge of the hysterical type, which commenced a little below the shoulders and terminated a short distance beneath the buttocks. Reference to the diagram of a transverse section (Fig. 40, d.), will make evident the curious shape of this bulge, which was particularly prominent along the middle line.

N., a poor miserable looking woman came to be inspected in May, 1915. She was sixty-two years of age and had never been robust. Lately there had been some family trouble, and at the same time she was worrying about the war, and in consequence had a complete breakdown. Whether sitting or standing she felt that she must fall as the room was going round and round. She complained of pain in the head, nausea, strange sensations all over the body, and inability to sleep properly. Her appearance at times was very peculiar, giving the impression that she was going out of her mind. Her mother had been insane. Upon examination no organic mischief could be found to account for the symptoms, so her ailment was considered to be pure neurasthenia. Under treatment her health rapidly improved, and she was able to leave her bed in a few days and do little things about the room. In a week or two she regained her health.

Upon inspection both auras were found to be well marked. The outer showed an approach to the spatulate type and had a huge bulge at the small of the back, beginning at the shoulders and finishing just below the nates. This part was highly character-istic of hysteria. The inner was coarsely striated, distinct, but of a most singular appearance. It seems extremely probable that the aura was in an intermediate stage between the normal and spatulate shapes.

Behind, the c.c. band disclosed two yellow patches on the back, the upper being by the left side of the spine, from the fourth to the sixth dorsal vertebræ, and the second upon the two lower lumbar vertebræ and the higher part of the sacrum, and there was a third patch on the right thigh where the patient complained of peculiar sensations. In front there was a light yellow patch over the epigastrium, due evidently to digestion, as there was no other condition to account for it. A dark spot was also seen on the lower part of the abdomen on the right side. In all these places she suffered pain and tenderness.

The colour of her aura was a bluish grey, and to the naked eye looked alike on the two sides, but the different coloured screens revealed a dissimilarity, as the right side was blue through the green screen, while the left was greenish and more opaque ; through the blue screen the inner aura on the left side was a yellow ochre, but on the right lighter and less yellow.

Besides being associated with spatulate auras, dorsal bulges occur under different circumstances. Varieties of these curves are met with in cases of organic mischief ; others denote that the patient may be excitable but not necessarily neurotic. All cases of organic change of the central nervous system are attended by the dorsal curves of some description, and the absence of these is an indication against the presence of organic mischief. In one characteristic form, which may be termed " Bow-shaped," the aura usually commences to enlarge at the head and proceeding downwards attains its full width at the small of the back, and then diminishes reaching its narrowest extent not above the level of the knees, but more commonly by the ankles.

When the aura of a patient who is standing with his face or back to the observer, presents asymmetrical irregularities, the healthy side affords a good gauge for measurement and for texture, etc. ; but when the patient is turned sideways, the want of a fixed unit for measurement for any increase or diminution is a serious drawback. Allowance has to be made for the variations presented by healthy subjects, and it is obligatory to fall back to a large extent upon experience, and mentally compare the aura with one known to be healthy. Speaking generally, no great trouble will be experienced when dealing with the auras of males and young girls before puberty, as they are fairly uniform all over the body. With women and girls of fourteen years and upwards the case becomes more complicated and a standard for measurement is almost essential. The best that can be devised, although open to many objections, is to take some ratio having the widest part of the aura by the sides of the trunk as the unit, in which case the breadth of the aura at the front or the back of a patient will usually be represented by a proper ıraction. In a healthy adult woman the ratio of the aura in front of the body with that ot the sides is about one-third, and occasionally may be as large as one half ; while the value of the dorsal aura rarely reaches two-thirds, except in neurotic females ;

certainly any higher figure is pathological. In girls the transitional state of the aura vastly aggravates the difficulty, as special allowances must be made according to the progress of the aura towards the adult form. Up to the present time no diminution in the aura on a large scale, has been recognized either at the back or the front of the body, this condition, if it occurs, is rare.

Case 37. (Fig. 39). B., an unmarried woman forty-six years of age, who had been unwell for a long time came to have her aura inspected. This was found to have a grey blue colour, as she stood facing, was of an average shape and size, being about eight inches by the head and trunk, and contracting to about four inches by the ankles. When she turned sideways, the outer aura made a bulge at the back commencing at the

Fig. 39.
Bow-shaped bulge.

top of the head and ending at the feet, where it was four inches broad. At the widest part it was just double this width. In front it was four inches all the way down. The inner aura was narrow being only two inches wide over the whole body, very indistinct, so much so, that striation could not be defined on the right side, and was only just perceptible on the left. The c.c. band showed a dark patch over the sixth and seventh dorsal vertebræ, a second, yellow ochre in colour, from the tenth to the twelfth dorsal vertebræ, and a third, a narrow one, on the sacrum. In front there was a patch over the right hypochondrium, dark but not so dark as those on the back. Finally the left thigh had a deeper shade all round than the right.

This patient was a school-mistress. Her illness (disseminated sclerosis), commenced, according to her own account in 1911, after an attack of influenza. She had been an in-patient at the University Hospital a short time before inspection. The disease was progressing. At the time of examination she was weak, swayed about when her eyes were closed, and had a tendency to do the same when walking. Knee jerks excessive. No nystagmus, but her pupils did not react to light or accommodation. Her left thigh and leg were wasted. She slurred her words when speaking. This, she said " she had done from a child," but a friend who accompanied her declared that the defect had increased considerably of late.

Although the aura can only be perceived for any particular position of the body as a lateral extension in the same plane, yet in health and in a considerable number of pathological states, it is not difficult to plot a diagrammatic transverse section. This has been done. Fig. 40, a and b, are those of a healthy man and woman, and the sections are supposed to be about the level of the second lumbar vertebræ. In other cases it is far from easy to draw the diagram. Take for example the spatulate aura at the waist of a patient, when the measurements are known. Here it is simple enough to make a diagram as far as the front and sides are concerned, but when it comes to the back the perplexity commences, as although the total thickness is known, yet many curves can be made from the sides of the trunk to the extreme point

Transverse sections

Males   Females

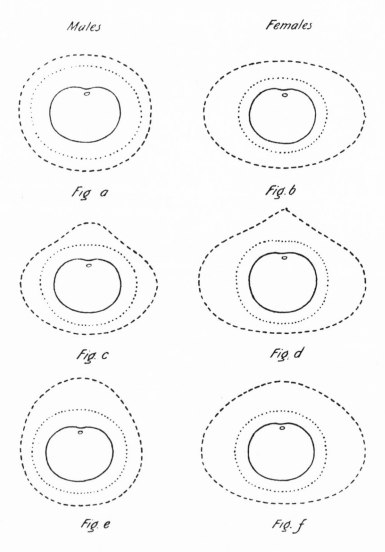

Fig a   Fig. b

Fig. c   Fig. d

Fig. e   Fig. f

Figs. a & b normal auras.   Figs c & d spatulate auras.
Figs. e & f auras with dorsal bow-shaped bulge.

Fig 40

of the aura at the back. The most likely are Fig. 40, c and e, for a man, and Fig. 40, d and f, for a woman. Personally the writer thinks that the Fig. 40, c and d, are correct for hysteria, and his opinion is founded upon a common aspect of the aura, which

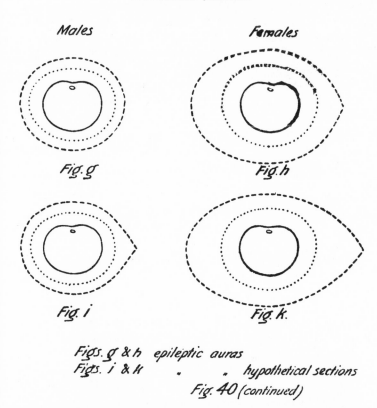

Transverse sections

Males

Females

Fig. g

Fig. h

Fig. i

Fig. k.

Figs. g & h epileptic auras
Figs. i & k   „   „ hypothetical sections
Fig. 40 (continued)

does not look as dense at the outer projecting part as near the body, when a patient is standing sideways ; besides, the angle of the shoulders and nates, is quite as acute as has been drawn in the diagram, which makes the transverse curve somewhat similar to the vertical.

In cases where the dorsal curve commences by the head and finishes by the feet, the writer has never noticed this apparent difference of the thickness of the aura near the body and at the edge of the bulge, and consequently imagines that the shape differs from the spatulate aura in horizontal as well as in vertical sections. (Fig. 40, e and f). Of course future observations may prove this idea to be incorrect. There is a third distinct shape of the transverse section of the aura, most pronounced in epileptics, as will be seen below. (Fig. 40, g to k).

Asymmetry of the aura on two sides of the body is not a particularly uncommon occurrence, and either the outer alone or both auras may be concerned. Epilepsy, which always seems to be associated with a want of symmetry, will be taken as the first example of the asymmetrical aura.

The aura of epileptics has a complete character of its own, quite unlike the hysterical type. The latter has been just described as wide and symmetrical, while the former is peculiarly unequal. The irregularity extends from the crown of the head to the soles of the feet, and is obviously due to a contraction of the aura on one side rather than to augmentation on the other. The change is not merely one of width, but also of texture. It is singular that in every case the diminution has been on the left side, but further investigation may show that the decrease can occur on the right also. The patients who have been examined have, without exception, been right-handed, and it is highly probable that a left-handed epileptic would have his aura affected on the right side. Patients not suffering from this disease occasionally have auras simulating to some extent the typical epileptic aura. These will be considered later on, but do not in the least detract from the diagnostic value of the type in doubtful cases.

The first thing to attract the attention when the

aura ol an epileptic is inspected, whether the patient
has had a recent attack or not, is the marked decrease
on one side of its width, and this is necessarily more
conspicuous in women than in men. The observer
will at once notice that the outer aura on the right
side of the head is two or three inches broader than

the shoulder, while on the left it
will generally not much exceed the
breadth of the shoulder and may
be even less. It is narrower all
down the left side of the trunk,
thighs, and legs than by the right.
A careful examination will always
show that the inner aura is correspondingly affected, not being as
wide on the left as on the right—
a sign of great importance. Besides, its appearance is more
opaque than normal, and striation, when not entirely absent, is
generally difficult to detect. The
texture of the outer aura is
almost, if not always, dissimilar
on the two sides. With the patient
sideways, the auras do not present
any abnormality in front, but at
the back a bulge may or may not
be seen. The colour of the haze
is usually grey with a deficiency
of the usual blue tinge.

Fig. 41.
Epileptic aura.

Case 38. (Fig. 41.) N.W., a
man aged forty-five years, had been strong and never
had any serious illness until a few months previous
to inspection, when he had an epileptic fit, and
subsequently several others. None of his brothers
or sisters have suffered from this complaint, nor, as
far as could be ascertained, were they in any way
neurotic. His children were all healthy and strong.

He has had no injury to his head to account for these attacks.

Neither aura reached the healthy standard in distinctness, as might be expected. The outer aura on the right side was clearer and wider than on the left, where it was coarser in texture. The inner aura on the right side was broader than on the left, and lineation could be easily seen, being normal ; on the left side srtiation was not only difficult to detect, but when seen was coarse. With the patient facing the observer, by the head the outer aura on the right side was ten inches against seven on the left ; by the trunk on the right side it was six inches wide, while it barely reached five on the left. Viewed sideways it was five inches in front, and six at the small of the back, where there was a slight but appreciable bulge. The inner aura was four inches on the right side of the trunk, and three by the lower limbs. On the opposite side it was a good inch less. The c.c. band was even over the whole body. The different coloured screens did not disclose any abnormality, except that the aura showed a yellow colour through the dark blue screen. The hue was more marked and deeper on the left.

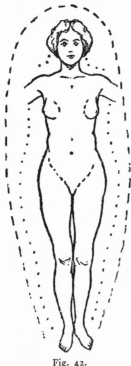

Fig. 42.
Epileptic aura.

Case 39. (Fig. 42.) I.E., thirty-nine years of age, had been an epileptic for over a quarter of a century, and the number of fits had gradually increased until now for months together they had been two or three a day, and never less than three or four during the week. Her family history was bad, as her mother and sister were afflicted with the same disease, whilst the intellect of another sister was considerably below par. For the last year or two her mental powers had been failing, and she complained greatly of loss of memory. Except for the fits she had always enjoyed good health. As might be expected, her aura was typical of epilepsy. A first examination was made in 1910, and a second in 1915, the appearances on both occasions being exactly similar. The colour of her aura was decidedly below the average width for a woman. The outer was in-distinct and the inner still more so, but there was no difficulty in seeing either, though their margins were ill-defined. On the left both auras were narrower, coarser and more opaque than on the right, Striation on the right could be easily observed, while on the left it remained doubtful whether any existed.

On the right side by the head and trunk the outer aura was seven inches wide, and four by the thigh and three by the leg. The breadth of the inner aura was three inches. On the left side the aura only measured five inches by the head and trunk, and by the leg three, while the inner aura was only two and a quarter inches in width. The outer aura was three and a half inches in front, four and a half at the small of the back, and three and a half by the legs. These figures show that the outer aura was narrow for a woman on the right side, and still more so on the left. The c.c. bands gave no results worth mentioning. When seen through the different coloured screens the aura did not exhibit the same hues on the two sides ; the left con-tained more yellow.

The patient was placed upon the insulated stool and electrified, receiving several charges of positive and negative electricity alternately. The effect, though definite, was not nearly as pronounced as usual, the eventual increase being only two inches on the right and a little less on the left, while at the same time the margins became still less marked, making it to be impossible to be sure of the exact amount of enlargement. The aura on the left side still continued to look coarser than on the right, and the comparative difference seemed to be equal, in spite of the loss of distinctness on both sides.

Case 40. X.T., a schoolboy thirteen years of age. A friend saw " the dreamy attacks," and asked his father to bring him for examination. He came in 1909, and purposely no questions were asked before inspection. The aura was obviously asymmetrical. The colour was a greenish grey. The outer aura was six inches wide by the side of the head, and the inner three inches on the right, while on the left it was four and two inches respectively. With his hands on the back of his neck, the outer aura on the right side of the trunk was four inches in breadth, narrowing about half inch lower down, and the inner was half an inch less than the outer.

On the left side the outer aura was only three inches wide, and the inner barely two and a half by the trunk, and not quite as much by the lower limbs. Sideways, the inner was about two and a half inches in breadth down the whole of the front and the outer a trifle wider. At the back the inner was the same, but the outer bulged to about six inches in the dorso-lumbar region. Elsewhere it was only three inches. The c.c. band was uniform over the whole body, but the extension on the right side of the head was darker than that of the left. Strange to say there was an admixture of brown in the c.c. band beyond the body, especially on the left side. The extensions by the sides of the trunk were very similar, but the brown colour was not as well marked. When the examination was ended, his father said " that the boy was under treatment for Petit Mal, and that he never had a grave attack."

Two questions naturally arise in connection with the differences in the size of the auras on the two sides of epileptics. The first is whether the asymmetry is congenital, or whether the aura is symmetrical at birth and commences to alter with the onset of fits, and the second is whether the disparity once produced, is permanent.

There are so many difficulties in the way of determining whether the asymmetry of the epileptic aura is congenital, that it is impossible at present to arrive at a definite conclusion, but the writer is inclined to think that such is not the case.

If congenital, the shape should occur in persons who are predisposed to the malady, and it might have been expected that occasionally cases would be met with where an existing variation in the size of both the outer and inner auras on either side would point to such predisposition, although no fits had yet occurred. Up to the present time no person has been examined whose aura was suggestive of epilepsy, but undoubtedly never had a fit. When possible, the auras of near relatives of epileptics have been searched for this defect, but always with the same result.

Another important fact is, that some children who own perfectly symmetrical auras, have had convulsive seizures during the first two years of their lives. It must be remembered that it is by no means easy to examine the haze round children until about the age of six or seven years, because apart from the shyness and the difficulty of keeping them still, their auras are narrow and slight differences in size are hard to detect.

An instance (case 44), which rather militates against the theory of congenital asymmetry is that of a woman who had puerperal eclampsia. Subsequently to the seizure the auras were dissimilar on the two sides. She herself was strong and healthy before marriage, and not one of her brothers or sisters had ever exhibited the slightest of any neurotic tendency.

If the inequalities be not congenital, they probably commence at the time of the first attack. A chance of settling this question would be afforded by observations on an individual who at first showed a normal aura, and later, after the development of epileptic seizures, manifested the typical asymmetrical alterations or no particular changes, as the case might be. It is more than likely that this point will be definitely settled in this way.

There is little or no doubt that auras which have developed typical epileptic characteristics are permanently affected, as the following example illustrates :

Case 41. B., a fresh-looking woman, thirty-nine years of age, came to have her aura inspected on account of a fall six months previously, when she injured her left shoulder, arm, and side. Pain had been continuous since the accident. If she lifted any weight she had a dragging sensation in the left side of her abdomen. She had been losing her spirits and becoming weak from the time of her accident. The observer did not expect to find any alteration in the shape of the aura, or at the very most, a slight tendency towards the spatulate type, and was quite unprepared to see the changes that were actually present.

With the patient facing, the outer aura on the right side was ten inches by the head and trunk, and six by the leg, which was rather wide for that part. It was natural in appearance, of a grey blue colour, and its outer margin was fairly distinct. The inner aura was three inches wide and definitely striated. On the left side the outer was no more than eight inches by the head and trunk, and not quite four by the leg. It looked coarse and its edge was indistinct. The inner aura was two and three quarters inches in breadth, and roughly striated. The latter emitted a short ray about four inches long from the injured shoulder. In order to make perfectly sure that the light did not induce disparity in size on the two sides, the patient was asked to turn completely round, but no alteration was visible. A side view showed the aura to be four inches wide in front, and the same width at the back except that there was a bulge commencing at the level of the shoulders and finishing just below the nates. Its broadest part was eight inches thick. The contraction of the aura on the left side of the head indicated that the diminution in width over the whole of the left side could not have been produced by the accident, as the injury was lower down. It is unnecessary to enter into the further details of blemishes demonstrated with the c.c. bands, etc., as they do not throw any light upon the subject under discussion.

The patient was placed upon the insulated stool and negatively electrified for five minutes. An enlargement of the outer aura developed, and as far as could be judged, was proportionately even all over, making the inequality of the outer aura still more conspicuous than before. The inner aura remained constant.

The above being a typical epileptic aura, the patient was asked immediately after the examination, whether she had ever suffered from fits, though there was nothing in her general appearance or the history she had given to suggest epilepsy. Without a moment's hesitation the answer was, " that she had had no fits since she was twelve years old, but previous to that age for two or three years, she had had two or three a year, and she believed also that she had suffered from infantile convulsions."

Here was an instance of the permanence of the epileptic type of aura, although the seizures had been in abeyance for twenty-seven years. If not congenital, the asymmetry must have developed during childhood.   The writer does not think it possible that apart from the fuller history a suspicion of epilepsy would have arisen.

Case 42.   In October, 1915, N.E., a woman thirty-four years of age, came to have her aura inspected. She complained of being very languid and unable to do her work properly for some time.   She often fainted.   These fainting attacks came on when she was standing, sitting, or lying.   Sometimes she gradually lost consciousness, and at times was able to ward off an attack by voluntary efforts, and in several instances she had not known about the seizure until it was all over.   Her heart was rather irritable, but there was no organic mischief.   Her father had had a fit fifteen years earlier, which at the time was considered epileptic, otherwise she appeared to be the only neurotic member of a large family.   It was thought that the inspection of the aura would have been a commonplace affair, and would decide whether the so-called faints were of nervous origin or due to the general state of health.   The whole aura was so different to any seen before, that a detailed description will be interesting.

The first thing to attract notice was, that the whole aura did not come up to the average in distinctness, although sufficiently clear to be easily seen and examined.   The second that the external margin was extremely ill-defined, and on cursory examination the aura appeared wide on account of a very evident ultra-outer aura.   After prolonged and careful investigation it was concluded that the ordinary outer aura was of average width by the trunk, but was broad by the lower part of the thighs and legs.   It was estimated to be nine inches by the head and trunk, six by the legs, while a side view showed it to be six inches in front, eight at the small of the back, and six by the legs.   Here the symmetry ended, as the aura, which was blue with an admixture of a little grey,

differed on the two sides, the right being of a purer
colour. Further the haze was coarser on the left side
than on the right. In order to make sure that there
was no inequality in the lighting, etc., during any part
of the inspection, the patient was requested to turn
completely round several times, but no alteration
could be detected. When the inner aura was examined through the red screens (several different
shades of the colour were employed), on the right side
it was obviously broader by quite an inch, more
distinct, and more markedly striated than on the
left. It was four and a half inches by the right side
of the trunk, and half an inch less by the thigh and
leg, and was the same width at the back and front,
while over the left side it was only three inches all
the way down. The c.c. bands did not make any
disclosures that need be mentioned here.

The most uncommon feature of this aura was the size
and clearness of the ultra-outer aura. In aspect it
was about half way between the ultra-outer aura,
as generally seen, and the effect of the enlargement
induced by static electricity.

After a metal brush connected with the positive
pole of a large Wimshurst machine had been moved
up and down the spine a few times without touching,
a considerable portion of the ultra-outer aura was
more distinct, but it still faded away gradually until
it became unrecognizable. However, it gave a
decided impression that the right side was a good deal
broader than the left. After the patient had been
placed upon the insulated stool and charged alternately positively and negatively several times, the
same condition was maintained.

With hands placed on the hips and elbows extended,
the aura in the interspaces between the arms and the
body, when examined through the different screens,
showed dissimilar hues on the two sides, the left having
a larger addition of yellow.

Screens.	R	O	Y	G	B	V
Right.	Red.	Yellow & Blue.	Blue.	Blue.	Blue.	Blue.
Left.	Red & Blue.	Yellow.	Yellow.	Yellow & Green.	Yellow & Blue.	Yellow & Blue.

The dissimilarity of the aura on the two sides was further enhanced when the back was fumed with iodine. Instead of affecting the two sides equally, it made the aura on the left side a red-brown, while on the right it was only slightly altered.

In this case all the characteristics of an epileptic aura were present, except that a diminution of the outer aura on the left side could not be satisfactorily determined, on account of the ultra-outer aura, but after electrification it gave the impression of being narrower, or if not really smaller, the distal portion was more faint.

Eight months later the patient was inspected a second time. The general appearances were the same. Nothing that could assist in the explanation of the unusual features was discovered.

Case 43. A somewhat analogous case was examined in 1918. The patient, S.J., was an old soldier who had become epileptic, and attributed the fits to a blow on the head received during the South African War. Some hesitation may be felt in admitting the sufficiency of the cause assigned, as the blow was not a severe one, not even keeping him from his work, while the attacks did not commence until a long time afterwards. Lately the fits have been increasing in frequency, and there are generally several within a few hours of each other, succeeded by a lengthy interval of freedom.

Inspection showed a well marked ultra-outer aura, extremely wide for a man. The margins were so ill-defined as to make the true dimensions of the outer aura uncertain. There was a considerable difference in the appearances on the two sides, the left being coarser and more opaque than on the right. Omitting the ultra-outer portion, the outer aura looked less wide on the left, but owing to indefiniteness of the edge the exact size could not be ascertained with accuracy. The inner aura on the left side was roughly striated and narrower than on the right, where it exhibited a more normal lineation. At the back there was a big bulge beginning just above the shoulders and ending a little below the buttocks. The different screens showed more yellow on the left side than on the right. The patient showed no surface electricity, but after having been charged negatively, his aura expanded to a greater extent than the writer had ever seen in a man.

This patient and the previous one are the only two epileptics who have displayed an ultra-outer aura, as generally this type of aura is considerably below the average in breadth.

Up to the end of 1918, only four cases which were not definitely epileptic, had upon investigation presented both outer and inner auras on the left side of the body smaller than those on the right. All these cases had brain disturbances ; one was suspected of masked epilepsy ; another had puerperal eclampsia ; a third was a man who had just been discharged from Bethlem Hospital ; and the last was a healthy woman. (Case 51.)

Case 44. Fortunately, instances of puerperal eclampsia are by no means common, so that it was a long time before an example could be obtained for inspection. This case was supplied by a friend. Mrs. S., twenty-seven years of age, mother of three children, had convulsions in the early stage of her fourth confinement, and was delivered as quickly as possible of twins. The mother made a rapid recovery, and the children were strong and healthy. She was inspected three weeks after the birth of her infants. The aura was of a bluish grey colour, and barely up to the healthy standard of distinctness, but could be easily examined. On the right side, the outer aura was eight inches by the head and trunk, five by the thigh and three and a half by the leg. The inner was two and a half inches all the way down. On the left side, the outer aura was seven inches by the head and trunk, and lower down it contracted to three by the ankle, while the inner was two and a quarter. The outer aura on the left side was not so plain as on the right, and the margin ill-defined, making it just possible, but not probable, that it was of the same width although looking narrower. The inner aura was not as perceptible on the left side as on the right, and striation was very faint. In front the outer aura was four inches by the trunk, five by the back, and by the thighs and legs three and a half, while the inner aura was two and a half inches back and front. Both auras were more pronounced in front of the breasts and to a lesser extent before the lower part of the abdomen, from whence a ray of the second order proceeded. The c.c. band was even all over the body, except the mammæ, where it appeared to be lighter in tint. When she put one of the infants to the breast, the colour became duller. Examined through the blue screen, the aura was a dirty ochre, but it was still more muddy looking over the left side.

This was an exceedingly interesting case, as it was impossible to predict whether any changes in the aura had taken place.

Case 45. I.X., a bootmaker by trade, fifty-eight years of age. His father and uncle had both been confined in an asylum, the latter until the day of his death. The patient was always dreading the same fate. He frequently became sullen, and without reason very depressed. These attacks of depression lasted for some hours, days or even weeks at a time. They did not, however, prevent him from following his trade. He was also liable to nervous attacks, dread, etc. Some years later he committed suicide.

His aura was inspected in 1910. The colour was

grey, and coarse in texture, especially the inner aura on the left side. The outer aura was round the head seven inches wide, and four by the trunk and leg on the right side, while the inner was two and a half inches. On the left side the outer aura was five inches round the head and by the body and leg three, the inner being two. Personally the writer considered him to be epileptic long before he commenced to study the aura, and the result of the investigation strengthens that opinion.

Case 46. This is an extremely sad case of a young man of great ability, who after a distinguished school and university career, when working for a Fellowship of his College, suddenly collapsed. He was placed in Bethlem Hospital, where he remained six months. A short time after leaving the hospital, his aura was inspected. At the time he looked dull and peculiar, and answered questions quite correctly, but slowly. He said, " he could study for an hour or two a day." The auras had the usual distinctness, were of a nondescript colour, showing blue and green without their blending. The outer aura round the head was eight inches on the right, against six on the left ; four and a half inches on the right side of the trunk, and half an inch less by the thigh and leg ; but on the left it was three and a half inches all the way down. The inner was two inches wide by the whole of the left side, and two and a half by the right. It showed striation everywhere, except over the right side of the head, where it was granular. The c.c. bands were even all over the body, but the right extension was darker than the left. The most conspicuous changes in the aura were concerned with its colour as seen through the different screens. The colours were so mixed without any actual blending, as to make it impossible to give an accurate description, and their distribution was also peculiar. Right side, when the red, orange, yellow, and green screens were employed, the auric colours looked as if they were mixed with an opaque white, which was absent with the blue and violet screens, and also on the left side.   Above the shoulder, with the orange screen, the aura looked blue and more distinct than by the trunk; with the green the hue was an even blue all down the body; but with the blue and violet screens, the aura showed green and yellow, and was more intense by the trunk than by the head.   Left side: through the orange, yellow, and green screens, the colour of the aura was blue and yellow, the latter colour being more pronounced by the body than by the head.   With the blue and the violet screens the hue was more marked by the head, being a greenish blue, but there was an addition of yellow by the side of the body.

At times the outer aura is found to be unequal on the two sides while the inner aura remains symmetrical, but this does not preclude great alterations in the latter as regards colour, texture, etc.   While the inner remains normal the patient may be in good health bodily, but mentally not quite sound, as the following example will show.

Case 47.   In this instance the patient has been under observation for many years, making it more than usually interesting.   N.D., in April, 1907, when she was twenty years old, overworked herself at a school, teaching all the day, and studying for an examination at night.   She did not retire to bed until the small hours, getting no proper sleep, as she was obliged to be up early.   She went home for the Easter holidays feeling ill, and two days later developed a high temperature, the first stage of meningitis, which affected both sides of the brain.   She was so ill that during one night, the nurse thought she had passed away; however, she recovered bodily, but was a changed person mentally.   Instead of being rather studious and amenable to reason, she became perverse, selfish, and unable to concentrate her thoughts.

It may be interesting to note that Kernig's sign was well marked during her illness, and continued evident to a slight extent for a year and a half, but six months later could not be detected.   In September, 1908, her aura was examined.   This was bluish in colour, plain, and much wider on the left than on the right side.   The blue c.c. band was even over the whole body, but its extensions on the right were considerably darker than on the left side.   The inspection was made before the aura could be divided into outer and inner sections.

June, 1909.   Bodily health was still good and mental powers much improved.   The girl had given up teaching, doing housework instead.   She was able to read a little but only light literature.

In November of the same year she was again examined.   The general characters of the aura were unaltered, but the *inequality had lessened*.   The etheric double was plainly visible on both sides, being a little over an eighth of an inch in width.   The outer aura was five inches on the right against seven on the left by the head ; by the trunk it was seven inches on the right and eight on the left ; by the thighs and legs there was very little difference, the breadth being about four inches.   The inner aura was about three inches wide and symmetrical.   In profile, the outer aura was about three and a half inches in front, and another half inch at the back, while the inner was two and a half back and front.

The important point to notice was that the inner aura was alike on the two sides.   Whether this would have been the case shortly after her illness must, of course, remain uncertain.   Here we have an instance of partial recovery of the aura after a severe illness.

September, 1913.   The patient, who for some months had been doing secretarial work, broke down again, and was obliged to give up her post.   For the last few weeks severe headaches prevented her from concentrating her mind upon work. She was very depressed, and had frequent burning sensations on the outer part of her thighs, the right being worse than the left. The same kind of discomfort sometimes attacked her right shoulder. All the pains were more acute when she was tired. There was great loss of sensation over the whole of the right thigh, and over a large patch on the abdomen, while at the back the right side was more affected than the left, and there was also a partial loss of sensation in the two feet. The strength of the right hand was perceptibly diminished, but there was no tremor. Both legs seemed equally strong. The tongue when protruded deviated to the right. The left eye was more prominent than the right, and showed internal squint but no nystagmus. Pupils reacted slowly both to accommodation and light.

Upon inspection neither aura was as distinct as in 1909, when she was in good bodily health. Although it was difficult to determine the exact size of the outer aura, there was no doubt about the right side being smaller than the left, and the inner equal on the two sides. Striation could be detected, but not easily. The c.c. band disclosed several discoloured patches on the body, all of which were tender to the touch. With arms akimbo, the aura displayed a larger amount of yellow than normal in the interspaces between the arms and trunk.

The next case is of more than ordinary interest, as it affords an example, firstly of a diminished outer aura on the whole of the right side while the inner remained unaltered in size; secondly of the quick return of the outer aura to its natural dimensions; and lastly an appearance of the outer aura almost identical with that of the ultra-outer aura, which was evidently originated by statical electricity, the effect of which persisted a long time.

Case 48. The patient was a woman thirty-seven

years of age, who had been twenty-one years in the same situation as a domestic servant. She had been in good health until three months before her inspection, when she had a severe attack of influenza, and four days afterwards began trembling. Her head and all her limbs were affected. The shaking became worse directly she tried to do anything, but ceased when lying down.

Upon examination neither aura was found to be normally distinct. The outer aura on the left side had a very perfect shape and was of average width. It was eight inches and a half by the head and trunk, six by the upper part of the thigh, and four and a half by the leg. On the right side it was narrower, being only seven inches by the head and trunk, five and four by the thigh and leg respectively, and at the same time was not as clear. The inner aura was the same size all over the body, but not so plain on the right side, where striation could be only made out with difficulty. There was a light patch over the four upper dorsal vertebræ, and by the left side of the sixth a small dark spot when the c.c. band was used. In front this band was even in colour.

In due course she was placed upon the insulated stool and negatively electrified. She, at once, complained of pain over the whole of her body. This was a very unusual occurrence as the charging rarely arouses any sensation. The machine was stopped almost immediately, but curious to relate, when she got off the stool she said " she felt brighter," and the shaking had greatly diminished. The hyperæsthesia which existed all over the body was lessened. As she thought she had benefitted she wished to be again electrified in spite of the pain. It was certain that a great improvement had taken place. This was the first case the writer had ever met with where real benefit had been derived from the action of statical electricity when applied to a patient standing upon an insulated stool. The aura enlarged in the usual manner.

As the woman seemed so much better the writer offered to try the further effect of statical electricity. She came again on August 7th, 1917. She looked better and the tremor was considerably less. She was able to pick up a pin more easily. This time the application of electricity caused no sensation whatever. Her third visit was on the 10th of the same month, when she exhibited a marked improvement. The aura looked equal in breadth on the two sides, although there was a difference in brightness, which was less on the right. She had developed a well marked ultra-outer aura, which was evidently the result of the electrical treatment.

On the 24th she returned nearly well in health. The aura, however, continued less plain on the right side, and the patch seen by the aid of the c.c. band on the dorsal vertebræ had almost disappeared, but the ultra-outer aura remained still unaltered although she had not been electrified for a week. In order to find out the length of time this condition lasted, she was requested to come again after three weeks. This she did. The proper outline of the outer aura was distinct, but beyond the ultra-outer aura was still in evidence. There was a sharp line of demarcation between the latter and the ordinary outer aura, the two not passing gradually into one another. Probably the distal portion would have vanished in another week's time.

Case 49. (Figs. 43 and 44.) N.U., thirty-four years of age, a lady who had never been robust nor had suffered from serious illness, had lately passed through a very trying time, which had affected her health, and made her depressed and thoroughly run down. She complained of pains in her head, shoulder, and thorax on the left side. Upon examination the great occipital nerve was found to be very sensitive, and there was a tenderness by the left side of the spine as far down as the lower dorsal vertebræ. This was especially marked at the places where the nerves emerge, and also in front at the corresponding spots on the thorax and abdomen. She was inspected for the

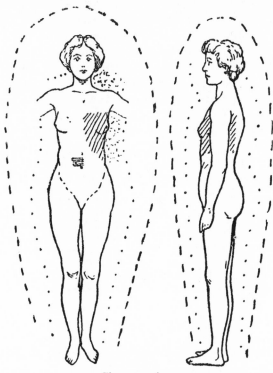

Figs. 43 and 44.
.... Granular aura.
≡ Dark with c.c. band.
////// Light ditto.

first time in 1908. It was noticed that the aura was considerably wider on the right side than on the left, as there were two inches by the trunk, but not so much by the head. Viewed sideways the aura was normal. The blue c.c. band was of a much lighter shade over the left side of the thorax than the right. The line of demarcation was the median line of the body, but the change from the one side to the other was gradual. The yellow c.c. band showed a corresponding modification. In front of the abdomen the tint was even all over. When the back was examined the left side was lighter than the right, the spines of the vertebræ marking the boundary of the change.

In the following November she was again investigated after having regained fair health. As she faced the observer, it was found that the inner aura measured three inches by the side of the head and trunk, and everywhere else it was a little more than two inches. The outer aura had become symmetrical on the two sides, being eleven inches round the head, ten by the trunk and five by the legs. Sideways the outer aura was five inches in front of the body, at the small of the back seven, and down the lower limbs four inches. Although the aura was equal on the two sides, yet it exhibited a curious dissimilarity, inasmuch as the exterior margin on the right side was more sharply defined than on the left, giving the impression of being narrower.

Other changes could also be distinguished. The inner aura on the left side of the thorax, as far down as the lowest ribs, was finely granular, and more opaque than on the right. Below this level there was no difference on either side. The blue c.c. band still showed a large patch in front on the left of a lighter shade than on the right side. The demarcation lines were distinct and sharp, the upper running along the superior border of the mamma, the inner the medium line of the sternum, and the lower with the costal cartilages, and about an inch above edges. On the abdomen the band was even all over with the exception of a dark patch over the right hypochondrium, lying a little above the level of the umbilicus. On the back it was even all over, except for two small spots, one lighter in shade than the rest of the band, situated just below the spine of the scapula on the left side, and the other darker over the sacrum. The former was tender to the touch.

Another interesting shape of the aura remains to be considered, the existence of which might have been foretold. It is characteristic of hemiplegia. In different cases that have been investigated slight variations have, of course, been detected. The following is a fairly typical instance.

Case 50. (Fig. 45.) E., a rather stout man, sixty-nine years of age, had an apoplectic fit in March, 1916. He remained unconscious for some days but had no unusual symptoms. His right arm and leg were paralysed, and he was aphasic. In a comparatively short time he regained a fair amount of power in his limbs, but his speech did not improve commensurately. He was able to understand what was said to him, but his answers were incongruous as he could rarely utter the words he wanted.

In August his aura was inspected. The outer on the right side of his head was nine inches wide, while on the left it only reached six and a half. By the trunk on the right side it was about four and a half inches, diminishing to about three and a half by the leg. On the left side it was six and a half by the trunk and contracted to six by the leg. Although more indistinct than if he had been in good health, on the left side the aura was still less plain than on the right,

Fig. 45.
Hemiplegia.

making it extremely difficult to determine the exact width. Sideways, the aura was five inches in front, and at the back quite natural in shape, being straight down, and four inches at the shoulders and buttocks.

The whole of the inner aura was below the ordinary standard of brightness. Above the shoulders, it was massed on each side and granular, but was broader and finer on the right. On the left side it was very coarse and dense. By the same side of the trunk and leg it was three inches wide, but on the right side it was about an inch narrower. Striation could be just detected on the left but not on the right.

Examined with screens the colours were alike on the two sides, with the red, orange, and violet screens. Contrary to all expectations the hue was blue on the right, and yellow and green on the left through the green screen, while through the blue screen it was blue on the right and yellow on the left. This peculiarity, for which no explanation can be offered, is the main reason why this case has been selected as an example for hemiplegia.

A most important question arising here is whether healthy people ever have asymmetrical auras ? Perhaps, it would be more to the point to ask " if the aura be not symmetrical, can a person, although apparently in good health, be so in reality, or is there present some local or constitutional defect ? " Unfortunately, sufficient data are not available for arriving at a definite conclusion, because so far, only one unequivocal case that could come under this heading, has been seen. This instance occurred before the aura could be divided into the outer and inner, and consequently loses much of its interest. A careful search is made whenever an opportunity presents itself, so that this peculiarity must be far from common. It has, however, to be borne in mind that a slight difference in the size of the aura on the two sides is difficult to distinguish, especially in males and young girls before puberty, and the detection is not made easier should, as sometimes occurs, when a person is not in good health, the outline of the aura on one side be less distinct than the other. Accordingly this investigation has had to be restricted to a great extent to women.

Case 51. C.N. was a tall and healthy woman twenty-nine years of age, whose only serious illness had been an ulcer of the stomach some few years previously. She was inspected in 1908. Her aura appeared as a light blue mist, broad by the trunk and coming down to the lower part of her thighs before it finally contracted to follow the outline of the body. For some unaccountable reason it looked wider on the right side, being twelve inches at the broadest part and three inches at the ankles. On the left it did not seem to exceed nine inches at the widest. As she stood sideways, it was nearly five inches in front of the body, and about three inches down the lower limbs. At the back it was broad down to the middle of the thighs, where it contracted.

The limits of the asymmetry and the shape of a transverse section of an aura showing the change must now be ascertained. Theoretically, in examples of inequality in shape, or dissimilarity in texture of the lateral halves of the aura, arising from systemic in contra-distinction to local causes, it would be natural to expect the junctions of the affected and unaffected aura to be situated along the median lines of the body, front and back. This has been found to be correct in several instances, of which two will be quoted.

Case 52. In April, 1912, an examination of the aura of K.N. was made. She was a young woman who had just reached her majority, and who had occasionally suffered from epilepsy since childhood, but had not had any fit prior to inspection for four years, and in spite of her long freedom from an attack, her aura still retained the epileptic type. It is unnecessary to enter into details of its shape and size, further than to mention that they were typical. During the inspection of this patient the colour of the aura was at first a grey with a slight tinge of blue, similar to that seen at a previous and a subsequent examination. While the back was being investigated with the c.c. bands, the aura on the whole of the left side of the trunk suddenly, without any obvious cause, became darker than the right, the line of demarcation being the spine. The white background was replaced by a black one, and the colour of the aura on the left side was seen to be an ochre, very unlike the grey tint on the other side which remained unaltered. The dissimilarity was so marked that there was no difficulty in determining the junction of the two halves of the aura, by turning the patient to different angles against the background, when the vertical lines back and front were seen to be the limits of the two colours. Coincidently with this change of colour the aura on the left side appeared to have become coarser in texture than that on the right, yet it was impossible to decide whether the coarseness had really increased, or was an appearance due to the alteration of colour.

Case 53. R.F., a young lady, was inspected in 1914. Her intellect was quite up to the average. It was known that she had had three fits, the last being two days before she was brought for examination. After questioning her there could be no doubt that she was subject to numerous slight attacks (Petit Mal), which had escaped the notice of her friends. She was a tall well nourished girl, but her spinal curves were exaggerated. The first thing to attract attention was, that the aura had a different hue on the two sides of the body, the right being a blue with a little grey, and the left a green-grey. The want of resemblance was such as to make it quite easy to ascertain that the different colours came into contact with each other along the vertical median lines, back and front. The outer aura on the left side of the head was seven inches and by the trunk eight, while by the leg it was only three and a half. On the right side it was eight inches by the head and ten by the trunk, and four and a half lower down. A profile view showed the outer aura to be four and a half inches in front, seven at the back, and four and a half by the legs. The inner aura was four inches wide on the right and three on the left.

There was a curious void space between the body and the inner aura at the small of the back, the widest portion being about an inch in breadth, and the length from seven to eight inches. The cause of this peculiarity could not be ascertained. As the patient stood facing, with her hands resting on her hips and her elbows extended, the aura was examined through different coloured screens, and showed a bluish grey through the red, orange, yellow, and green screens on the right side, while that on the left was a greenish grey. Through the blue screen the right was blue, and the left a blue and yellow unblended; lastly, through the violet screen the right showed violet and the left blue.

These two cases prove conclusively that in some instances, and perhaps in all, when the aura is not symmetrical the inequality starts at the median lines of the body front and back. If a hypothetical section of an epileptic aura be made transversely, the median lines must be taken as the points where the contraction of the aura commences. Fig. 40, g and h (page 180), show the shapes of the male and female epileptic auras as they usually appear. In some instances of epilepsy, as will be seen in cases 42 and 43, the aura on the contracted side has an exceedingly ill-defined margin, and occasionally gives the impression of extra width resembling in appearance an ultra-outer aura beyond the normal haze. From this circumstance and from want of sharpness of the edge, it seems just, and only just, possible, that in some epileptics the outer aura may be equally wide on the two sides, and that on one side the aura may be so attenuated, as to produce the effect of contraction. Of this thin aura, Fig. 40, i and k, are suppositious transverse sections.

Case 54. (Fig. 46.) H., a married woman, was

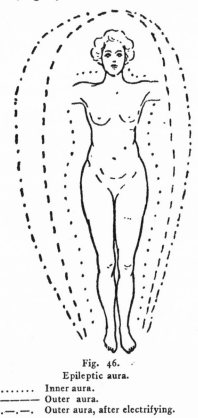

Fig. 46.
Epileptic aura.
.... Inner aura.
————— Outer aura.
—.—.—. Outer aura, after electrifying.

subject to fits. The first was noticed when she was two years old, and she knows that she has had seven others within the last two years. Before and after each attack she suffered from severe headaches, and the last one caused her temperature to remain high for four days. She was a dull-looking woman, and evidently her mind had weakened.

She was inspected in the latter half of 1915, when both auras were distinct and their colour grey. On the right side the outer aura was nine inches by the head and the same width by the trunk, and by the leg four. On the left side the aura was opaque in appearance, and coarse in texture, while the margin was not as defined as on the right. It was six inches by the head and trunk, and became three by the lower part of the thigh and leg. A side view showed the outer aura to be four inches in front, and at the small of the back seven and by the legs four. The inner aura was three inches on the right, and on the left two inches wide, being not merely narrower but considerably less plain.

The woman was placed upon the insulated stool and negatively charged, when the inner aura vanished first, and the outer massed on both sides of the trunk in the early stage, subsequently disappearing. After the charge had been dissipated, both auras soon returned, but it was quite ten minutes before expansion had reached its full extent. There was not the usual loss of distinctness, and the right aura looked natural in texture, while the left remained dense. The outer aura on the right side had increased to fourteen inches by the head and trunk, and six by the leg. On the left side it was nine inches by the head and trunk and four by the leg. On this side the margin had become more definite. To make sure that there was no inequality in the illumination, which might be the cause of disparity on the two sides, the patient was turned with her back to the observer, but no change could be detected. The inner aura did not seem altered.

These results assisted in arriving at the decision that the aura on the left side was not as large as on the right, by making the inequality even more conspicuous than it was previous to electrification.

If the outer aura be contracted on one side of the body, and the diminution begins at the median lines back and front, it will of necessity be lessened all over one side of the trunk, back and front, as well as beyond the body. Try as hard as possible, no occular demonstration of this phenomenon has been obtained, nor does there seem much chance of its ever being done, because the aura can be only perceived as a silhouette so that the wider portion precludes sharp definition of the latter.

Diminution of the aura, either when absolute or apparent only, must be produced by a lessening of the auric forces. If the decrease of these forces be merely quantitative, the aura will be only contracted or attenuated. (Fig. 40, g to k.) But it is more likely than not that changes in the auric forces involve some alteration in the character as well. This question will be discussed in the next chapter.

Seen during health the aura seems to be so symmetrical in size, shape, and texture, that the possibility of the existence of differences between the two sides might easily have escaped realization had not the question arisen as the direct consequences of the findings in certain pathological states.

The following is a resumé of the facts which seem to throw light upon the matter :—

1. Asymmetry in size. During the consideration of the haze surrounding epileptics, mention has been made that both the outer and the inner auras were broader on one side than on the other (page 182), in every instance with the exception of the two cases 42 and 43, where the equality of the outer is apparent, not real.

2. Asymmetry in texture. Accompanying the disparity in size, an alteration of the texture of the aura is usually present on the smaller side. (Page 182.) The vertical median lines, anteriorly and posteriorly, have been shown to be the two most likely positions

for the meeting of the asymmetrical auras, which are usually well defined. (Cases 52 to 54.)

3. Asymmetry in colour. Patients, even in perfect health, have occasionally been seen with colour differences on the two sides. In neurotics and people in indifferent health such differences are by no means uncommon, and whenever the lines of junction can be detected, they are the vertical median lines. Sometimes screens may be necessary to discover the difference. (Case 42.) For this purpose a blue screen is generally the most useful.

4. Asymmetry discovered by means of c.c. bands. Long before the question of the possibility of the existence of differences between the halves of a normal aura had arisen, it had often been noticed that the patches disclosed during examination with the c.c. bands were unilateral, especially in front, and when near the centre of the body sharply limited at the middle line.

5. Asymmetry of chemically induced changes. It has been frequently observed that when one side has been tinted by chemical vapours while the other side has been left in a natural state, the junctions of the two colours are at the median lines. The same happens when the aura on the two sides has been treated with different chemical agents.

Once or twice when the back had been fumigated by a gas, e.g., iodine vapour, to a very slight extent, the colours of the aura on the two sides did not correspond.

Asymmetry due to voluntary effort. Similarly, whenever changes have been initiated by voluntary effort, they have ceased at the central lines or, if they have, contrary to intention, extended to the other half of the body, they have been different in quality on either side of the middle line.

These considerations taken all together afford strong presumptive evidence that there are some differences in the constitution of the aura on the two sides of the body of persons in good health, but that they are too delicate to demonstrate with our present means of investigation. Nevertheless, there is hope that in the near future this interesting question will be satisfactorily settled by further experiments.

APPENDIX TO CHAPTER VII

(CASE 55.) The following example of delayed development is extremely interesting and instructive, as the patient, S.K., displayed an aura unlike any previously noted. The woman was twenty-two years of age, constitutionally healthy, but had been suffering a short time from anæmia, but not of a severe type. She had never menstruated, for which reason she wished to have her aura investigated. In figure she was tall, large, and strongly built, and inclined to stoutness. She was well proportioned except that her mammæ had retained their infantile form, the glands not being more pronounced than those of a child of six to eight years old. On the pubes there was a small quantity of hair, about as much as might have been expected at the approach of puberty. She seemed bright and intelligent for a woman of her age and occupation.

Before examination it was thought that any departure from the adult type would be in the direction of the form normally found amongst girls between the ages of fourteen and eighteen years. The result did not fulfil these anticipations.

The first impression received at the examination was, that the aura was broad round the head where it measured at least nine inches, while round the trunk it appeared not more than seven to seven and a half inches, and to descend straight to the ankles, consequently being rather wide by the thighs and legs. The margin, too, did not look as defined as usual. Careful inspection, however, showed the edge, just mentioned, not to be the true one, as the haze was in reality two to three inches broader by the trunk, but not quite as distinct.   In appearance this portion of the aura looked like an ordinary outer aura rather below the average in brightness, but not less plain than what often occurs when a patient is in ill health. It differed in character from the ultra-outer aura. This addition caused the aura to become almost spatulate in shape.   In front and by the back, the outer aura was wider than usual, and had a bulge in the lumbar regions which commenced near the level of the shoulders and ended just beneath the nates. The inner aura, too, was wide, inordinately so, if the outer aura had only been seven inches in breadth, while it corresponded in size to what would most likely be found with an outer aura ten inches wide by the sides of the trunk.

After a negative charge of electricity, the outer aura became enlarged and took on an almost perfectly spatulate shape, and the bulge at the back became very pronounced.   At the same time the difference in the two parts of the outer aura by the sides of the trunk grew less marked but did not entirely vanish. Unfortunately, the woman showed no signs of surface electricity, and so it was impossible to ascertain whether the maxima commonly found in females were present.

It would be useless attempting to draw any conclusion from a single case, but comparison between the above case and others in which bodily development was delayed is extremely interesting.   Every girl so affected, with the exception of one, had a transitional aura narrower than usual at her age, and in one exceptional instance of an infantile type. Besides in every example which has been inspected from time to time the aura has been noticed to assume the transitional stage before the onset of menstruation. It has also been observed that the aura, although exceptions occur, is generally narrow when the sexual organs, after having commenced to function, temporarily cease to do so from any cause. Thus there would have been nothing unusual had the aura in the case just related been from seven to seven and a half inches in breadth. The addition of the outer part is where the interest lies. A study of similar cases may possibly throw light upon the origin of the spatulate type in hysterical people.

CHAPTER VIII

The Inner Aura in Disease

In the last chapter an account was given of the deviations of large portions of the aura from normal, and it was seen that the outer aura was affected, while the inner might or might not escape derangement. In the present chapter local changes will be considered, which will be noticed most frequently to affect the inner aura alone, though in a few cases the outer, too, is altered. In no instance, however, is there a local change of the outer without participation of the inner.

Circumscribed alterations in the shape of the aura are not so conspicuous as those described in the last chapter, and consist of either a local diminution, or occasionally of an obliteration of a part or the whole breadth of the inner aura, while external and contiguous to the deranged portion, the outer also may be to some degree affected. The inner aura besides is liable to alterations of texture, resulting in appearances completely at variance with any observed during health. The chief local modifications in structure are : (a), coarse striation of the inner aura ; (b), loss of striation of the inner aura ; (c), granulation of the inner aura. The last change may also affect the outer aura.

The simplest form of a local diminution is met with when a fair size of the inner aura remains in normal contact with the body, but becomes narrower from the loss of its distal portion. Usually the whole width of the impaired portion of the inner aura will be fainter, and the lineation less marked, while at the same time the free edge will not be as sharply defined as that of the adjacent healthy areas. These changes seem to be the result of a quantitative decrease with little or perhaps no qualitative alteration of the inner auric force. The following is a typical example, which is, besides, interesting in other respects.

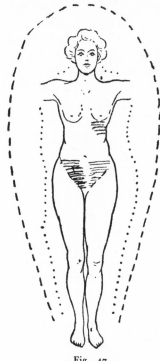

Fig. 47.
Locally contracted inner aura.

Case 56. (Fig. 47.) X.A., a childless married woman, thirty-seven years of age, had been ill several years. Within the last four she had undergone operations for a floating kidney, double hernia, and appendicitis. As the kidney remained very moveable another operation had been suggested.

When inspected, the outer aura reached the healthy standard of distinctness. The shape was good with the exception of a wide dorsal bow, which commenced at the head and finished at the feet. The breadth was nine and a half inches round the head and by the sides of the trunk. It was six by the thighs and four and a half by the ankles. Down the front it was four and a half, while at the widest part of the bow at the back it measured nine inches. The inner aura was not quite as plain as the average, but exhibited striation all over the body. On the left side, at the front and at the back it was three inches throughout. On the right side above the level of the umbilicus, and also from the upper third of the thigh downwards it had the same breadth, but between these two points it was only two inches wide. Here lineation was visible, inclined to be a little coarse, and the outer edge not properly defined. There was no gap between the outer and inner auras. As was expected, the c.c. band presented several discoloured areas. On the back the usual sacral patch was present, a yellow one three inches in length was perceptible above the crest of the right ilium, and a third over the right lower ribs. In front the greater part of both iliac regions was dark, but the lower part had a deeper hue than the upper. The colour was also darker on the right than on the left. There was, besides, a dark patch on the left hypochondrium. She complained of pain at each of these discoloured areas, but strange to say, both it and the tenderness were more intense in the left iliac region, although the colour here was lighter than on the right. The excessive darkening on the right side was atrributed rightly or wrongly to descent of the kidney. Periodically she had acute suffering in her back, which accounted for the well marked discoloured patch.

Other variants of the contracted inner aura are the funnel-shaped and the cylindrical depressions, which often entail a complete breach of the haze. The mode of formations is probably as follows :—In chapter v., it was demonstrated that the auric forces proceed from the body in direct lines at right angles to it. If from any cause a circumscribed area be deranged in such a manner that no auric force emanates from it, while all around the affected spot the healthy parts are emitting auric force in the ordinary way, a cylindrical hollow space with its long axis at right angles to the body will be the outcome. (Case 59.) More frequently than not the deranged area, instead of being separated from the healthy portions of the body by a sharp line of demarcation, will be surrounded by zones of gradually inrceasing auric forces. (Cases 57 and 58.) The result of this condition will be the formation of a conical defect, with its apex towards the body. It may be difficult to detect unless large in area, as in case 58. The effect of these void spaces in the aura upon the c.c. band has already been described.

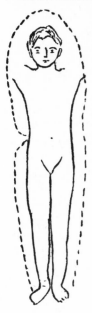

Fig. 48.
Funnel-shaped depression of aura.

These breaks in the inner aura can only be perceived under favourable circumstances, and in sections. Up to the present time only two or three of them (see cases 58 and 60), have been observed except at the side of the body. The reason is obvious ; the void intervals by the side of the body when the patients stand facing the observer, have not to be viewed through the same thickness of aura as when they occur either in front or at the back, and must be looked for with subjects standing sideways. In like manner any increase of density or opacity of the aura helps to obscure these spaces. A suitable background is absolutely necessary for their detection, and the one, par excellence, for this purpose is a dead black ; light colours are entirely useless. Taking all these circumstances into consideration, for every one of these spaces detected, it is not at all unlikely that several elude recognition.

The following case occurred before the two auras could be separated, and is quoted as it was the first instance in which an aura affected by local disease was observed. As, however, the difference in size between the outer and inner auras in children is so slight, it is probable that an observation through a red screen would not have seriously affected the result.

Case 57. (Fig. 48.) H.H., a boy ten years old,

had been suffering from herpes zoster for five or six days before an opportunity of examining him presented itself. The part affected was the right lumbar region in front ot the abdomen, and there were also a few spots upon the flank. The rash had reached the stage of desiccation. His aura was plainly marked, being, as he stood facing the observer, six inches by the head, and two and a half inches by the sides of the body. It was quite normal but narrow for a boy of his age, with the exception of a portion on the right side from the level of the sterno-xiphoid plane to the crest of the ilium. From the upper level just mentioned the aura curved inwards reaching the body by the twelfth rib. From this point it bent outwards, regaining its full width at the crest of the ilium. The apex of this blank space apparently touched the body, and the adjacent part of the aura did not look in any way affected either in texture or colour. Upon examination with the blue c.c. band employed transversely, the right half of the body seemed to be darker than the left, and as might be surmised, the left extension was lighter than the right. When the c.c. band was used on the back the colour was normal above the eleventh dorsal spine, but below darker, the transition between the two being abrupt. All traces of the void space vanished if the boy stood in any position except facing the observer. The aura looked perfectly normal, both at the back and front of the body.

The aura in the next case displayed a funnel-shaped depression, and when the two constituents were separated by the carmine screen the inner was seen to be more deranged.

Case 58. (Fig. 49.) B., an old lady, seventy-three years of age, the mother of ten children, had been suffering for some time from pain in the epigastrium and abdomen, and coincidently losing flesh. It had been suggested that an exploratory operation would be probably required. As neither her aura nor subsequent ordinary examination showed any definite signs of organic mischief, she was advised to wait a short time before undergoing any operation. Under treatment all pain vanished, and she regained her proper weight. Three years later she was in good health.

At the commencement of 1914, her outer aura was found to be of good shape, and normal in clearness, being nine inches by the head and trunk, four by the legs, six at the back and four in front and down the legs. The inner aura was not nearly as conspicuous as it would have been had the patient been in good health. Striation could only be detected with difficulty, and above the shoulders was almost invisible. It was three inches broad by the head and trunk, and half an inch narrower lower down. In profile, it was at the back three inches and two and a half by the thighs and legs. In front, wherever normal, it was three inches. It had, however, nearly vanished about the level of the umbilicus, but regained its proper width about four inches above and below, making a funnel-shaped indentation. It was coarsely granular by the sides of the trunk. The c.c. band exhibited three

Fig. 49.
Funnel-shaped depression of inner aura.

yellow patches on the back, one on the left side of the spine between the fourth and seventh dorsal vertebræ, another on the left shoulder blade, and the last on the small of the back. In front there was a yellow patch over the epigastrium, a second over the lower part of the abdomen, while the band was dark over the right hypochondrium. Had there been any growth it would have been beneath the dark patch, and this probably would have contained a smaller and still darker spot. Yellow patches usually indicate no serious organic mischief. It was confidently expected that the funnel-shaped depression of the inner aura would have definitely discoloured the c.c. band, but on the contrary there appeared only a small ill-defined

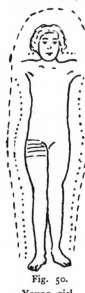

Fig. 50.
Young girl.
Hip disease.

spot, lighter in colour than the remainder of the band, which might have been easily overlooked. This patch would probably have had the same depth of colour as the other yellow spots except for the absence of a part of the inner aura.

Case 59. (Fig. 50.) This is an extremely instructive case of a delicate looking girl, H.M., seven years of age, who in May, 1908, complained of pain in her right hip, which was diagnosed as a very early stage of tubercular hip disease. Calmette's tuberculo-ophthalmic test gave a decided reaction. As soon as possible she entered a children's hospital, where she remained an in-patient for several months, and was afterwards transferred to a convalescent home.

During February, 1909, within a day or two of her arrival home, she came to have her aura inspected. She was then looking exceedingly well, had no pain, and complete movement of her hip joint. Her aura was fairly developed, but narrow, of a greyish colour two inches wide. It was normal for a girl of her age except, that as she faced the observer, there was a complete gap two inches in length by the right trochanter major. This void space was so plainly visible and well marked that her mother noticed it immediately. Instead of the edges curving outwards, as they did in the last case, they were quite straight, presenting a punched out appearance. The area could not be detected when she stood sideways. The c.c. band was even all over the body except where a side view exhibited a light patch over the void space.

She removed to Scotland, but in 1912, returned to London for a few weeks, when a second examination was allowed. She had grown a tall, strong, healthy girl. Her aura was a grey bluish colour, six inches wide by the head, four at the small of the back and three everywhere else. The inner aura was one and a half inches all over. Both auras looked natural for a child of her age, except round the right hip. The aura when investigated without the intervention of a screen was less distinct near the trochanter, especially close to the body. When the carmine screen was employed, the inner aura was almost completely absent at this place, and no striation could be discovered, though it was perfect above and below. The c.c. band appeared even over the whole body, back and front, except that over the right hip, it had a deeper shade, which was prolonged into the extension. Viewed sideways the band was lighter over the trochanter. Both her mother and a lady nurse who were present during the examination, were able to distinguish the abnormality without the slightest trouble.

Case 60. A woman, D.S., thirty-four years of age, had been suffering from ulcer of the stomach. She had left a hospital two months before inspection. Her complaint, which dated back five months, was her first severe illness. The outer aura, rather above the average in breadth, was a good shape and measured by the head and sides of the trunk ten and a half inches, and by the thighs six, contracting gently as it approached the ankles. A profile view showed the aura coming down straight at the back, and four inches wide at the shoulders and nates. In front the aura ought to have been six inches in breadth before the body and lower limbs. However, there was a diminution in width from the level of the lower border of the manubrium to about the umbilical plane. This depression could not be termed funnel-shaped, but looked as if it might have been so once, and was filling up on its return to a normal condition. Here the haze was not so bright as elsewhere. The inner aura, too, was below par as regards clearness, but showed striation. The indistinctness was due to the patient not having recovered her strength. In front of the epigastrium it was *narrower* and fainter than over the remainder of the body, to which it was still contiguous.

The c.c. band exhibited on the back a light yellow patch by the left side of the spine from the fourth to the eighth dorsal vertebræ, and also a dark one over the two lower lumbar vertebræ and the upper part of the sacrum. In front of the body there was a patch over the epigastrium, nondescript in colour, which was more marked over the place where the pain had been previously most intense. A long dark mark running down by the rectus abdominis on the left side, and two others one in either groin, the left being deeper than the right, also came into view. In all these places the patient complained of tenderness and pain.

The different coloured screens showed no modifications, except that through the blue screen the aura looked green and yellow unblended.

The main interest in this case lay in the condition of the aura in front of the epigastrium, where a transitional stage between a void space and a healthy state had been reached, showing how the restoration of the aura takes place gradually from the body outwards.

The next change of the inner aura to be described is most difficult to understand. It consists of a diminution in breadth at the expense of the part nearest the body, leaving an apparently vacant space between the two.

A former chapter has been devoted to the etheric double, which appears as an empty space intervening between the body and the aura. It rarely exceeds three-sixteenths of an inch in breadth, and usually passes unobserved during the inspection of a patient. Sometimes, however, when wider, it is recognized at the first glance, over the whole body, while occasionally it seems to be more clearly defined on one side than the other. The last condition is generally accompanied by some alteration of the inner aura. At times the blank space will be seen to be broadened locally, while the inner aura is proportionally narrowed with its outer margin remaining in its normal place. At present it is impossible to decide whether this vacant space is an enlarged etheric double or arises from a complete disappearance of a portion of the aura. The appearance recalls the clear space between the visible steam and the spout of the kettle from which it has issued when the water inside is boiling freely.

In well marked cases this phenomenon can hardly be missed, but in slight instances it is difficult to determine whether the gap between the body and the aura is or is not normal, and what makes it still more perplexing is, that an alteration in the texture may also be present. In many cases these empty spaces may be invisible, being obscured by the surrounding healthy aura, so probably they are really not uncommon.

No part of the body is exempt. The change has been noticed over the trunk, front, back, and sides, and upon the upper and lower limbs. It occurs most frequently in neurotic people, and also accompanies or results from various conditions, *e.g.*, injury (case 68), growth (page 287), muscular atrophy (case 61), herpes zoster (case 62), disseminated sclerosis (case

37), etc. The duration of the change cannot usually be determined, but in a case of injury to the ribs proved to be purely temporary. (Case 68.)

In case 61 (figs. 51 and 52), an account is given of some very curious changes in the aura, including a local vacant space.

N., a woman lately married, twenty-seven years of

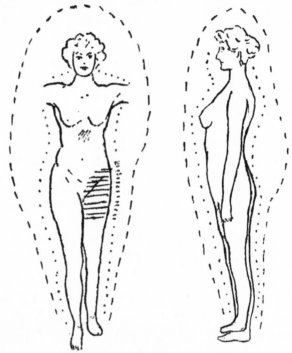

Figs. 51 and 52.
Old hip disease. Spatulate aura.
≡ Dark with c.c. band.
/// Light ditto.

age, had suffered with hip disease when two years old. She had been an in-patient several times in a hospital, where she had undergone four operations, the wound of the last one only healing when she was nineteen. She was obliged to use a crutch, as her left leg was two inches shorter, and the left thigh was four inches less in circumference than that of the right. At the time of inspection she looked a perfect picture of health.

Her aura, when examined in 1912, was blue in colour. On the right side the outer aura had a normally defined edge, and was typically spatulate, being nine inches round the head and by the trunk, curving inwards just below the lowest level of the body, becoming four inches by the knee. On the left side the aura gradually shaded off to its margin, and as far as could be verified, was eight inches by the trunk, but on a superficial examination looked less, and bent inwards at a sharp angle just below the crest of the ilium, from whence it proceeded downwards at a width of three inches. Viewed sideways, the aura was four inches in front of the trunk, the right thigh and leg, but was one inch narrower by the left thigh and leg. At the back there was the usual large lumbar bulge seen with this type of aura, being eight inches wide at the broadest part ; lower down along the thighs and legs the haze had the same width as in front. The inner aura was equal in breadth over the whole body, except from the crest of the ilium to the middle of the thigh on the left side. The aura looked quite natural above the affected part, over which there appeared a dark void space three quarters of an inch deep, resembling a wide etheric double. It was impossible to determine how far round the thigh this blank space extended. External to this void the aura was coarsely striated. The outer aura here was also correspondingly coarse, and the alteration of texture was limited by the vertical median lines of the body back and front. The c.c. band was dark between the crest of the ilium and the middle of the thigh on the left side. It also disclosed a dark patch on the epigastrium due to indigestion. Otherwise the band was uniform over the whole body.

A unique phenomenon of great interest was associated with multiple changes of the kind under consideration in a patient suffering from herpes zoster. The rash was so extensive that some derangement of the aura, short of complete absence over the entire affected area, was expected. Although the patient's aura was not very distinct, and was below the normal in clearness, the following extraordinary aspect could be easily detected :

When the patient extended his arm, the aura adjacent to the rash presented a most remarkable appearance ; it seemed to be honeycombed with vacuoles beneath the arm and beside the trunk. At first the phenomenon was hard to explain, but the difficulty vanished directly it was recollected that the lines of the auric forces are at right angles to the body, and that in this instance some of them would proceed from the trunk, others from the arm, and again others from the axilla, all at different angles, causing them to be continually intersecting in the almost empty space. As the auric forces over this part of the body were, owing to the complaint, considerably below the usual strength and irregularly distributed, the haze was correspondingly small, and a cellular or spongy appearance was thus produced. This effect would also be enhanced by a more or less healthy aura at the back and in front of the pathological portion.

Case 62. F.F., a shoemaker, twenty-two years of age. When a boy of seven he had hip disease, and for years suffered from abcesses due to sequestra. He had undergone several operations, but for the last five years had enjoyed good health until a week previous to his inspection, when he noticed a rash upon the side of his chest followed by an eruption in the axilla and inner side of the arm, and another similar patch on the back accompanied by severe pain. When examined there was a herpetic patch about one and a half inches square just below the clavicle. The whole of the right axilla and three quarters of the right arm, as well as another small place on the back near the spine at the level of the third dorsal vertebræ, were covered with the rash. The blebs were very large, some being half an inch in length. There could be no mistake about its being a severe case of herpes zoster. Inspection showed the aura to be less distinct than normal, and of a grey blue colour. On the left side it was quite natural, but very narrow, the outer being three inches in breadth and the inner two and a half. At the front and the back it was the same width, and showed no departure in shape from what would be found in health. On the right side, however, the aura was normal round the head, but as soon as the arms were raised, the appearance under the right arm and a little way down the trunk was very peculiar. It was granular but not as plainly so as usual. Against a black background, it looked as if it consisted of a haze honeycombed with dark holes. The effect produced is difficult in the extreme to describe, and the diminution of the intensity of the granular part of the aura resulted evidently from a loss of substance. Besides, the outer and inner auras appeared to be completely amalgamated, since not a vestige of differentiation could be detected. Below this disorganized portion, the aura seemed to have regained its proper condition for a short distance. Opposite the ilium, from the crest downwards, for about five inches, the haze showed a condition similar to that described, only less marked. This was contiguous to the formerly diseased joint.

The next example is one displaying an alteration of the configuration of an aura due to local disturbance, and recovery from immediately the patient began to improve in health. Fortunately the woman allowed an examination from time to time, and thus diagrams illustrating the gradual recovery could be made. For the sake of simplicity the outer aura alone has been depicted in the diagram. Although at intervals other cases have been seen in which auras impaired in shape have been noticed to return gradually to their natural forms, not one has shown the same amount of alteration, and none could be so closely followed.

Case 63. (Fig. 53.) D., a spinster, forty-seven years of age, whose occupation was housework, was

inspected for the first time at the end of July, 1908. For several years she had been subject to indigestion. For some months she had suffered great discomfort and pain, accompanied by a good deal of flatulence which commenced about an hour and a half after meals, and continued another half hour or longer. She was constipated and her stomach was dilated.

The aura on the left side proceeded downwards in the ordinary manner for a woman, reaching the middle of the thigh before it commenced to contract permanently. It was about seven inches at the widest part. On the right it was very peculiar. Around the head it was similar to that on the left, but at the level of the nipples, being then about six and a half inches wide, it suddenly curved inwards to a point a trifle above the level of the umbilicus, where it was only one and a half inches in breadth. From this place downwards it did not alter in width. Sideways, there was no peculiarity either at the back or in front of the body.

Fig. 53.
Recuperation of aura.
—— Dark with c.c. band.

When the c.c. band was employed, a dark quadrilateral patch was seen over the right hypochondrium.

It started at the median line and extended round the body, having its upper edge level with the xiphoid cartilage, and its lower margin at the level of the umbilicus. This space was several shades darker than the rest of the band, and its lines of demarcation were sharply defined. Upon palpation tenderness of the liver was found, and one spot two inches above the navel and the same distance to the right of the median line, was exceedingly painful to deep pressure. The patient improved greatly under treatment.

In October, 1908, another inspection was made. The aura was unchanged except on the right side. Its curve was not so deep as formerly, and it began to widen before it finally contracted at the same level as on the left side, viz., about the middle of the thigh.

Six months later the inward curve of the aura on the right side could still be plainly seen, but had greatly diminished, otherwise there was no alteration. As the aura seemed to be gradually regaining its natural state, it was inspected once again in October, 1909. The patient had been suffering from indigestion for about six weeks, but after treatment for the last three had vastly improved. The aura had become quite symmetrical on the two sides of the body, but the previously affected area still continued to have a different aspect to any other part.

This modified portion of the aura commenced about the level of the xiphoid cartilage, and terminated a short distance above the crest of the ilium. It had a dull look and was coarse in texture, and its colour was not quite as blue as the healthy part. To the right it was bounded by streaks of a lighter shade proceeding straight from the body. These differed from the ordinary rays in their opacity. Here the inner aura was slightly narrowed, showed no striation and was coarsely granular. Elsewhere it was even all over the body, being two inches wide and was fairly lineated. The etheric double was well marked as a dark space one eighth of an inch in breadth. This showed that while the aura had regained its proper shape, it had not resumed its natural condition. With the blue c.c. band the quadrilateral space in the hypochondriac region still was darker than the rest of the band, but the difference was not so pronounced. The extension band on the right side also remained of a darker hue than on the left, but the difference was less marked. Fig. 53 shows the gradual amendment in the aura from time to time.

Some months later, as the patient was in fair health, her aura was again inspected. The outer was natural in size all over the body, and symmetrical. However, the inner aura had not wholly regained its proper texture on the right side, as it remained coarse and opaque, but it showed signs of striation although the lines were unlike healthy ones. The upper and lower margins of the unhealthy aura were the sterno-xiphoid plane and a level a little higher than the crest of the ilium.

With the blue c.c. band the large dark patch was still in existence but had become less distinct than on the previous occasion. It was continued round to the back. The band also brought to view a well marked patch having ill-defined edges, on the left side, partially in the lumbar and partially over the iliac region. She had pain in this place on the previous day, and the spot was tender to palpation.

After a long lapse of time her aura was finally examined in the early part of 1917. There was nothing of special interest except that the aura on the right side had completely recovered its proper texture, leaving no trace of its former abnormal condition.

Local enlargements of the aura must now be considered. Such are always present in pregnancy, but only temporarily, and must be regarded as physiological. In fact, as will be seen in a later chapter, the increase in front of the breasts and abdomen constitute one of the signs of that state. The two following instances are exceptions to the rule, because although in both the increase was similar to that occurring in pregnancy, this condition was not present.

Case 64. E., was the mother of two children, of whom the first was still born and the second two and a half years old. For some time after the birth of the latter child she had flooding and a polypus was removed in the succeeding year. Since the operation her periods had occurred at intervals of fourteen days, and were copious. She had missed three times. Her abdomen was very slightly enlarged. She had been feeling well, but far from strong. Her aura was bluish grey colour. It was nine inches by the head and the sides of the trunk, and four by the ankles. In profile the aura was five inches in front of the abdomen, but only three above and below, and by the thighs and legs four. The inner aura was two and a half inches over the whole body with the exception of the front of the abdomen, where it was wider. Pregnancy was diagnosed, but, as it turned out, incorrectly.

Case 65. N., a married childless woman. She was very nervous and depressed, as she had been growing thin for the last twelve months, and complained of vague pains in different parts of her body. Three years before inspection she had undergone an uterine operation. Her aura was blue, spatulate, seven inches and a half by the head, nine by the trunk, and not quite four by the ankles. Seen sideways, the outer aura was nine inches at the small of the back, and elsewhere four, and in front it was four all the way down, except the portion in front of the lower part of the abdomen, which was three quarters of an inch wider. The inner aura was two and a half inches all over the body, with the exception of the part in front of the abdomen, where it was three inches. Omitting this broader portion which was granular, the inner aura was striated throughout.   This want of lineation was evidence against pregnancy.

Nearly allied to this alteration in texture, which will be described almost directly, is the indistinctness of the inner or both auras simultaneously.   A less defined striation of the inner aura than normal may be looked upon as presumptive evidence that the patient is not naturally robust, or is in a temporary or permanent state of ill-health.   The only common exception is among women during pregnancy, when the inner, or more frequently both, auras, are decidedly more shadowy than is to be expected in good health. So numerous are these instances in which this condition of the auras occur, that diminution of visibility may be numbered among the less important signs of being enceinte.

A very good example of this condition is the next case, that of a strong, well-built, tall man who, having lumbago, took it into his head to cure it by fasting. When seen, although he had taken no food for nine days and only water to drink, declared that he felt quite fit, and that on the previous day, after attending to his bees all the morning, had been gardening the whole afternoon, doing, as he termed it, "navvy's work."   When in his usual state of health, his aura would be pronounced wide, especially round his head, as his intellectual powers were considerably above the average.   He was a barrister and a wrangler.

Case 66.   H. G., aged forty-eight, was inspected in 1915.   The outer aura was quite up to the normal in distinctness, and of a good shape.   The inner was almost invisible, however, striation could be just detected.   The c.c. band was uniform over the whole body, except that there was a yellow patch in front of the stomach.   The patient owned to having discomfort at that place for the first time since he had commenced fasting, and attributed it to want of food.   There was nothing worth mentioning about

the aura. It is interesting to note that his surface
electricity was almost nil, while a month or two
previously it had been unusually great.

Case 67. A lady thirty-four years of age, who
had never been strong but never had any serious
illness, was examined in 1913. A short time before
she had complained of indigestion from which she
had completely recovered. She was thin but that
was natural to her. Several members of her family
had died of consumption, but she had shown no signs
of that complaint. She was regarded as a healthy
but delicate woman. The colour of her aura was
blue tinged with grey. The outer aura barely reached
the average standard of distinctness, while the inner
was far below, though striation could be detected
with difficulty. The dimensions of the outer aura
were nine inches by the sides of the trunk and round
the head, four in front of the body, seven at the back,
and by the lower limbs three and a half. The inner
aura was two and a half inches by the head and
trunk, and two by the legs. The c.c. band only
revealed slight marks, one in front and one at the
back. The colours of the aura when observed through
the different screens were curious, but hardly worth
mentioning here.

This condition is constantly met with in girls and
young women when anæmic, but the aura returns
to its normal brightness as they become convalescent.

Directly the outer and inner auras could be differentiated, it became reasonable to surmise that
each of these at times would display alterations in
size and structure. It has been incidentally noted
that in a large number of instances, a variation in the
size of the inner aura has been accompanied by a
modification of substance, so that the two conditions
may be conveniently studied together.

To understand the changes that take place in the
texture of the inner aura, it must be borne in mind

that when healthy it is composed of an exceedingly fine haze, apparently made up of fine granules which by their arrangement impart a striated appearance. This aura keeps so nearly the same breadth over every part of the body, that it is probably the outcome of one and only one force emanating from the body, viz., the inner auric force. (Page 133).

Any departure from health is liable to derange this force, and to induce some change in the substance of the aura. One that can be frequently distinguished without the intervention of any screen, is the loss of natural striation. This is the earliest morbid modification of the inner aura.

As an adjunct to this want of striation, the incomparably fine granules constituting the inner aura in health, will be replaced by others more coarse and opaque. Apparently each of these large granules is formed by the coalescence of two or more small ones. The sizes of these granules vary greatly, but there is generally a predominance of one size which imparts a distinctive feature to the affected part. The granular state may be conveniently classified as *fine, medium, and coarse*, as the case may be. With the appearance of these granules, lineation first becomes coarse, and ultimately disappears. It would appear from the infrequency of alterations in breadth of the inner aura, that the intensity of the forces originating it is usually preserved, but what part, if any, it plays in the production of the abnormal granules is not known. When once the granular appearance is established, especially if coarse, a long time generally elapses before the aura returns to its pristine state. An example may be cited of a lady, who showed this peculiarity seven weeks after suffering from a stiff neck. After an interval of another five months her neck was again examined. When investigated in the ordinary manner there was a small deranged patch emanating from the lowest part of the neck. This patch was about two and a half inches wide at the base, and two in height. The outer margin consisted of a number of points, one taller than the other until the highest was reached, and on the other side of the peak it fell away in the same manner. With a light carmine screen the spot looked finely granular, having been on the former occasion much coarser. When the c.c. bands were employed, the blue and the green on the right side were darker, while the yellow was even on the two sides. The change from the large to the small granules was obviously the precursor of a return to the normal.

The next case is extremely interesting as the patient was inspected during bad health—after an injury— and again when she was in perfect health. It was thus possible to determine whether the alterations in the aura were transient or permanent.

Case 68. U., a shop assistant, twenty-four years of age, who throughout her life had been healthy and strong, recently became the victim of indigestion, which under treatment soon disappeared. At the time of her inspection she was far from strong. Her outer aura was natural in shape, and of a greyish blue colour. By the sides of the head and trunk it was nine inches in breadth, six by the thighs and four by the ankles. In front it was four inches all the way down, and at the back showed a slight bulge seven inches wide, and by the thighs and legs it was three and a half inches broad.

The inner aura measured two and three-quarter inches by the body and a little less by the limbs. Natural striation could be recognized all over the body, except in the left hypochondriac region, where it had become coarsely lineated. The c.c. band showed the very common change on the sacrum, while over the epigastrium there was a large dark patch extending round the left side as far as the spine.

Two years later she became anæmic, always felt languid, and had a return of indigestion accompanied by dilatation of the stomach. While in this condition she was inspected a second time. the outer aura, with the exception of being *enlarged* in front of the abdomen, had not changed. The inner aura had lost considerably in clearness, and was decidedly below the average in distinctness, yet lineation could, without much difficulty, be perceived. It remained unchanged, except that it had increased in front of the trunk, from the level of the nipple line to a short distance above the umbilicus. Here striation was visible, but was coarse and had a tendency to become granular. Examination with the c.c. band disclosed a large yellow spot over the left hypochondrium.

As this enlargement of the aura was not present in front of the abdomen during the first inspection, it is evident that it could have been in existence only a comparatively short time, so it was thought that another examination would prove whether the augmentation was temporary or permanent, and thus be instructive. The woman kindly assented, but unfortunately was unable to fulfil her promise for a considerable time, as during the interval she married and her new home was in the north of England.

Her third inspection took place in the autumn of 1916, when she was still feeling the effects of a fall which resulted in two fractured ribs on the right side. It is unnecessary to enter into the details of this examination, as for the most part the auras remained the same, and there was no alteration in the enlargement in front of the abdomen, while the inner aura had regained its proper distinctness. However, near the site of the recent injury from the level of the sterno-xiphoid plane to the crest of the ilium, there was a void space about an inch and a half between the body and the inner aura. As owing to the injury she could not be regarded in perfect health she came when feeling absolutely well.

In March, 1917, she was examined for the last time. Her outer aura looked unusually distinct and appeared larger than at the former inspections. After making all allowances for its indefinite margin, the outcome of a slight ultra-outer aura, there was no doubt about a true increase in size. The measurements were, by the head eleven inches, twelve by the trunk, six and a half by the thighs, and four by the ankles. Back and front of the trunk it was eight inches, and down the thighs and legs it was the same as by the sides. The enlargement in front of the abdomen of both auras remained constant. The inner was coarsely striated near the seat of the injury, (where also the c.c. band looked dark), otherwise it appeared healthy over the whole body, being three inches and a half wide, and a trifle narrower by the limbs. The former blank space between the body and the haze was occupied by the inner aura in the ordinary manner. The extra width of the auras in front of the abdomen in this case must now be considered a permanent feature.

As the inner auras of persons in good health are more extensive in the robust than in the constitutionally delicate, it is extremely improbable that the broader side will prove to be abnormal when asymmetry occurs. Usually there is no difficulty in coming to a decision, as some other modification on the affected side can always be detected either directly or with the c.c. band. It will be found that whenever a contraction of the inner aura exists, a corresponding change in the outer will have taken place ; but the reverse does not hold good. It is worth remembering that in every instance in which a contracted inner aura has been observed over a large surface, the patient has suffered from a grave malady.

The inspection of an epileptic shows the inner aura on the left side to be narrowed, while on the right it retains its full size. The modifications do not stop here, as invariably on the left side the texture of the aura is coarse in appearance, or even granular, causing striation when distinguishable to be detected only with difficulty. This one-sided diminution of the inner aura is far more diagnostic of epilepsy than the contracted outer aura, although the latter is considerably more conspicuous and was first discovered.

The permanence of the granular state of the inner aura reaches its zenith in one place, where it almost ceases to be pathological. This is over some part of the lower lumbar and sacral regions of many women between the ages of twenty and fifty years. In some it is the lowest part of the sacrum, in others higher up, but although in every instance the median line is affected, the patch usually extends more to one side than the other. When this condition is present an unvarying tale is told, of pain, or at least discomfort, at that place in the back during the menstrual periods. The recurrence of these cycles at short intervals does not permit sufficient time for the aura to return to its natural state before a fresh onset commences, thus making the abnormal condition perpetual. Another interesting fact is, that this patch is generally more pronounced when the pain has been severe. The granular condition may as a rule be recognized by the aid of a deep carmine screen, but before this was used, dark patches had been discovered in the c.c. bands, and their cause had been a great puzzle, until the influence of local changes had been realized. It had also been noticed that this dark patch was non-existent in men, and did not appear in girls before puberty, nor in women who had passed their grand climacteric, and that it generally vanished during pregnancy unless it was produced by a known cause such as lumbago. An additional proof of its intimate connection with menstruation was forthcoming, when on one occasion a young lady who presented not the slightest sign of any discoloured patch over the sacrum, upon being interrogated, stated, " that she had never suffered the least pain or ache in that region during her periods." At the same examination the c.c. band exhibited a small light discoloured spot, about one and a half inches in diameter over the first lumbar spine. When questioned whether there was pain or tenderness in that place, she replied that there had been none for the last fortnight, but previously she had a good deal of pain, on one occasion so acute that she had to retire to bed. This is another instance of the long time sometimes taken by the aura before a return to normal after being granular.

Besides the very crude variations in texture which are easily perceived, such as the granular conditions, there are others of a more refined nature, imperceptible to the naked eye but distinguishable by the c.c. bands. The use of these bands will form the subject of the next chapter.

Physiological enlargements of the inner aura are of two kinds. The first only persists a short time, is very great and sometimes extends beyond the limits of the outer aura ; these are the rays which have already been discussed. The second is also temporary, but of longer duration ; occasionally it may persist for weeks or even months. A good illustration of this condition is seen over the front of the abdomen in pregnancy.

Pathological enlargements of the inner aura do indubitably occur, as in case 68. Whenever the inner aura look broaders locally and the texture has not been sufficiently altered to abolish striation throughout the whole width, there can be no doubt about a real increase if present. At the same time the outer aura will probably also show some augmentation.

In many cases the extension of the inner aura is only specious and a result of an alteration in the adjacent outer aura, consequently it is necessary to take into consideration the structure of this aura when estimating the size of the inner. During health the portion of the outer aura lying just outside the inner has larger granules than the more distant parts. The layers of the different sized granules imperceptibly graduate into one another. When a local disturbance arises in the inner aura causing it to become granular, the grains of the outer are liable to be similarly affected to a less extent. As the derangement of the inner aura progresses there occurs *pari passu* a change in the outer, which frequently can be verified by the chromatic alterations in the c.c. bands over the affected portions. Besides, the charging of the patient with static electricity will sometimes be of assistance in determining the true width of the inner aura, and consequently the extent of the derangement of the outer, as this proceeding causes the inner aura to vanish before the outer, leaving a void space. However, it is not always easy to decide whether there has been an increase of one of the auras at the expense of the other.

The following case affords a very good illustration of a similar change affecting both auras, making the inner aura appear widened; and of the separation of the two auras by the help of static electricity. There are, besides, other peculiarities which make the case worth quoting.

Case 69. (Fig. 54). I.W., a girl twenty years old was lately examined. Twelve months previously she had an attack of influenza complicated by pleurisy, on the left side, and subsequently she had undergone an operation for empyema. A few months later enlarged glands were removed from the right side of her neck. When eleven years old she was a patient in the Hospital suffering from paralysis of both legs, and was discharged as incurable ; but two days after reaching home she had suddenly regained the use of her legs.

When inspected both auras were normal in distinctness. The outer was spat-ulate in shape, rather wide, ten inches by the sides of the head, eleven by the trunk, six by the thighs and five by the ankles. The inward curve was sudden, and just below the level of the body. The inner aura over the right side of the neck showed a void space quite an inch wide, and the remainder was coarsely granular. This occurred over the situation of the diseased glands. Over the rest of the right side of the body the aura was natural, and striation clearly defined. On the left side from the axilla to the middle of the thigh the aura was very coarsely granular, while by the neck and leg it was nor-

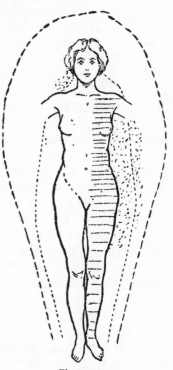

Fig. 54.
Granular outer and inner auras.
Void space by neck.

mal. The inner aura on the left side of the trunk appeared to be six inches wide, but over the rest of the body, including the affected portion on the right, was not more than three. It was taken for granted that the wide granular aura on the left side included a portion of the outer aura. Later on, when the patient standing on the insulated stool received a sufficiently large positive charge to cause the inner aura to vanish, but not enough to abolish the outer, the void space could be seen as nearly as possible of the same width as the inner aura in other places, viz, three inches, thus proving that the outer aura to a depth of three inches partook of the same granular alteration. With a larger charge it was noticed that the granular outer aura was the last to depart.

The c.c. band also presented some abnormalities. First of all the whole of the left side from the level of the clavicle downwards looked darker than on the right. This deepening of colour commenced in the middle of the spine at the back, and extended round to the front to about an inch to the left of the median line. As the girl stood facing, the right extension of the c.c. band was normal, while the left extension appeared darker, but it was difficult to obtain the true colour as the band was projected on to the aura itself on a plane in front of the trunk, and seemed to be mixed up with the granules. This was a unilateral instance of a phenomenon already mentioned. (Page 158). A dark spot was also discovered upon the nape of the neck.

To sum up, the inner aura does not vary in shape and size to the same extent as does the outer, and the chief morbid changes manifest themselves as alterations of substance. It is plain from the cases quoted, that variations in shape and size of the outer aura occur frequently and extensively, while in general structural modifications are either so slight or so delicate as to be almost imperceptible.

Nothing much can be said about the hue of an aura seen without a screen. The colours are for the most part limited to blue or grey, or to the mixtures of the two in different proportions. Temperament and mental powers seem to be of more importance in this direction than are temporary changes in the health. In the following table compiled from the first hundred examinations made, auras have been classified according to their colours under the different headings. I. Blue auras. II. Blue mixed with grey auras. III. Grey auras. (N.B. The table originally published in the first edition of this book has been retained unaltered, as the overwhelming majority of the people examined since have been in ill-health).

I.   Blue series.   Forty cases.
   No individuals below, some above the average in mental power.

II.   Blue with more or less grey.   Thirty-six cases.
   Some individuals below, none above the average in mental power.
   One case of hemiplegia. ⎫
   Two epileptics.   ⎬ included in this class.
   One case of meningitis. ⎭

III.   Grey series.   Seventeen cases.
   All below the average in mental power.
   Two eccentric people.   ⎫
   Six epileptics.   ⎮
   One case of general   ⎬ included in this class.
      paralysis.   ⎮
   Three mentally dull.   ⎭

In the remaining seven cases no note was taken of the colour of the aura.

This table shows conclusively that the owners of blue auras are generally best endowed mentally.

A congenital grey aura indicates a deficiency of the intellectual faculties, but it has not been ascertained whether the loss of brain power through disease would change the colour of the aura to grey, which seems not unlikely.

N.B. It should be remembered that in all cases the colours of auras are faint and delicate.

CHAPTER IX

The Use of the Complementary Coloured Bands in Disease

The theory of the complementary coloured bands has already been discussed in a former chapter. There still remains the consideration of the practical use of these bands both in health and disease. Like most other scientific methods of research, a certain amount of proficiency, which only practice can give, is required. After the technique has been mastered with the help of the instructions previously given, there arise difficulties of interpretation. It is essential to acquire rapidity in recognizing the alterations of the tints, not merely to save time, but also to prevent excessive strain upon the eyesight. Immediately after the eyes have been sufficiently (but not too much) colour-fatigued, the first glance is the most sensitive to any slight alteration of the c.c. band, and the more that can be perceived with it the better; later whilst the image is changing colour, rather than when constant, follows the next best opportunity for noticing modifications. The more habitually the band is employed, the more numerous will be the variations recognized. The most that can be hoped for in this chapter, is to give some slight assistance to other workers on this subject, as experience alone can supply the requisite knowledge.

Generally it is inadvisable, even if possible, to examine the whole body minutely at one sitting, especially if it be necessary to employ several complementary colours, as the observer's eyes become fatigued and therefore incapable of appreciating the slighter differences. Fortunately it is rarely necessary to use all the c.c. bands over the entire body, and the procedure in many examinations may be considerably curtailed, if the history of the patient be sufficiently detailed to direct immediate attention to the actually affected organ or part of the body. Again while the shape and general characteristics of the aura are being investigated, abnormalities may attract notice and point to the position of a derangement that needs investigation by the help of the c.c. bands. The following remarks, unless otherwise stated, refer to the blue c.c. band, as in previous chapters.

The colour of the c.c. band when used vertically upon the thorax and abdomen of healthy men and children will be uniform throughout its whole length, unless there is some irregularity in the pigmentation of the skin. This statement is not always applicable to girls above the age of puberty, and seldom to adult women under the age of fifty, in whom the colour will at one time be evenly distributed throughout, while at another time it will be of a darker shade from a short distance below the umbilicus downwards over the lower part of the abdomen. The region where this change becomes most pronounced is about three inches above the pubes. This modification will be found to coincide with the monthly activities of the sexual organs.

One of three conditions is indicated by a vertical c.c. band monochromatic over the whole of a woman's abdomen : (1) most commonly that the last monthly period finished not less than three or four days previously, or that the next is not to be expected within four or five days ; (2) amenorrhœa ; (3) pregnancy. At the approach of the menstrual period, the c.c. band will be darkened low down, at first slightly and later as the time draws near more deeply. The colour advances from lighter to darker imperceptibly without any definite line of demarcation, so that a comparison is best made between distant parts of the band. This gradual deepening of colour is of great importance, as it usually serves to discriminate between an alteration incidental to the natural sexual functions and one that should be ascribed to derangements of the abdominal and pelvic organs.

Darkening of the c.c. band in the lower part of the abdomen from other causes is occasionally an insuperable impediment to calculations relating to menstrual periods. Allowance for the pigmentation on this part of the body may sometimes have to be made if the patient has already been a mother, but generally there is no difficulty of any consequence when proper care has been exercised. An interesting instance connected with this subject is that of a women thirty-three years of age, who manifested an incipient darkening of the c.c. band just above the pubes. When informed that she might expect her next monthly period within the following six or seven days, she replied that it was not due for a fortnight. However, at our next meeting she suddenly exclaimed, " do you remember telling me that my monthly courses would take place in about a week? Well, they did seven days afterwards, being a week sooner than anticipated." In another instance a young woman expected to menstruate within three or four days. With her there was no change in the colour of the band above the pubes. It eventually turned out that her period was delayed for a week.

The acquisition of such information concerning the sexual functions is generally unimportant and obtained while other observations are being made, because during the same projection of the band, all modifications of colour in different parts of its length and their limits can be ascertained, and it can also be noted whether the changes be gradual or abrupt, and the line of demarcation sharp. The band will be found wide enough in most cases for the observer to determine any differences in colour which may happen to occur on the two lateral halves of the body, and to note roughly their position. Subsequently the transverse band should be employed to verify all minutiæ. This latter band has the advantage over the vertical, that during the greater part of the inspection the central portion only need be used, making it easier to watch and freer from errors of observation than when the ends have to be used. Cases 49 and 71, figs. 43 and 56, are instructive and will serve as examples. In the first case when the c.c. band was employed vertically down the middle of the thorax and abdomen, the left side of the former was seen to be lighter than the right for a considerable distance and the upper margin of the discoloured portion lay on the superior aspect of the mamma, while the inferior border was over the lower part of the sternum. The line of demarcation was sharp, corresponding to the median line of the body. Lower down, the band on the abdomen disclosed a small patch of a different shade on the extreme right edge a little above the level of the umbilicus. This gave a useful indication for further investigation with the c.c. band transversely, the result of which has been described elsewhere.

When the examiner begins to scrutinize the spinal column with the c.c. bands he will find it advantageous to divide the inspection into parts, as the band is rarely sufficiently long to cover the whole space simultaneously. Before commencing it will be prudent to take particular notice of the colour of the skin over the vertebral spines, where it has frequently a different tint from the neighbouring portions of the epidermis. This may be a natural pigmentation, or an alteration in colour produced by constant pressure of the clothes. Directly the observer looks at the spine, he will most likely detect some variation in the shade of the c.c. band should derangement be present. The commonest irregularity exhibited on the back are patches seen on the spine itself, either lighter, darker, or of a different colour as the case may be. These spots may be situated on any part throughout its length, but most frequently over the two lowest lumbar vertebræ and the sacrum in women, where the colour of the band is constantly altered. The reason for this has already been stated. Two other common positions are over the lower dorsal and upper lumbar vertebræ, and over the seventh cervical and higher dorsal spines. Here, usually, some shade of yellow, or else a paler tint of the c.c. band is generally seen, but over the sacrum the shade is dark or the colour often approaches ochre. It is not uncommon to find two or more different coloured patches on the same patient. Another fairly frequent abnormality is the appearance of a coloured streak by the side of the spinal column, while the aura over the spine itself remains natural.

Such spots are invariably attended with pain or tenderness, not necessarily just at the time of inspection, as even weeks may elapse before pain-marks disappear finally. Of this occurrence a good example has been mentioned on page 240. A patch on or near the spine of a light yellow colour, or of a lighter tint than the rest of the band, is a sign that there is no organic mischief, and almost always that the cause is only temporary, not seldom having a nervous origin. The darker patches and those in which the colour tends to ochre seem to point to more important or prolonged disorders.

The next case is of interest as an illustration of the remarks just made and also showing a hysterical type of aura.

Case 70. (Fig. 55.) S., a married woman twenty-eight years of age, childless, complained of vomiting during the previous six weeks, which was increased by any worry, was first examined in 1910.

For three months she had been losing flesh. Her

menses were regular. She suffered occasionally from globus hystericus. Her thorax was peculiar in shape, being straight down, and the sternal notch was as high as the nipples, although her breasts were not pendulous. There was tenderness in the epigastrium, and pressure there induced pain between the shoulders. The aura was ten inches round the head, and the same width by the sides of the trunk, but it suddenly curved inwards a little below the level of the pubes, contracting rapidly. It was a typical specimen of a spatulate aura. The outer aura barely reached the normal standard of distinctness. A side view disclosed a bulge at the back in the lumbar regions about eight inches deep, which bent inwards a short distance beneath the buttocks, from which level contracted quickly to the full extent. All down the front and limbs it was about four inches wide. The inner aura was about two and a half inches in breadth, all over the body. There were faint rays proceeding upwards from each shoulder, and another perpendicular to the right lower ribs.

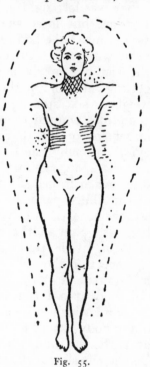

Fig. 55.
Exophthalmic Goitre.
·∴· Granular aura.
≡ Dark with c.c. band.
xxx Peculiar pink with c.c. band.
| ≡ Void space of inner aura.

Over the fourth and fifth lumbar vertebræ and the sacrum the inner aura was granular, and the adjacent outer aura partook of the same alteration. The c.c. band was even over the whole of the thorax and abdomen; on the back the band showed close to and parallel with the spine, a strip on the left side lighter in colour, reaching from the third to the ninth dorsal vertebræ, having all its margins distinctly defined. This was considered to be a case of nervous vomiting and was treated accordingly.

She was lost sight of for three years as she had left London, but later she returned with a new set of symptoms. She had remained in good health for two years without a recurrence of her old complaint. For the last five or six months, however, she had been getting thin, and at the time of examination she only weighed six stones, seven pounds. All her new symptoms pointed to exophthalmic goitre—slight enlargement of the thyroid gland—prominence of the eyes, especially the left, sufficient for her friends to remark upon, rapidity of the pulse and palpitation, often when in bed, debility and nervousness, tremors of the limbs, particularly of the right hand and leg, strange sensations in various parts of the body. She had also pain in the right side of the thorax, culminating at the tip of the eleventh rib.

Inspection showed both auras to be distinct. The measurements of the outer were identical with those obtained at a former examination. The inner had the same width as before, and was striated over most of the body except by the right side of the thorax and over the sacrum, where it was coarsely granular. On the left side of the thorax it had disappeared close to the body leaving a void space about half an inch in breadth. On both sides of the neck, more especially the right, it was finely granular. The c.c. band revealed a dark patch on the spine between the fifth and the ninth dorsal vertebræ, another over the sacrum, whilst in front there was a third over the right lower ribs. All these places were tender. The extensions by the sides of the neck had a deeper shade than elsewhere.

It will be interesting to compare this patient with

another woman who had been afflicted with Graves'
disease for some years, and had been under treatment
at different hospitals.

Case 71. (Figs. 56 to 58.) K., a woman thirty-
seven years of age, the mother of two children, was

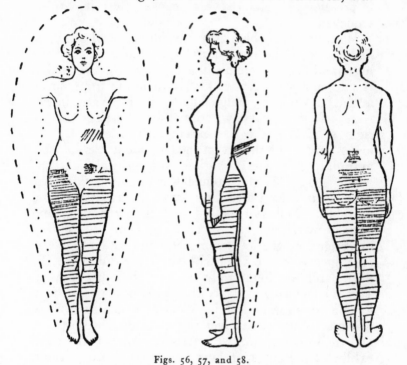

Figs. 56, 57, and 58.
Exophthalmic Goitre.
—— Dark with c.c. band. Intensity according to shading.
////// Light ditto.

inspected in 1911. Until marriage she was delicate
but had never exhibited any signs of hysteria. Between
four and five years ago her illness was diagnosed as
exophthalmic goitre. At the time of examination her
symptoms were : slight enlargement of the thyroid
gland, protruding eyes, pulse fairly normal, no palpitations, and great nervousness. She did not feel so

strong as she did a short time previously, and was depressed. A week before examination a severe thunderstorm frightened her, and immediately afterwards she felt a peculiar sensation in her thighs and legs, the left thigh being the worst. This singular impression continued several weeks before it entirely vanished.

Her aura was a blue grey in colour, and of good size and shape. The outer aura was nine inches by the head and trunk, diminishing to three by the ankles. A side view showed it to be five inches in front, seven at the back with no bulge, and by the legs three inches wide. It was coarsely striated by the neck on the right side, and to a less extent on the left. By the lower part of the thorax on the left side it was coarsely granular, otherwise striation was natural over the whole body. As the woman was standing sideways, a ray was seen proceeding from the twelfth dorsal vertebra. This ray caused a dark patch when examined with the c.c. band. Later on during the investigation the ray vanished, and the place was examined a second time with the c.c. band, when the dark patch was found to have completely disappeared. This is conclusive evidence that a ray and a patch may have a common underlying cause. In addition there was a large dark area over the lower lumbar vertebræ and the upper part of the sacrum. In front the band exhibited a light spot over the left hypochondrium. The band was much deeper in shade over the thighs and legs, being darkest in the places where the sensations reached their maximum. The shading in the figures is proportional to the depth of colour.

She was inspected a second time in the following February. Although the lower limbs were free from the peculiar sensations, the right side of the thorax was now attacked.

Neither aura showed any alteration in size or shape since the previous investigation. However, the c.c.

band was darkened all over the right side of the thorax. The inner lines of demarcation between the normal and abnormal colours were the vertical lines back and front. The left thigh was still deepened by the c.c. band but not to the same extent as before. This was evidently a continuation of the former condition.

Shortly after this examination the patient became pregnant, and while in that state her health improved greatly. In October, 1912, she was inspected a third time. The only change in the shape of her was, as might be expected, in front of her abdomen. Here the outer aura was seven and a half inches, while the inner was three and a half; both were conical. In this case pregnancy caused the outer aura to be diminished in distinctness to a slight extent, while the inner aura was more affected, and had lost much of its clearness. Striation was only to be detected with difficulty. Late in December she gave birth to a healthy girl; both mother and daughter did well. Soon afterwards she removed to another neighbourhood.

With our present imperfect means of investigation, the observer must not expect to see discolouration of the c.c. band over every painful or tender place of which the patient complains. Some of these patches are so distinct that a very cursory glance will detect them, while others differ from the rest of the c.c. bands so slightly that keen sight and a trained eye are required to isolate them. As practice makes perfect, a larger number of these discoloured patches will be discovered.

It is by no means easy to understand why some local disturbances should induce sufficient change in the aura to produce a chromatic alteration in the c.c. bands, while others seemingly similar in every respect give negative results. Intensity of the disorder, especially if acute, appears to be one of the chief factors in the auric change. It is instructive to notice that these discoloured spots in the c.c. bands projected upon the spinal column are not nearly as common among males as females, and are especially marked amongst hysterical, nervous, and excitable girls and women.

As soon as the examination by means of the c.c. bands, when used vertically, has been concluded, having noted as far as possible the positions of local abnormalities, the transverse band will complete all the information to be gleaned by this method. It will enable the investigator to examine the two sides of the body, and with the same projection to observe if one of the extensions has been affected. As a rule the band will be found wide enough to include the whole of the disordered area, but occasionally further observations will be needed. This is, too, the best opportunity for ascertaining whether a discoloured patch spreads over the whole breadth of the body, or only over a portion, also to determine whether it is situated, in toto, on one side of the median line, or crosses it, or whether again it is only a small spot surrounded by the unaltered c.c. band. A large area chronically affected has usually a deep hue, but exceptions are by no means rare. For examples see cases 49 and 69. Although large patches may be discovered on any part of the body, yet they occur more frequently in some positions than in others. A common situation is over the hypochondriac and epigastric regions. The following is a good illustration and demonstrates the length of time an alteration may endure, as the period between the first and last inspections was more than five years.

Case 72. A childless woman who had been married several years suffered for more than twelve months with pain in the stomach, which increased after a meal and was often relieved only by vomiting. She was constantly sick, had pyrosis, but no hæmatemesis. Dread of pain, which she described as agonizing,

prevented her from taking any proper food ; consequently she was emaciated, weak, and anæmic. From
these and other symptoms an ulcer of the stomach
was diagnosed, and under treatment she gradually
improved and became convalescent. When first
examined in 1909, her aura was blue in colour, over
eight inches by the head and by the sides of the trunk,
and four by the legs. In front it was four inches wide,
and at the back nearly six in the lumbar regions,
coming straight down. The shape was good. The
inner aura was two and a half inches in breadth.
There were several rays projected from different
parts of her body, one from each shoulder, one from
each flank, and on the right side one streaming downwards. As she stood sideways, a sixth was noticed
emitted from the lower lumbar vertebræ upwards
and outwards. The c.c. band disclosed no patches
on the back. In front a dark spot over the epigastrium was present, with its upper border on the
sterno-xiphoid plane, and the lower two inches
above the umbilicus ; the inner margin was at the
middle line, and the outer edge on the side of the
trunk. This area was several shades darker than
the rest of the band, and the left extension was
darker than the right.

Unfortunately, after being apparently well for some
months, she had a relapse in January, 1910, and as
proper attention could not be obtained at home, she
entered a hospital for treatment. Finally she was
discharged cured, as she had lost all pain, and was able
to eat solid food without discomfort. Shortly after
her return home she was again examined. There was
no difference in the outer aura, but the inner was
granular on the left side from the nipple line to the
crest of the ilium, front, back, and side. When the
transverse c.c. band was used over this part of the
body, the large discoloured patch could be distinctly
seen, but was not perhaps quite as plain as it had been

previously. The extension still remained darker than on the right side.

There were two discoloured patches on the back, one by the right side of the third and fourth dorsal vertebræ, where she had previously suffered pain. The second spot was over the lower lumbar vertebræ. The writer thinks these patches may have been present at the first examination, only that not being as proficient with the c.c. bands as later on, he missed them.

In 1914, her aura was inspected a third time. There had been no recurrence of any symptom of ulcer. Although in fair health she had never completely regained her full strength, and just lately had been feeling run down. The size and shape of the auras remained unchanged. By the lower ribs on the left side there was a void space between the inner aura and the body, but lineation in the constricted portion could be distinguished. With the c.c. band the same dark patch over the epigastrium was still in existence, but it had altered inasmuch as the dark portion had lessened in width, and the upper part had become lighter in colour. This was one of the few instances that have been seen of a dark spot turning paler, and the change was exceedingly interesting as being probably the first step towards complete disappearance.

Another example in regard to which it would be superfluous to enter into details as it is so like the preceeding one, is that of an unmarried woman twenty-nine years of age, who was brought by Dr. Merrick. Examination with the c.c. band showed that the abdominal area affected was almost identical with that of the last case, but there was one important difference, viz, that the colour of the patch was lighter instead of being darker than the remainder of the band. Experience having taught that pale coloured spots are generally indicative of temporary disorder, the opinion was expressed that the patient's ailment was slight and fleeting, which turned out to be correct. A word of explanation is necessary. The writer had intentionally not investigated this case in the ordinary manner, as this had been done by Dr. Merrick, and it was looked upon as a test of the value of the auric changes.

These two are instructive cases in which the c.c. band gave directly opposite colour effects, although the regions under observation were the same in both instances. In the latter example, whatever the malady may have been, there was in all probability a nervous element at work, and very likely the derangement was entirely functional. In the former case the woman was suffering from chronic gastritis with the corresponding tissue alterations.

Analagous changes may occur over the right hypochondrium and are generally also bounded by the middle line of the body. The upper edge is usually somewhere about the level of the sterno-xiphoid plane, while the lower boundary is about the level of the costal plane. These limits are only approximate, and variations constantly occur. When a patch is seen in this position an invariable accompaniment is tenderness of the liver, with or without superficial hyperæsthesia. Persons addicted to imbibing too much alcohol almost without exception show this patch, which in such cases is dark, and generally associated with another discoloured spot over the epigastrium. These two patches may join and make a single large one. Occasionally when the c.c. band exhibits the large dark patch just mentioned, a small area still darker or one of a different tint may be seen within it. Such a small dark spot is invariably of serious import, through which the presence of malignant disease, before it could have been detected by ordinary means, has been discovered, the diagnosis, unfortunately for the patient, turning out to be only too correct.

Case 73. (Fig. 59). I., a married woman sixty-four years of age, who had always been delicate, had her breast removed in 1901. She was gouty and for five years had been a martyr to neuralgia of the face and neck, the sequel of herpes zoster. In December,

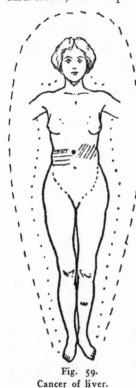

Fig. 59.
Cancer of liver.

≡ Dark with c.c. band.
///// Light ditto.
Showing position of the coming growth.

1911, she was losing flesh rapidly, and suffered pain in the abdomen commencing from a quarter to half an hour after meals and lasting from an hour to an hour and a half, with frequent vomiting. These and other symptoms gave rise to a suspicion of cancer, and it was anticipated that the seat of mischief would be the pylorus. Time after time a search was made for a growth, but none could be found. A medical friend kindly saw the patient and felt confident that malignant disease was present, but he too was unable to locate the site of mischief. Just at this time she was obliged to keep her bed. About ten days later when she had rallied a little she came to have her aura inspected.

The outer aura was distinct, of good size and shape, and greyish blue in colour. It was eight inches round the head and by the sides of the trunk, and four by the legs, as she stood facing. When she turned sideways, it was four inches by the back and front, except in the lumbar regions, where it was six. The inner aura, which was not nearly as plain as it should have been, had the patient been in good health, was two and a half inches wide all over the body and faintly striated. The c.c. band was uniform over the whole body, except in front on the right side, from the pyloric plane to the level of the umbilicus where there was a dark patch, limited by the median line, whilst to the right it went as far as could be seen. There was a still darker spot just over the ninth costal cartilage. Over the epigastrium the c.c. band exhibited a light coloured patch. A diagnosis of growth near the gall bladder was made.

She improved for a short time and went into the country for change of air. At the end of May, 1912, she returned home as she had suddenly developed jaundice. Examination of the abdomen disclosed a hard tumour about the size of a pigeon's egg, which could be felt near the gall bladder, exactly in the place where the very dark spot had been previously seen. The tumour grew rapidly, and other nodules soon made their appearance. She survived only five months.

As an antithesis to this case, a woman asked to have her mother inspected as she had cancer of the liver.

Case 74. N., a woman, seventy-three years of age, was examined in December, 1914, *without a single question being asked*. The colour of her aura looked a greenish blue with an admixture of white—an uncommon appearance. The outer aura was quite up to the average in distinctness, and of a good shape. It was nine inches round the head and eight by the trunk, and four by the ankles. In front it was four inches, and at the back seven at the widest place. The inner aura did not reach the standard of clearness for health, but striation could with a little difficulty be distinguished, and in no place did it exhibit the slightest sign of being granular. When the c.c. band was employed upon the back, a small patch was perceived on the left side, by, but over, the third and fourth dorsal vertebræ, slightly darker than the rest of the band. In front there was only one faint patch about two and a half inches by two, just over the gall bladder. The other c.c. bands did not assist in any way.

Taking into consideration that the aura was healthy, and that the changes disclosed by the c.c. bands were insignificant, the writer felt confident there was no malignant growth. Palpation revealed the presence of gall stones. The patient then gave the following history : she had been suffering from bouts of sickness for several years, and had been growing thinner for three. There had been pain and tenderness over the gall bladder. Two years previously she had entered a hospital, when an operation was recommended, she believed, for gall stones. She would not allow it to be performed, being timid on account of her age. As a result of the examination she was advised to go at once and consult a surgeon. In this instance the aura did not disclose any facts that could not have been ascertained quite easily by ordinary methods of examination, but it is none the less interesting on that account.

Examination of their aura has been the means of reassuring not a few people who had come up under the impression that they were suffering from cancer.

Another common situation for a discoloured patch is over one and sometimes both groins in women mostly over twenty-five years of age. In no instance has a patch over one groin only of a man been recorded, but in a few cases there have been found dark bands stretching right across the lowest part of the abdomen. The upper margins rarely reach as high as the anterior superior spines of the ilium.

The colour of these patches may be either darker, lighter, or of a different hue, to the remainder of the c.c. band, and if there be two patches, one in either groin, they are seldom of the same shade, but should they join and form a complete belt across the lowest part of the abdomen, then the colour will generally be uniform throughout its whole length. After tabulating the different cases it was found that sixty per cent. of these discoloured areas were on the left side, about five and twenty on the right, and the remainder on the two sides, while of these latter about half were joined in the centre.

These patches are invariably diagnostic of pain or tenderness, and according to the depth of shade these symptoms vary in intensity. They are usually accompanied by discoloured places on other parts of the body. Their position in women is sufficient to make it probable that they may have some connection with the genital organs, and, if so, are more commonly than not associated with activity or functional disturbance of the ovaries. From this point of view the next case is very instructive.

Case 75. Mrs. N., forty years of age, had her aura inspected during the autumn of 1918. The outer aura was proportionately rather narrow round the head; otherwise it was of good shape, and exhibited no abnormality. It was nine inches round the head, ten and a half by the trunk, six by the thighs, four and a half by the ankles, and the same width at the back opposite the shoulders and nates, coming down straight behind from the head to the feet. Striation of the inner aura was visible all over the body, but by the left side of the trunk and at the small of the back it was coarse. Neither aura quite reached the proper standard of distinctness for a perfectly healthy person. With the c.c. band, a dark patch was observed upon the sacrum, and in front there was one in either groin. The one on the right side extended nearly as high as the crest of the ilium and continued downwards but with lessened depth of colour to the middle of the thigh. On the left groin the spot was smaller and not so plain, and there was no darkening of the band on the thigh. Besides these she presented other discoloured areas, one by the left side of the dorsal vertebræ, another on the epigastrium, and a third over the right hypochondrium. These may be neglected, being unimportant for the present purpose. In addition to the outer aura which is universal after a person has been electrified, the inner aura by the lower part of the right side of the abdomen and the thigh became augmented.

The patient was a childless married woman who had never been really strong, but who had never suffered from any serious illness. The marked difference in the size and shade of the patches seen with the c.c. band was suggestive of more disturbance on the right side than on the left during menstruation. On being asked whether she suffered an equal amount of discomfort at each period, the following facts were elicited. She had only menstruated a few times in her life, but each month she experienced a considerable amount of pain which was more intense every other time. On the occasions when she had the severer pain, the right thigh always participated in the discomfort as far down as the middle. The lower part of the back always ached.

The alternating violence of the menstrual prodromata points to ovulation taking place successively first in one ovary and then in the other, and more intense functional disturbance when the right was involved.

A discoloured area is of common occurrence over the epigastrium, both in males and females, so common indeed as to seem almost physiological, in the majority of cases where there seems no sufficient reason for suspecting any abnormality. These spots are always light in colour, or of a pale yellow, and are mostly of a fleeting character. The darker shades and hues denote true gastric derangements of some description. Should the light coloured patches prove to be physiological, they are the only known instances, but the only possible alternative is, that a pathological change so slight as to be imperceptible both to the patient and the observer, exists.

Besides these large affected areas, small discoloured spots may be visible which are usually indications of purely local disturbance, and are accompanied by pain or tenderness. These small areas are frequently coloured, yellow of some shade being the most common, and next in frequency a pinkish tinge, which as a rule denotes a more severe disorder. The greater number of them are completely isolated, but may be included within a larger patch, when they point to a focus of considerable mischief. All parts of the body are liable to them, and position may sometimes determine their importance.

A striking example of the foregoing observations was seen in the following incident. Dr. Merrick, wishing to see the aura, brought a patient with him for examination. Knowing that this woman was suffering from ulcer of the stomach, the writer stated that it was extremely probable that the most painful spot or the position of the ulcer could be detected by the help of the c.c. band. No question was asked. Dr. Merrick was able to see the aura distinctly but not the coloured spot, as he was not accustomed to the use of these bands, and could not keep them fixed on the right place.

Case 76. T., a married woman thirty-three years of age, had been suffering from ulcer of the stomach for a long time. She had already been in a hospital and was advised to re-enter for an operation as she was greatly emaciated, and bloodless as a result of repeated vomiting and hæmatemesis. Her aura was well marked and of a bluish colour. A yellow spot about the size of a shilling was visible by the aid of the c.c. band on the left side two and a half inches from the median line, and a little below the ensiform cartilage. This coincided with the most painful place, and was so tender that the patient would hardly allow it to be touched. The rest of the epigastrium was sensitive but not nearly to the same extent. Further examination could not then be made. It was curious that no large discoloured patch, as might have been expected, could be seen.

During March, 1910, she was again inspected. She had not been to a hospital as advised, but had, however, improved greatly, having gained weight although still remaining anæmic. Most of the pain had disappeared and only a slight tenderness in the epigastrium persisted, vomiting had ceased, and she was able to eat ordinary food. Some little pain and tenderness still continued in the lower part of the right hypochondrium. Her outer aura measured nine inches round the head and by the sides of the trunk, and gradually contracted to four by the lower limbs. A side view showed the aura extending four inches in front of the body, while at the back it was seven inches in the lumbar regions. The inner aura was two and a half inches all over the body. Through the dark carmine screen this aura looked granular on the left side between the line of the nipples and the crest of the ilium, and when viewed sideways, the same effect was noticeable over the thorax, which was lighter in shade. The change commenced at the median line of the body, the upper margin being at the level of the mid-point of the sternum, and the lower following the outline of the costal cartilages. In this patch there was a still lighter spot coinciding with the yellow one seen at the first inspection. The second discoloured place consisted of a small mark on the right side where the aura was granular.

Occasionally a patient may have considerable bodily disturbance, and yet the aura may be only slightly involved. As an illustration the following example has been selected.

Case 77. (Figs. 60 and 61.) S., a bright sturdy woman, twenty-seven years of age, was inspected at the end of 1913. Twelve months previously she had

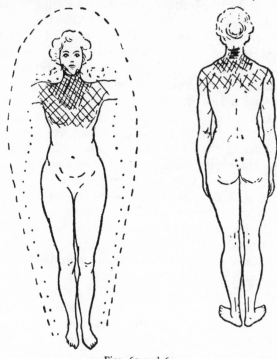

Figs. 60 and 61.
Raynaud's disease.
×××
××× Parts turning red.
∴∴ Granular aura.
≡ Dark with c.c. band.

lost her mother after a short illness, the shock of which, together with the extra cares of the house and the charge of a motherless child, produced a slight break-down. For nearly a year the lower part of the face, the neck, and the upper portion of the trunk constantly turned a very deep crimson, and below this region in front to the level of the inferior borders of the mammæ, and not quite as low down at the back, the red tinge was well marked but not to the same extent. The deeper colour had an irregular outline, and the limits and comparative depths are shown in figs. 60 and 61. A phenomenon corresponding to tache cerebrale could be obtained over the whole of that part of the body which was affected. The attacks occurred at any time, whether the woman was alone or with company. A slight change of temperature was sufficient to excite an onset. Each paroxysm only lasted a few minutes, but the average was between twenty and thirty per diem. When flushing, she felt a burning sensation but no absolute pain. The skin over the most affected area was scaly, and over the remaining portion where the tache cerebrale could be induced was dry, being elsewhere normal. The case was considered to be allied to Raynauds' disease, and an exceptional interesting aura, especially with the c.c. bands was expected, but nothing of the kind was found.

Both auras attained the usual standard of distinctness and had a blue grey colour, and were normal in shape. The outer aura was eight inches round the head and by the sides of the trunk, while in front it was four, and behind at the shoulders and nates it had the same width, descending without any bulge. The inner aura was three inches all over the body, with well marked striation, except just above the shoulders where it was granular. Contrary to expectation when there was no flush the c.c. band was even over the whole body with the exception of a small dark patch on the third and fourth cervical vertebræ.

Case 78. A second case showing a very similar condition came up for examination in December, 1914. The patient was a young woman who had never been robust, and at the time of inspection was anæmic.

For some few months her neck and upper part of her thorax were constantly turning crimson without any obvious cause, while the lower parts of the cheeks participated to a less extent. Paroxysms only persisted a short time and then passed off slowly. They were by no means as severe as in the previous case. Her mother had been for years a victim of Raynaud's disease. When the patient was examined the colour of her aura was uncommon, viz., green and blue not blended. The outer aura was wide and of average distinctness, ten inches by the head and twelve by the trunk. It had, however, an ill-defined margin, and gave the impression that an ultra-outer aura existed. A profile view showed the aura to be six inches in front, eight at the small of the back, and by the legs five, being slightly bow-shaped. The inner aura was plain and lineation obvious. The c.c. band exhibited three yellow patches on the back. The upper was small and situated over the third and fourth cervical vertebræ, the middle one over the second, third and fourth dorsal vertebræ, and lastly there was a large patch in the lumbar regions. In front there were two dark areas, one in either groin, separated from each other by an almost colourless interval. These two patches seemed raised about an inch from the body, and the aura between was massed. This was an unique phenomenon, as no other instance of this effect has ever been noticed, and the reason could not be determined. The three last patches were evidently due to ordinary functions, while for some undiscovered cause there was pain where the patch in the dorsal region existed. The most interesting point was the existence of the small spot on the nape of the neck, which occupied *exactly the same position* as did the one in the previous case.

A very remarkable case presented itself in September, 1916, and a second time a few months later. As certain points were of great interest and seemed likely to furnish a key for the solution of several difficult problems, it will be fully described.

Case 79. P.B., a young Belgian woman of Flemish extraction, complained of deafness following on a relaxed throat. The uncovered part of her chest, which was triangular in shape was very conspicuous as it was of a deep crimson hue, far deeper than would result from mere exposure. In a few minutes it lost a good deal of its colour. After a remark upon its appearance she said that the slightest touch or rub on any part of her body would cause a red mark within a couple of minutes, which would last a considerable time. This had happened ever since she could recollect, and was accompanied by no abnormal sensations, so that she would be perfectly unconscious of the flush except for seeing it. Her skin was smooth and normal with no liability to rashes. She, as might be expected, bruised very easily. The mind did not seem to have any influence as an exciting cause.

When a nail was drawn lightly across any portion of the skin, a red line appeared on the part touched in from one to two minutes, a wheal formed and its colour gradually deepened to dark crimson. The blush spread upon each side of the wheal to the depth of half an inch or more according to the pressure used. This redness then declined slowly, leaving the wheal white. This would often persist half an hour or more. A slight flick of a pencil produced the same effect. A rub induced redness but the surface remained smooth. Every part of the body was similarly affected. Sensation on the wheals, as tested by the prick of a pin, was more acute than on the adjacent skin.

She was a small, well proportioned, very fair woman, twenty-two years of age, quick and intelligent and as far as could be ascertained did not evince any neurotic signs. Her health had always been good. She was the only child, and her parents were both alive and strong. Slight wounds did not bleed abnormally.

She believed herself to be more sensitive to tactile sensations than most women. Knee jerks were normal, and there was no abnormal response when the soles of the feet were tickled. The superficial reflexes were much exaggerated. With the sphygmometer a pressure of 118 mm. of mercury was required before the pulse was obliterated.

Both auras were of normal distinctness. The colour was peculiar—a whitish grey-blue mingled with a little green. The white imparted an opaque look, which was increased in the interspaces between the arms and the body, as the girl stood with her arms akimbo. As she faced the observer, the aura was nine inches round the head, the same by the sides of the trunk contracting to four by the feet. Seen sideways, it was four and a half inches in front, and the same width at the back by the shoulders and buttocks, coming down straight. This aura was perfect in shape and of average size for a woman. The inner aura was three inches over the whole body, with natural striation. The blue c.c. band disclosed a small purple patch, which was darker with the red band, on the neck from the third to the fifth cervical spines and nothing more.

After this preliminary investigation, various parts of her body were rubbed or lightly scratched, and the aura was examined during the time the changes were proceeding. As in each instance similar alterations took place, one description will suffice.

The central line of the body between the ensiform cartilage and the umbilicus was gently rubbed for a few seconds. For the first minute or so no change occurred, but gradually both auras seemed to widen, and become more distinct and opaque, and at the same time the etheric double, which was not noticeable before, became very clearly marked. It was half an inch in width. The outer aura soon enlarged to its maximum, which was eight inches, just twice its normal breadth. The inner aura when seen through the red screen was about five inches broad, coarsely granular, and had completely lost its lineation. It had not the slightest resemblance to any ray. This condition lasted a few minutes, after which the auras gradually resumed their natural state, keeping pace with the fading of the red colour.

In the next experiment, with the hands resting on the hips and the elbows extended, the aura in the diamond-shaped spaces so formed with the body, was examined with screens before and after gentle friction had been applied to one side of the chest. The following were the results.

Screen.	RED	ORANGE	YELLOW	GREEN	BLUE	VIOLET
Aura.		Before rubbing.				
	R–bGy	R–bGy	R–bGy	White blue	B–G	B
		After rubbing.				
	RW–B	Opaque B	Opaque B	B–G	B–G	V
Note.	R–Red.	B–Blue.	G–Green. W–White. V–Violet. bGy–Bluish grey.			

Up to the present time, with the exception of this patient, although the aura has been constantly examined for it, no local change has been detected over parts where redness has been induced by friction. This may, perhaps, be attributed to the fact that ordinarily only the most superficial layers of the skin are affected, while in the case above described the deeper layers of the corium were probably also involved. It is more likely than not that even in a normal subject if the force used were sufficient to cause slight bruising, the aura would be influenced immediately or within a short time.

In another experiment the cervical spines were gently percussed with the finger in the region where the purple patch was seen with the c.c. band. It was not expected that this proceeding would have any influence upon the aura, but almost instantaneously a general enlargement took place, yet not to the same extent as when static electricity had been used on a previous occasion. The width was eleven inches round the head, twelve by the trunk, and six by the feet, and when she stood sideways it was six by the shoulders continuing straight down the back.

This case differs from the last two inasmuch as the previous patients had only the upper part of their bodies affected. In them the skin frequently became red without any appreciable cause, while at other times the colour was induced by emotion, or some slight change in temperature, etc. The epidermis was deranged in the affected parts, which were dry, and in the worst places, even scaly. The urticarial reaction could always be produced over, and was wholly confined to, the abnormal areas. The colour changes, too, never attained the same depth as in the last instance, and only at the very darkest portion in the case 77 did they approach those usually induced by the slightest friction at any point in the affected area in the woman P.B.

It is certainly a curious coincident, if a coincident it be, and it hardly looks like one, that in all these three cases the c.c. band disclosed a coloured spot on the nape of the neck. In the last instance this was the only patch that could be detected over the whole of the body, with the exception of a very faint one on the sacrum. The presence of other patches over the different parts of the spine had been expected whether or not one occurred on the neck.

Case 80. E.D., a woman twenty-seven years of age, was inspected for the first time in 1913. She had been nursing her mother through a long illness, and immediately afterwards her father required great attention on account of his health. As a result she became greatly depressed and run down. For some months at intervals, her lips, both hands, and to a variable extent her foreams, became deeply cyanosed.

The attacks were sudden in onset, and often continued a considerable time. She experienced no pain but her hands were always cold. Although there was no heart diease, she suffered constantly from palpitations. Tache cerebrale could always be obtained on the chest and the back, almost as far down as the waist.

With the patient standing facing the observer, the outer aura was well marked, being seven inches by the head, eight by the trunk and three and a half by the ankles. A side view showed it to be three and a half inches in front, while at the small of the back it was seven inches, exhibiting a bow-shaped bulge, which commenced at the top of the head and finished at the feet. The colour was a blue-grey. The inner aura, as might be expected from the state of her health, was indistinct, nevertheless lineation was present, but was coarse in the lumbar regions. Three yellow patches were seen with the c.c. band on the back, the two lower being very plain but the upper not so definite. The highest one was situated on the third and fourth dorsal vertebræ, the central one over the twelfth dorsal and first lumbar, and the third over the sacrum. In front there were also three patches, all of a yellow colour with the blue c.c. band, and of a peculiar indescribable hue with the red band. The highest was over the epigastrium and left hypochondrium, the second was on the right side level with the umbilicus, and the lowest on the left groin. She had pain and tenderness in all these discoloured areas, especially the lowest on the back and the one in the groin during menstruation, at which time the pain was always severe. Indigestion accounted for the upper spot in front.

In February, 1915, after recovery, she was inspected a second time. Of late there had been no cyanosis of the hands, and no palpitations. The only trace of her former trouble was an occasional duskiness of her lips, seen not once a week. The c.c. band showed two patches on the back precisely in the same positions as before, but the central one was missing. The upper one had grown faint, and the lowest continued quite plain. In front there was a pale yellow patch over the epigastrium, smaller and less conspicuous than it had been at the former examination, while the dark patch in the groin remained unaltered. The fading spots will probably soon disappear. (See page 257.)

When considering the shape of the aura in ill-health, it was remarked that in cases of hysteria, the outer aura takes a very characteristic form quite different to that seen in non-neurotic persons, while at the same time the inner retains its natural configuration. This statement is correct but does not go far enough, as subtle alterations also frequently occur in the inner aura, some of which can be detected only by the aid of the c.c. bands. In hysteria the number and size of these patches reach their highest, and are rarely equalled or exceeded in other diseases.

The following is an exceptional case which is almost phenomenal as regards the number of spots.

Case 81. (Figs. 62 and 63.) S., an unmarried largely built woman, thirty-six years of age, was, from her appearance, one of the last persons likely to be hysterical. She, however, had always been nervous, and a few years before had a breakdown after the death of her mother, but had recovered in a comparatively short time. In 1913, after returning from a holiday spent at the seaside, she began to complain of vague pains in different parts of her body which continually shifted from one place to another, and varied in intensity. She had slight mastitis which quickly got well. The upper part of the right thigh was also painful and continued so for a long period. Another time she had pain in the epigastrium with indigestion, and occasionally globus hystericus. On a different occasion she complained of acute pain in the left shoulder and upper part of the left thorax. No satisfactory causes could be discovered for all these troubles.

At the end of the year her aura was inspected, and was found to be of a grey-blue colour. Both auras

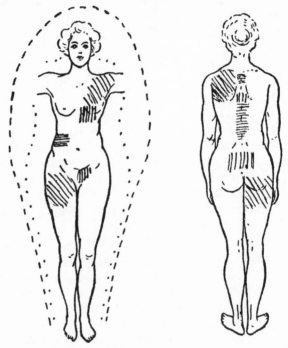

Figs. 62 and 63.
Multiple patches.
≡   Dark with c.c. band.
|||| Dark yellow ditto.
//////   Light yellow ditto.

reached the healthy standard of distinctness. The outer was a typical spatulate aura, eight inches round the head, nine and a half by the sides of the trunk, and four by the legs with the usual curve. In front it was six inches wide, which was broad consider-

ing the breadth at the sides, and in the lumbar regions
it was nine inches, as there was a big bulge commencing
at the shoulders and terminating just beneath the
nates, below which it was four inches wide. The
inner aura was three and a half inches by the trunk,
and about an inch narrower by the lower extremities.
The whole of this aura was plainly lineated except
where it was granular. This latter condition existed
by the right side of the neck, thorax, and at the small
of the back.

The c.c. band showed a large lemon coloured patch
on the left side in front, from the shoulder to the nipple
line, the inner margin corresponding to the median
line of the body. It extended round to the back
where the edge took the outline of the scapula. A
continuation of the lower part of the patch in front
was dark to the level of the ensiform cartilage. There
was a deep yellow spot on the left groin, and another
dark one on the right hypochondrium. The upper
part of the right thigh was a pale yellow in front and
round to the back. On the back there was a dark
patch on the second and third, a yellow one on the
sixth and seventh dorsal vertebræ, and a third one
continuous with the last but dark and extending as
low down as the second lumbar vertebra. Lastly
there was a dark yellow area over the sacrum. Wherever the c.c. band exhibited discolouration the patient
had either pain or tenderness at the time of inspection
or shortly before.

The patient referred to in chapter vii (case 47)
exhibited a good many patches, and this was only
what might have been expected after the severe illness
she had suffered from a few years previously. In
front there was a light yellow spot a short distance
beneath the right clavicle, another on the epigastrium,
and a third darker yellow on the upper part of the
right thigh below Poupart's ligament. On the back
there was a yellow patch under the left scapula, a

second on the spine from the fourth to the tenth dorsal vertebræ, and lastly a large one over the sacrum.

There does not seem to be as great a tendency to the development of patches in males as in females, but occasionally one or more may be seen. In almost

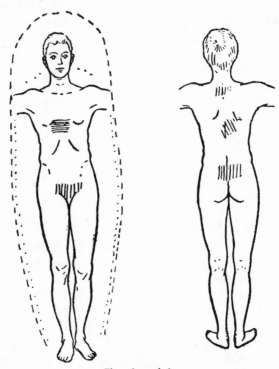

Figs. 64 and 65.
Locomotor Ataxy.
||||| Dark yellow with c.c. band.
////// Light ditto.

every instance where a man has shown more than three discoloured areas, he has been the victim of a grave malady, which would among women have produced far more numerous patches. The following cases of locomotor ataxy exemplify this statement.

Case 82. (Figs. 64 and 65.) H., a man of fifty-four

years of age, contracted lues when he was twenty-two years old. Twelve years later locomotor ataxy was diagnosed, and since that time he has attended several different hospitals.

His unsteadiness when standing made it difficult to examine his aura. All the symptoms of his illness were those usually met with in that disease, so they hardly need description. His aura was inspected in 1914. The outer aura did not reach the good health standard of distinctness, and was grey in colour. It had nearly the size and shape commonly found in a man, being seven inches round the head, five by the trunk, and four by the legs, five in front of the trunk and four lower down, while at the back there was a bulge commencing a little above the head and terminating a short distance beneath the nates. The widest part was eight inches. The inner aura, as anticipated, was decidedly below the normal in clearness, and had a granular appearance by the right side of the trunk and at the small of the back. Its breadth was two and a half inches, and at the back in the lumbar regions was a trifle more pronounced.

Three discoloured places were brought to light by the c.c. band on the dorsum, first an ochre coloured patch on the upper two or three dorsal vertebræ, a light yellow one over the eighth to the twelfth dorsal, and a third over the sacrum, which was a dark yellow. In front there was a dark patch over the thorax, and a second dark yellow, on the right hypochondrium.

Case 83. (Figs. 66 and 67.) X., an inmate of St. Joseph's Home, sixty-two years of age, developed tabes dorsalis several years ago. At various times she had been an in-patient of four London hospitals, ot most of them more than once. She was a thin miserable-looking woman, who from her worn appearance had been a great sufferer. She had all the customary symptoms of the disease in a more advanced stage than the last case. She experienced frequent bouts of pain, often agonizing, and sometimes was compelled to keep her bed for days together. She was quite ataxic, but at times with help could walk a little.

Her outer aura, contrary to expectations, was perfectly normal in shape, showing nothing indicative

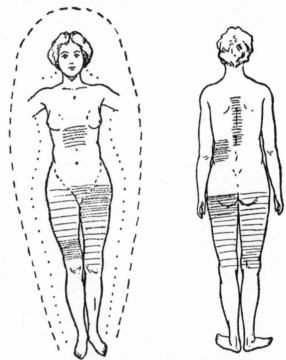

Figs. 66 and 67.
Locomotor Ataxy.
Dark with c.c. band according to shading.

of a nervous disease. The inner had an average width all over the body, although far less distinct than during health. It was granular a short distance above the crest of the ilium on the left side but nowhere else. It was only with the greatest difficulty that a faint striation could be anywhere detected.

With the c.c. band a long dark patch about two inches wide reaching from the fourth dorsal to the first lumbar vertebræ, and a second in the lumbar regions, was seen. In front there was a dark area over the epigastrium and another over the hypochondrium. The most noticeable feature was an uneven darkening over the whole of both thighs back and front. The colour of the band on the upper part of the left thigh, and the middle third of the right thigh was several shades deeper than over the rest of the limbs. The legs exhibited no discolouration. The depth of colour corresponded to the severity of the pain, which was more intense in some places than in others, and has been indicated in the diagrams.

Since diseases of the chest form a large proportion of cases seen in every day practice, it might have been expected that they would offer a good field for the study of the aura, but as a matter of fact they have assisted very slightly in the investigations, and conversely the aura does not afford much aid in their diagnosis. There are several reasons for this. A very important one is that when a patient is suffering from an acute illness, he would of a necessity have to remain in bed. It is obvious that besides the difficulty of a background and the arrangement of the light, etc., it would in most of these cases be inadvisable, if not absolutely improper, to trouble a patient in such a condition with an investigation which must be unavoidably prolonged and fatiguing, while in the present state of knowledge the benefits derived from it could only be problematic. Chronic cases, on the other hand, can be inspected with impunity, and show changes in the aura, but none that have much diagnostic value. Although the examination might be interesting, attention has been mainly devoted to other conditions thought more likely to give results of practical importance. However, a description of one or two examples will give a good idea of the changes likely to be found.

Case 84. T., a married woman forty-three years of age, complained once that when coughing she brought up some bright blood. According to her account it was quite a teaspoonful. Although a very careful examination of her lungs was made, the affected spot could not be ascertained. Two days later her aura was inspected prior to the usual examination by auscultation, etc. The aura had the proper size and shape for a woman of her age, and showed no abnormality until the c.c. band was employed across her chest. A light spot about the size of a florin, on the left side in the intercostal space, about an inch from the sternum, was immediately noticed. As soon as a stethescope was placed over this spot, fine crepidations could be heard deep down, and the writer believes, rightly or wrongly, this to be the part of the lung from which the blood exuded. Even if he had not seen the pale patch in the c.c. band, he hardly thinks the physical signs would have escaped his notice. From subsequent experience he is certain that the band would have shown some alteration had it been employed directly after the hæmoptisis. This was the only part of the lung in which any disease could be discovered.

Of all chest complaints, the one *par excellence* in which changes of the aura could be of assistance, is incipient phthisis, but at present there is no distinctive case to bring forward, as in fact there has been only disappointment with those that have been examined. Of course, if bronchitis or emphysema be present, since the whole or the greater part of the lung is affected, it would be unreasonable to expect the detection of a small tubercular focus by some slight alteration in the aura which would inevitably be masked by the changes due to the more general disorders.

The next instance is a good example of the changes which take place in the aura during chronic phthisis.

Case 85. G., a lady twenty-seven years old, became consumptive in 1905, and progressed unfavourably for a long time. She had pleurisy on the left side in 1906, pneumothorax in the early months of 1909, and in the middle of that year the right lung became affected. During the whole of that time she was in Scotland, but to the surprise of all her friends she gradually improved in health. She was inspected in 1911. Her condition was exceedingly good considering the state of her lungs. The outer aura was found to be of medium width, being eight inches by the head, and the sides of the trunk, contracting to four inches by the ankles. It was symmetrical, but its texture was not as fine on the left, between the jaw and the crest of the ilium, as on the right. The inner aura was three inches in breadth on the right side and only two on the left of the trunk, but was alike in size and texture over both thighs and legs. Striation was very distinct on the whole of the right side, but on the left above the shoulder and by the trunk as far down as the crest of the ilium, the inner aura was either coarsely granular or roughly lineated. Lower down it was normal. The c.c. band was darker over the whole of the left side of the thorax, back and front, while below the costal cartilages and ribs was a dark patch reaching from the median line to the side as far as could be seen. The latter fault was evidently due to indigestion caused by the overfeeding which had been part of the patient's treatment. On the upper part of the right side of the chest was a dark patch over the diseased area in the lung. It was considered that the aura revealed that the patient had great vitality, but that the left lung was completely disorganized.

As volition is a high attribute of the brain, through which the aura as a whole can be influenced, it may be confidently asserted that every cerebral derangement will affect the aura in some way or another. Probably such disturbances do produce some modifications of the whole aura, but the majority of the changes are of too refined a nature to be perceptible, and only the cruder ones can be detected. The coarse alterations that are recognizable may be so strange in appearance, that not even the most imaginative person would be likely to invent them. Who, for example, could have devised the hysterical aura ? The more one contemplates this prodigy the more inexplicable it seems.

Among women the ovoid shape (fig. 11) of the aura is evidently the highest form, and the nearer it approqimates to this figure the more perfect it is. As before mentioned, the main peculiarity of the hysterical aura lies in its being disproportionately wide by the sides of the trunk and in the lumbar regions of the back, when compared with its narrowness lower down.

It is not yet possible to follow the stages of alterations undergone by the aura during its transformation from the normal to the spatulate shape. At first the idea was that the development of the aura, which naturally occurs during the transitional period in girls, might have been arrested round the lower limbs. Although this theory seemed reasonable, it was shattered by the fact that spatulate auras are occasionally seen round children, and even more often round adult males. Another view which seems to embrace all known cases and therefore is more likely to be correct, is that a true increase of the outer aura by the sides of the trunk with little or no augmentation by the thighs and legs is present. This idea is supported by case 55, and also by the fact that all hysterical auras seen in males have been far wider than any ever met with round healthy men. The theory receives additional proof from the accompanying bulge of the aura at the back, which cannot be explained in any other way than by local increase.

It is useless to speculate in the present state of our knowledge why this peculiar configuration of the aura should occur amongst hysterical women. The practical question arises whether a normal aura ever becomes spatulate. It seems probable that this may occasionally happen. But intermediate forms are rare. Theoretically they might originate both during the evolution of the disease and during recovery.

When the aura is seen to be imperfectly spatulate, it is impossible to decide at a single sitting from its appearance alone, whether changes have reached their maximum or are progressive. Several further examinations must be made, and as yet the writer has never had the chance of obtaining them. Fortunately another method is available, viz., the artificial enlargement of the aura by static electricity. This agent often accentuates peculiarities which without its help are too ill-defined for accurate observation. Since the discovery of this property special attention has been paid to the subject.

The outer aura of the patient discussed in the appendix to chapter vii., was complex, and reasons were given why it was considered normal for that person. Its great width, it will be remembered, was thought to be due to a spatulate configuration rather than to the presence of an ultra-outer aura. The question was, however, definitely settled by electricity, as after the woman had been negatively charged, the haze at once assumed the true spatulate figure. This seems to be an example of an aura changing to the spatulate type, as owing to the low grade of bodily development, the woman's aura might reasonably be expected to have remained narrow.

In epilepsy a different variation of the aura is encountered. Here instead of the outer aura being alone or more particularly affected (as in hysteria), both auras seem to be correspondingly modified, being unilaterally contracted. No explanation of this diminution can be offered, and it is still more incomprehensible why the left side should be the one usually influenced. Patient's friends have been asked, whether during the attack one side was more affected, or whether the head was turned to one side ; as if the convulsions were more severe on the one side than the other, some light might be thrown upon the question. These interrogations did not produce any satisfactory answers, as with one or two exceptions all said that they were too much upset to notice. The mother of one girl said that the child had more spasms on the right side.

It is positively certain that the aura is influenced locally when there is a circumscribed disturbance of nerves, but whether the alteration is the direct outcome of the nerve disorder, as happens in the case of functional derangements of organs, or whether the change in the aura is secondary and dependent solely upon the actually affected organ, has not yet been decided. Probably each of these causes either alone or in combination with the other may be operative in various cases or at various times in the same case. One fact stands out prominently, viz., that a local disturbance influences the inner with greater frequency than the outer aura, but when the latter is affected the former rarely if ever escapes.

Neuralgia may be taken as an example of the manner in which the nervous system operates upon the aura. Case 49 is a very good instance. When seen in 1909, it was noticed that the whole of the inner aura adjacent to the painful spot was altered, as all striation had disappeared and it had become granular in aspect. The outer, too, showed signs of disorder, as the distal portions were less plainly visible than usual, appearing less dense. In other words, the outer auric force was not so potent as when in health, but at the same time retained its general characters. Had the force been still further reduced, the haze would have contracted.

This was the condition of the aura when seen in 1908 (*vide* page 200), and it is evident that at the latter date the auric force was regaining its natural energy.

In an acute case of neuralgia, a girl thirteen years of age, had a spot at the level of, and two inches to the right of the third dorsal vertebra, where paroxysms of pain came on suddenly and often lasted for hours. The most common time for its accession was at night shortly before going to bed, or else soon after, but anyhow the spasm prevented sleep. There was no tenderness over the place, and no cause could be found for the trouble. The ailment was very intractable for some weeks, and then slightly improved. She developed appendicitis, when pain suddenly vanished and never returned. Her aura was examined and seen to be quite natural all over the body, with the exception of a small spot just above the painful place where it was granular. It was only in the inner aura that any change could be discovered. As the disordered patch must have been small, it is unlikely that the outer would exhibit any alteration since the surrounding healthy portion must certainly have acted as a mask. In this instance the c.c. band showed a dark spot, while in the previous case the affected aura induced a light shade.

Two or three patients suffering from sciatica have exhibited very similar changes in the aura down the whole of the affected limb. When a local organic alteration of tissue is dependent upon nervous derangement, it is probable that the modification that takes place in the adjacent aura is partially due to the nervous element, and in part to the diseased tissue, but it is next to impossible to decide the proportion associated with each factor. Herpes Zoster is a very good example of the combined causes, but so much has been said about these alterations that the reader is referred to the cases 57 and 62.

As these cases demonstrate that the nervous system

can induce transformations of the aura, both with and without a corresponding change in the local tissues, it might possibly be thought that the modification would be entirely dependent upon the influence of the nervous system, and that the disordered tissues had no share in its production. The only method of disproving this hypothesis is to find a case where the change in the aura cannot be credited to the nervous system. Fortunately notes were made upon several cases in which it is extremely unlikely that any deranged nervous agency could be present. The patients had superficial tumours, and the examples chosen for illustration are a fibro-adenoid, a cystic tumour of the breast, a fatty one of the thigh, and an osteo-sarcoma of the arm. In none of these cases could any alteration of the outer aura be discovered, but in each there was a derangement of the inner.

The fibro-adenoid caused the inner aura to assume the appearance of a small ray, not more than one and a half inches in length, slightly wider than the breadth of the aura, and granular. When viewed with the blue c.c. band, it was seen as a spot lighter than the rest of the band, and with the yellow, darker.

The cystic tumour gave a somewhat similar effect, except that the inner aura was altered throughout its whole width, the change consisting of a coarse granular condition replacing the ordinary striation just over the tumour. Examination of this ray by the aid of the c.c. bands, showed a light area with the blue and a dark one with the yellow.

The fatty tumour was a moderately large one of several years standing, on the outside of the left thigh of an otherwise healthy woman, thirty-six years of age. Inspection did not show any perceptible change near the growth until the c.c. bands were employed. With each of these bands the haze over the tumour looked lighter than the rest of the band, indicating that some delicate modification had taken place.

The last example was an osteo-sarcoma of the humerus. Here the aura assumed the appearance of a coarsely granular ray without any signs of lineation. The blue c.c. band produced a discoloured spot of a most unusual colour, which can only be designated by pinkish-yellow.

From the above remarks it may be taken for granted, that although the nervous system has a very great, perhaps a predominant control over the auras, yet other tissues when in an unhealthy state do influence them as well. In this connection it will be interesting to compare case 72 with case 76. In the former the patient had an ulcer of the stomach which caused the c.c. band in front to be lighter than the natural hue of the band. The inner was also granular in the gastric region. It must be noticed that there was no change in colour of the band near the dorsal vertebræ. In the latter, although the woman was suffering from constant vomiting, there was only slight granulation in the gastric region, and the c.c. band did not disclose any alteration of colour on the front of the body, but on the back there was a narrow streak lying close to the spinal column on the left side, from the third to the fourth dorsal vertebræ, decidedly lighter in colour than the rest of the band, and with sharply defined margins. In the former of these examples, it looked as if the diseased organ was the factor producing the alterations, while in the latter the stomach only influenced the aura slightly, but the main change in the band was due to a nervous element.

Enough has been said in this chapter to show how important a part the c.c. bands play in investigations, and how great is the assistance they can give in diagnosis, both positively and negatively—positively, by demonstrating that the auras have undergone some alteration locally, the result of a disturbance at that place, and negatively, by proving that no appreciable change has taken place where an underlying disorder has been suspected. It is, however, necessary to remember that the c.c. band may occasionally not show alteration when it is known that the part beneath it is diseased. The help that this band can give is thus limited, but becomes greater and greater as the observer gains experience by practice in appreciating the finer differences manifested. The mischief in instances giving negative results is, almost without exception, of slow progress, such as takes place in contracted kidney, while the more acute and active changes will be more likely to induce alterations in the auras, and consequently in the c.c. bands.

CHAPTER X

The Aura During Pregnancy

It is not uncommon for a patient, after she has missed one or two periods, to ask a medical man " am I pregnant ? " Delay in answering is not always acceptable. The difficulties in arriving at a correct conclusion in very early pregnancy are great, so that any fresh method that can aid diagnosis will no doubt be appreciated. It must be understood that no single sign of pregnancy, as described below can be accepted by itself, but that when more than one sign points in the same direction, either one way or the other, an almost certain opinion may be expressed. There are three distinct signs made manifest by changes in the aura ; two are arrived at through the investigations by c.c. bands, and the third is a slight alteration in the shape of the auras and in their texture.

When inspecting an aura to determine whether an early stage of pregnancy exists, the first step in the examination is to ascertain if the shape of both auras be normal by the sides and back, and note their widths, especially the inner aura over the various parts of the body. This supplies a standard by which the measurements over the front of the body can be compared. As a rule a woman in good health and not enceinte, will show the two auras of the same width all down the front of the trunk, with the occasional exception that they may be a little wider in front of the breasts when a menstrual period is at hand. In almost every case of early pregnancy the outer aura is slightly but definitely wider at the lower part of the abdomen, the alteration commencing a short distance

below the umbilicus ; in the later stages this enlargement extends higher up. At the same time there is
always an increase in front of the mammæ, which is best
observed when the patient does not stand completely
sideways, but only sufficiently to permit the breasts to
be silhouetted one at a time against the background.
When the position of the woman is such that the best
view of the aura before the breast is obtained, a small
ray proceeding from the nipple is often seen. In
addition to the extra breadth, the aura frequently
appears denser in texture.

The inner aura also participates in the alteration
at the same places as does the outer. Its breadth is a
little increased in the early stages of pregnancy, but
not to the same extent as at a later period, and its
opacity is a trifle greater, and what is extremely
important, striation remains unchanged. Each case
must be fully investigated and judged on its own
merits, as owing to individual differences no fixed
standards for auras can be laid down.

It has been constantly noticed during the inspection
of a pregnant woman, that the aura is not so distinct
as is usually the case in health. For some time this
was attributed to various causes, such as bad light,
etc., until it had been observed so frequently that
there could be no doubt about its connection with the
patient's condition. Looking over the different
records, this decrease of brilliancy occurs in a considerable percentage of cases, so that it may be
accepted as an auxiliary sign of pregnancy, and its
presence may assist in forming an opinion in a doubtful
instance

After the preliminary inspection the observer next
proceeds to tests with the c.c. bands. For this part of
the examination the woman should first stand facing
the investigator. The vertical c.c. band will then
be perceived uniform throughout its length if she
be in good health and enceinte. Special attention

must be paid to the portion of the band upon the lower part of the band near the pubes. This is of importance in ascertaining that the woman shows no sign of impending menstruation. When the c.c. band is used transversely over the breasts, the colour in women, who are neither enceinte nor nursing an infant, nor suffering from any affection of the mammæ, is naturally even (except over the areolæ and nipples), not only on the breasts themselves but also on the adjacent parts of the body. During pregnancy and lactation, the colour not uncommonly becomes paler over the mammæ. The lighter tint is due to a modification of the aura similar to that already considered in chapter viii. This alteration has no significance in itself, but affords valuable corroboration that a change has taken place in the breasts. When a transverse c.c. band is projected upon the epigastric and hypogastric regions, an alteration of colour is rare, even though the patient may be suffering from nausea and vomiting, pointing to the fact that the gastric disturbance is not so dependent upon local derangement as upon some more general influence.

Case 70 is an instance somewhat analogous to stomach troubles during pregnancy. Should, however, a woman have been suffering from some definite gastric trouble previous to gestation the above statement will, of course, not hold good. No further assistance can be obtained from the c.c. bands when employed upon the front of the body.

Allusion has been made to the fact that the majority of women in the prime of life show a change in the aura over the lumbo-sacral region of the back, when the c.c. band is darkened or even changed in hue. *This patch nearly always vanishes* from the sacrum during pregnancy, *generally during the early stages*. However, if the prospective mother suffers from more than the average amount of pain during menstrual periods, the patch will therefore be usually darker, and in consequence will persist longer ; but in any case it generally disappears before the fourth month. But should this discoloured area be due to any other cause, such as rheumatism, gestation will exert no influence upon it. The presence of this patch rather militates against the probability of pregnancy. Absence of this mark in a woman who is known to have previously had it, or to have suffered from a considerable amount of backache during her monthly periods, is a very important if not an absolute sign of pregnancy, unless it was due to some other cause which has been removed.

When the transverse c.c. band is employed upon the lowest part of the abdomen, with the patient standing sideways, the colours of the extensions are often dissimilar. If this happens, the one in front of the abdomen is more likely to be lighter than that at the back. This is due to some such alteration of the aura as has been discussed previously, and is of positive value unless some change was detected in the preceding examination of the abdomen, with the patient facing, is the cause of the variance.

To sum up, the early signs of gestation as shown by the aura are :

1. A slight increase in the size of the aura at the lower part of the abdomen and in front of the breasts. The inner, too, may be a little wider, but it always retains its striation perfect.

2. The c.c. band shows no discolouration on the lower part of the abdomen. A coloured patch over the stomach is unusual, unless there was previous gastric trouble. The band is often lighter over the breasts.

3. Absence of the dark area on the lumbo-sacral regions.

4. A general indistinctness of the two auras may be added as an auxiliary sign.

The following is the earliest case of pregnancy the writer has had the opportunity of inspecting.

Case 86. C., a married woman thirty-three years of age, the mother of two children, having missed one period, was desirous of knowing whether she was to expect another baby. She was not a very strong woman, but at the time was in good health. There were good reasons for knowing that she could not have been pregnant for a longer time than thirty days at the most. She had been suffering from *pain across her loins* especially when tired, and even at the time of inspection was not quite free of it, but *usually had none during menstruation*.

The outer aura was distinct and the inner below the average, but striation could be easily distinguished. As she stood facing the observer, the outer aura was ten inches round the head, twelve by the trunk, and contracted to four by the ankles, being of a good ovoid shape. In addition a perceptible ultra-outer aura was present. When she turned sideways, the haze exhibited a slight bow-shaped bulge at the small of the back, commencing at the head and ending at the feet. In front of the trunk the general width was four inches, but before the lower part of the abdomen increased to six, and over the breasts to above five inches.

The inner aura was barely two and a half inches wide all over the body, except in three places, viz., in front of the lower part of the abdomen, at the small of the back where it was three inches, and in front of the mammæ, where it was nearly as broad.

The vertical c.c. band was uniform in front of the body, but the transverse showed paler areas over the mammæ. At the back there was a large dark patch on the upper part of the sacrum which reached nearly as high as the second lumbar vertebra.

In this instance all the changes from normal were those that might have been expected in early pregnancy, with the exception of the dark patch on the sacrum, which was accounted for by the rheumatic pain, so an unqualified opinion was given that the patient was pregnant. A child was born at the proper time.

Case 87. K., a lady twenty-nine years old, who had been married two years and hoped that she was pregnant as she had missed one period and a second was almost due. With the patient facing, the outer aura was ten inches round the head and trunk, gradually diminishing to five by the ankles. Sideways, at the back it was seen to be four inches at the level of the shoulders and nates, with a slight bulge in the lumbar region, and in front its normal width was four inches, but there was a small increase in front of the breasts, and another at the lowest part of the abdomen. In these places the inner aura looked opaque and in consequence more distinct, but striation was clearly visible. Over the whole body the inner aura was two inches in breadth, even, and displayed lineation. The extension of the c.c. band in front of the abdomen was lighter than at the same level at the back. When she again faced the investigator, the vertical c.c. band appeared uniform all down the front, except over the mammæ, where it was paler than the neighbouring portions of the body. There was no alteration in tint over the gastric region. Over the back the colour was not altered in any part. The lessons learnt from this case are, first, that the woman did not show any signs of approaching menstruation although it was just due ; next, that the aura disclosed the fact that there was physiological activity going on in the breasts, and under that part of the abdomen near the pubes. There was no doubt about the case being one of gestation.

The lady, whose aura was described in case 49, believed herself to be pregnant after missing two monthly periods. When examined a third was nearly due. However, there was no alteration in the haze in front of the right breast, nor any increase by the lower part of the abdomen, neither was the c.c. band deeper in shade above the pubes, while on the back a prominent dark patch was visible on the sacrum.

In this case the only sign of pregnancy was the absence of discolouration above the pubes when the abdomen was examined by means of the c.c. bands, at a time when such ought to be usually present. The diagnosis made was that gestation was out of the question, and that menstruation would not supervene for four or five days at least, but the date could not be foretold. As a matter of fact it commenced seven days after inspection.

As pregnancy progresses the changes in the aura in front of the mammæ increase, but vary in extent and do not altogether correspond with those in front of the abdomen. The expansion is not confined to the outer aura, as in most instances the inner becomes wider. Even when the inner aura remains stationary in size, it becomes more opaque than the neighbouring parts, showing that the glands are preparing to take on their special functions. There is very rarely any difficulty in determining whether the inner aura in the vicinity of the breasts has enlarged, because comparison is so easily made with the adjoining parts above and below. Although it may look to the naked eye finely granular, yet the intervention of a dark carmine screen will disclose the striated appearance of health. The auras of a woman who has reached the fifth month of gestation will be broader than during the early stages, and may continue to expand until the time for the birth of the child approaches.

The auras of women after the fourth or fifth month may be divided into two classes, which although not very unlike yet show a difference which is by no means artificial, and in the future may lead to important results. In one group the broadest of the aura is not so wide as in the second, while the shape is more regular, and follows with greater exactitude the contour of the body, but usually attains *its maximum size beneath the projecting abdomen.*   When such an aura is viewed with the patient standing sideways, through a deep carmine screen, it will be found that the inner aura is also slightly enlarged all over the abdomen.

In the second group the auras are wider and more distinct in *front of the most prominent part of the abdomen*, giving rise to the " conical aura," which often gives the impression that it is more extensive than really is the case.   When the two auras are separated in the ordinary manner, the inner will also be found to be more or less conical, being a little wider at the base in front of the most prominent part of the abdomen, but hardly to the same extent as the outer.   This is a good instance of the inner aura growing larger and subsequently diminishing, as it resumes its natural size after parturition.

With the c.c. bands the whole of the breasts, except the areaolæ and nipples, will usually appear lighter than the neighbouring parts of the body, in whatever position the patient may be placed.

This band when projected upon the thorax and abdomen may be even in colour, but when the inner is conical it is often lighter on the front of the abdomen. If a woman, who shows a conical aura, is examined with the transverse c.c. band (antero-posteriorly), the extreme point of the distended abdomen is generally paler, and the front extension is lighter than the back extension.   In the first group of cases the latter only occurs.

The paleness of the colour over the breasts and abdomen when associated with enlargement and definition of the inner aura, indicates the probability that some alteration in the aura itself has taken place, and is a good example of the statement that " a change in the texture of the aura is a sufficient cause to produce an alteration in the tint of the c.c. band." (Vide chapter vi.)   The following is a very interesting and instructive case.

Case 88. Mrs. T. was pregnant for the fourth time. Inspection took place soon after she had reached the sixth month of gestation. The history was that she had been feeling exceedingly well during the whole of the period until the last three weeks, when she was suddenly roused from her sleep by a row in the house. From that moment all movement of the child ceased, and the abdomen decreased in size, although previous to the upset the movements of the infant had been uncomfortably active. She was depressed thinking that the baby was dead.

The aura at the sides and back were normal in every respect. In front, as she stood sideways to the investigator, the inner aura was about three inches all down the thorax and lower extremities except that it was a little more pronounced in front of the nipples. Before the prominent abdomen it had increased in width. The outer aura was about four inches down the whole of the front, except over the abdomen, where it was conical and eight inches in breadth. The main interest was centered in the inner aura. This above the sternal notch and down the legs and thighs was finely striated in the usual manner. The part before the lowest part of the abdomen was distinctly and coarsely granular, while in front of the upper two thirds it was roughly striated and well marked. Here it was in the transitional stage between the granular and naturally striated states. Thus it could be seen that the aura was normal all round the body, with the exception of the part in front of the abdomen, where it was pathological. The c.c. band disclosed nothing unusual, but it may be worth stating that it was lighter on the left breast and darker on the right than the remaining portion of the band, while at the same time the extensions were even. The explanation of this effect happened to be quite easy, because the shade on the left breast is that which was common during pregnancy, but the right breast was distinctly pigmented. Being healthy it did not affect the extension beyond the body.

It was thought that in this case a diagnosis of a dead child would be justified. Subsequent to the inspection of the aura, the uterus was palpated, and was found to be softer than usual at the sixth month of gestation No signs of any uterine souffle nor of fœtal heart-beats could be distinguished. Two months later she was delivered of a dead child.

In conclusion the writer is conscious of many short-comings which he hopes his readers will overlook.. The whole subject is fraught with vast difficulties, not merely in practice but in description, as there are a large number of minutiæ, very important, which is almost impossible to put into words. He has tried to be as free from ambiguity as possible, but at the same time feels that he has by no means done justice to the subject. Time after time new phenomena have come to hand upsetting previous ideas, and compelling him to begin afresh. He is positive that some of the hypotheses which have been advanced to assist progress will have to be rejected. He is firmly convinced that the study of the aura physically will gradually come to the fore, as one of the aids to diagnosis. Investigations upon the aura open up a large number of questions for future observers.

To him the study of the aura has been a labour of love, but the main object, *which is to help medical diagnosis*, has been perpetually kept in view. He will be quite satisfied if true science has been advanced even a little.

He cannot finish without thanking his many friends for their kind aid, more especially those who have put themselves to great personal inconvenience to forward his researches.

INDEX

(Kilner: *The Human Atmosphere*)

Action, chemical: influence on the aura, v; *see also* names of compounds, e.g., Bromide

Alcohol, excessive use of, and the aura, 259

Alterations in complementary colour bands, causes of, 153

Ammonia, and the aura, 115

Anaemia, and the aura, 235

Antwerp Blue, 146

Asymmetry, of the aura, 204 ff., 210-12

Atmosphere, and the aura, 11

Attraction, mutual, between auras, 53

Aura, inner, *see* Inner aura

Aura, outer, *see* Outer aura

Aura, structure of, *see* Etheric double; Inner aura; Outer aura; Ultra-outer aura

Aura, ultra-outer, *see* Ultra-outer aura

Aura as ultra-violet phenomenon, v

B, *see* Screen, pale blue

Background, dead black, essential to perception of the aura, 5
relation of patient to, during examination, 6

Bands, complementary coloured, *see* Colours, complementary

Body, as source of forces producing the aura, 133 ff.

Brain, diseases of, and the aura, 193, 283 ff.

Bromine, and the aura, 113-15

Brush, electric, 101

C, *see* Screen, deep carmine

Ca, *see* Screen, light carmine

Cancer, and the aura, 260-61

Carbonic acid gas, and the aura, 115

Carmine, 146

Cells, glass, use of in perceiving the aura, 3-4

Central nervous system, and the aura, 139

Changes, temporary, in the aura, 51 ff.; by hypnotic suggestion, 126-33; voluntary, v, 77-78, 119-26

Chemical action, *see* Action, chemical

Chemical experiments, and the aura, 109 ff.

Children, characteristic aura of, 12

Chlorine, and the aura, 115

Clairvoyants, 58-59; ability to perceive the aura, 1; vision of, 59

Colour, of the aura, 9, 36-37, 72 ff., 77-78, 80-81 (table), 157-59, 245 (*see also* cases under Females; cases under Males); changes produced in, by use of chemicals, 109-19; voluntary changes of, v, 122-26

Colours, complementary, and perception of the aura, 11, 141-60, 246-90

Colours, personal primary, 142-43

Complementary colour bands, *see* Colours, complementary

Conditions essential to perception of the aura, 4 ff., 71, 84

Curtains, use of, in perceiving the aura, 6

301

Rays: phenomenon of, in healthy 23 - year - old woman, 25; − in healthy 25-year-old woman, 27-28; absorption and reflection of, 42-43; projection of, by the body, 52-56; size of, 54; colour of, 54-55; voluntary production of, 119-21, 122

Re-examination, importance of, 11

Screen: dark blue, 40, 58, 72; dark diacyanin, 4, 6-7, 8, 9; − use of in separating inner and outer auras, 11; dark red, 40-41; deep carmine (C), 41, 44-45, 72; green, 40, 72; light carmine (Ca), 44, 45, 72; light diacyanin, 4, 8; methylene blue, 58, 72; orange, 72; pale blue (B), 44, 45, 72; pale red, 41-42; violet, 72; yellow, 40, 72

Screens, coloured: use of, in perceiving the aura, 1, 3 ff.; − in study of the etheric double, 40-41; action of, 41-43; use of, in study of inner and outer auras, 44-45, 71; − in experiments on vision, 61 ff.

Sciatica, and the aura, 287

Sections, transverse, of auras, 179-82

Shape, of the aura, 9-10, 35, 161-62, 284; *see also* cases under Females; *see also* cases under Males

Size, of the aura, 9-10, 35-36; *see also* cases under Females; *see also* cases under Males

Skin, sensitive, 270-73

Spatulate aura, 162 ff., 284-85; *see also* Females: spatulate aura; *see also* Males: spatulate aura

Spectrum, solar, 66, 73-74

Still birth, prediction of, by examination of aura, 299-300

Surface charges, and the aura, 108-9

Surfaces, pointed, and rays, 55-56

Temperament: and the aura, 36, 139-40; hysterical, and the aura, 163 ff., 275-77

Tent, folding, use of in perceiving the aura, 5

Texture, of the aura, 9, 36, 155-76; *see also* cases under Females; *see also* cases under Males

Transformation, of the aura in females, 12, 14-15

Tuberculosis, and the aura, 281-83

Tumours, superficial, and the aura, 288-89

Ulcer, stomach, and the aura, 256-58, 265-66

Ultra-outer aura, 26-27, 47-51; *see also* Females: ultra-outer auras of

Undulations, ultra-violet, as source of aura, 85

Uranium-Nitrate, 88, 138

Vapour, improbability that aura is, 84-85

Variations, in the aura, 177-78

Venereal disease, and the aura, 278-81

Vision, normal, and ability to perceive the aura, 2

Wimshurst machines, 92-93; *see also* Electricity, use of, in perception of aura

Window blinds, use of, in perceiving the aura, 5-6